JEWISH CHRISTIANS AND CHRISTIAN JEWS
FROM THE RENAISSANCE TO THE ENLIGHTENMENT

ARCHIVES INTERNATIONALES D'HISTOIRE DES IDÉES

INTERNATIONAL ARCHIVES OF THE HISTORY OF IDEAS

138

JEWISH CHRISTIANS AND CHRISTIAN JEWS FROM THE RENAISSANCE TO THE ENLIGHTENMENT

EDITED BY

RICHARD H. POPKIN AND GORDON M. WEINER

JEWISH CHRISTIANS AND CHRISTIAN JEWS

From the Renaissance to the Enlightenment

Edited by

RICHARD H. POPKIN

University of California, Los Angeles, California, U.S.A.

and

GORDON M. WEINER

Arizona State University, Tempe, Arizona, U.S.A.

KLUWER ACADEMIC PUBLISHERS

DORDRECHT / BOSTON / LONDON

Library of Congress Cataloging-in-Publication Data

Jewish Christians and Christian Jews : from the Renaissance to the
  Enlightenment / edited by Richard H. Popkin and Gordon M. Weiner.
      p.   cm. -- (Archives internationales d'histoire des idées =
  International archives of the history of ideas ; 138)
    Includes bibliographical references and index.
    ISBN 0-7923-2452-8 (alk. paper)
    1. Jewish Christians--Europe--History. 2. Christianity and other
  religions--Judaism. 3. Judaism--Relations--Christianity.
  4. Europe--Church history.   I. Popkin, Richard Henry, 1923-
  II. Weiner, Gordon M.   III. Series: Archives internationales
  d'histoire des idées ; 138.
  BR158.J48 1993
  261.2'6'094--dc20   93-28326

ISBN 0-7923-2452-8

Published by Kluwer Academic Publishers,
P.O. Box 17, 3300 AA Dordrecht, The Netherlands.

Kluwer Academic Publishers incorporates
the publishing programmes of
D. Reidel, Martinus Nijhoff, Dr W. Junk and MTP Press.

Sold and distributed in the U.S.A. and Canada
by Kluwer Academic Publishers,
101 Philip Drive, Norwell, MA 02061, U.S.A.

In all other countries, sold and distributed
by Kluwer Academic Publishers,
P.O. Box 322, 3300 AH Dordrecht, The Netherlands.

printed on acid-free paper

Printed in The Netherlands

TABLE OF CONTENTS

CONTRIBUTORS

Dagmar Barnouw, *University of Southern California, U.S.A.*
Allison P. Coudert, *Arizona State University, U.S.A.*
James E. Force, *University of Kentucky, U.S.A.*
Jerome Friedman, *Kent State University, U.S.A.*
David S. Katz, *Tel-Aviv University, U.S.A.*
Bernard McGinn, *University of Chicago, U.S.A.*
*Richard H. Popkin, Washington University (St. Louis) and University
    of California, Los Angeles, U.S.A.*
Gordon M. Weiner, *Arizona State University, U.S.A.*
Arthur H. Williamson, *California State University, Sacramento,
    U.S.A.*

1. INTRODUCTION

Hopefully it is no longer the case that historical presentations of the main intellectual and religious developments from the Renaissance and the Reformation up to the Enlightenment treat Jews and their relations to Christians as just a minor side issue unrelated to the central concerns of the overall societies of the time. The view that was expressed by Erasmus around 1500 that Judaism ossified after the beginning of Christianity and has had no developmental history thereafter has, hopefully, been discarded or abandoned by serious scholars. Researches into the history of the Cabbalistic writings and their impact on European thought, into the revival of Hebrew studies during the Renaissance, into the immediate importance of the conversion of the Jews and of the location of the Lost Tribes of Israel in Millenarian thought and activities, into the effects of the Spanish and Portuguese expulsions of the Jews on Europe and the Colonial Empires, into the emergence of the so-called "Jewish question" in secular nationalist societies, and into the status of Jews in modern tolerant societies, all indicate how intertwined Jewish, Christian and secular histories have been during the last five centuries.

From the time of the First Crusade in 1095 there was a growing pressure in European Christian societies to drive out the Jews and to restrict the activities of the surviving Jewish communities. Jews had earlier settled throughout the territory of the Roman Empire, and had established many thriving communities and institutions in Europe, including important religious centers, such as those in France. From the end of the 11th century onward some of these Jewish communities were destroyed. Jews were blamed for almost every bad thing that befell Christians. Jewish usury was constantly attacked as a cause of all sorts of social ills. Jews were held responsible for plagues and pestilence. Jewish doctors were accused of trying to kill Christian patients. Blood libels were set forth claiming that Jewish religious practices, especially those of the Passover, required the use of Christian blood. Jewish learning was regarded as dangerously threatening to Christian believers. The Talmud was burned in Paris in the mid–13th century.

These various negative developments led to the expulsion of the Jews from England in 1290, and from France at the end of the 14th century. There were strenuous and somewhat successful efforts to forcibly convert the Jews first in Spain and then in Portugal. The unconverted Jews in Iberia were expelled from Spain in 1492 and from Portugal in 1497. In many parts of

R.H. Popkin and G.M. Weiner (eds): Jewish Christians and Christian Jews, 1–9.
© 1994 *Kluwer Academic Publishers. Printed in the Netherlands.*

Germany and Italy Jews were forced into ghettoes in order to limit their contacts with Christians, and the Jews were prevented from entering into numerous occupations and activities.

In spite of this growing antagonism on the part of the Christian world to the then living Jews in various parts of Europe, regarding them as sworn and implacable enemies of Christ, and as clear and present dangers to the life and limbs and souls of living Christians, there was also at the same time a growing involvement on the part of Christian thinkers and writers with Jewish ideas and concerns. Jewish mysticism, especially as expressed in the Cabbalistic form, and Jewish philosophical views, especially as expressed by such figures as Moses Maimonides, became of great importance to Christians. Ancient and medieval Jewish commentators on Scripture became of central interest to many Christian intellectuals. Hebrew scholars were sought out by Christians in the great rush to understand the sacred texts of the Bible in the original languages. Jews and converted Jews became advisers to theologians, Church authorities, and professors and printers, especially in Italy and Germany. Jewish religious ideas were considered anew and more favorably in the effort during the Reformation and Counter-Reformation to uncover the true nature of Christianity and the real Divine Message. Those who had doubts about the truth of the Doctrine of the Trinity started looking into Jewish views about the nature of God and of the Messiah. Not only the Old Testament, but also other Jewish texts as well as Jewish ways of interpreting God's Word became of genuine importance to Christian scholars and theologians. Anti-Trinitarian Christians starting with Miguel Servetus sought justification of their views in Jewish ideas.

The forced conversions of a great many Jews that took place in Spain during the period 1391–1492, and in Portugal in 1497, created thousands, maybe hundreds of thousands, of so-called New Christians. These people who were dragooned into Christianity by physical, social and economic force had many different reactions to their new situation as Christian Jews. Some were just fake Christians, that is, they were Christians on the outside, but were really Jews on the inside-the Marranos. Others were partial Christians adopting some aspects of Christian belief and practice. And still others sought features of Christianity that were compatible with their original Jewish beliefs. As the Spanish and Portuguese Inquisitions tried to ferret out the fake, partial and backsliding Christians, many of the suspect New Christians fled from Iberia, either seeking to return to the practice of Judaism in the Ottoman Empire and in some of the Italian cities, or to find Christian territories where they could live more comfortably as New Christians without fear of being arrested. Some of them brought along elements of Jewish learning and ideas. Some combined these with Christian ideas. And in the religious ferment of the Reformation and the Counter-Reformation, some played significant roles in the development of European Christendom. The New Christians were prominent in the early Reformation and in newly created Catholic groups such as the Jesuits and the Carmelites. Some New Christians such as Juan Luis Vives, were important both as Renaissance humanists and as liberal Christian thinkers. Within Iberia some of the New Christians explored and developed elements of Christian belief and practice that they found compatible with their remaining Jewish views. Many of the views and practices that the Inquisition branded as heresies (especially judaizing practices and mystical views) were espoused and advocated by New Christians, some of whom had become important figures in both the Catholic and Protestant worlds.

One important aspect of the religious discussion and controversy of the 16th and 17th centuries was the conviction that the *true* understanding of the Divine Revelation involved the realization that God was still active in human history, and was soon to bring about the culmination of Divine history, the Second Coming of Christ and the onset of the Millennium, the Thousand Year Reign of Christ on Earth. Growing out of the medieval prophecies of Joachim de Fiore, and out of new understandings that were being offered of the secrets contained in the books of *Daniel* and *Revelation*, various religious thinkers envisaged the Conversion of the Jews and the reappearance of the Lost Tribes of Israel as the penultimate steps before the grand finale of human history. These great events would be followed by, or be accompanied by, the return of the now converted Jews to the Land of Zion, the rebuilding of the Temple, and the re-establishment of Divine rule on earth from Jerusalem.

Those who were believers in the imminent onset of the Millennium saw living Jews as crucial participants in the events to come. Reformed Franciscans in Spain and New Spain, at the beginning of the 16th century, led by Cardinal Ximines, prepared for the Millennium by fostering Hebrew and Aramaic learning at the newly founded University of Alcala, by organizing and underwriting the production of the Polyglot Bible, and by "finding" the Lost Tribes in America, saving them from destruction by the Conquistidores, and converting them to "pure" Christianity. New Christians, especially ones who had Jewish training before 1492, played a central role in these projects. Christopher Columbus saw his voyages as part of a Messianic-Millenarian scenario that would lead ultimately to the liberation of Jerusalem and to the reconstruction of the Temple. He told Queen Isabella in his *Book of Prophecies* that he would use the gold found in the New World to reproduce the ancient building that would be the center of the world, the nipple of the universe.

Late in the 16th and early in the 17th century Protestant Millenarian theologians especially in England, Scotland, Germany, and The Netherlands determined to their own satisfaction that the great prophecized events would begin taking place around 1655–60. Various theoreticians figured out that they would start happening 1260 years after the Fall of the Roman Empire, which they dated as having taken place around 400 a.d. The prophecized denouement of human history would begin very soon, and it was now the duty of Christian states to take those actions which would help prepare for these great impending developments. The Millenarians read the histories that were unfolding around them in terms of the Scriptural scenarios. The success of the Reformation in Northern Europe, the defeat of the Spanish Armada, the success of the Dutch Rebellion, the Protestant victories, especially those of the Swedish king, Gustavus Adolphus, in the Thirty Years War, the Union of Crowns of Scotland and England, all were seen as Divine occurrences portending the final events of the 'end of days'.

England, which had no legal Jewish resident at the time, nonetheless saw itself as the New Israel. Many Puritan leaders saw it as England's special mission in the Providential world to recall the Jews to its shores and to lead them to convert to the pure Christianity that was being created in the British Isles, in contrast to the spurious kind of Christianity sponsored by the Church of Rome, or the fractious mixed-up Christianity of the various Continental Protestant groups.

Other European countries and cultures saw their own triumphs as part of the unfolding of the Divine Plan, and similarly read what was happening to them in terms of what would soon happen in Millennial history. A French oriented Millenarianism developed in which the Jews would be brought back to France, would be converted there. After this the King of France would then lead them to Jerusalem, and the Messiah would rule the world from there with the King of France as his governing regent. A Portuguese version of the Millenarian scenario was offered by the Jesuit, Antonio de Vieira, to the effect that the Jews would have to be brought back to Portugal. After this Jesus would then return first to Portugal to reclaim the Jews, and take them to the Holy Land. Millenarianism and Messianism thus became part and parcel of defining nations and their destinies. And in each and every one of these scenarios, the Jews, converted or unconverted, would play a critical role in the unfolding Millennial events.

In addition, given all of the excitement generated about Jewish learning, especially in the Cabbalistic form, in leading to the true understanding of God's Message, and the realization that the culmination of world history was on the horizon, it is not surprising that so many forms of Jewish Christianity and Christian Judaism, both as theories and practices, emerged. Christians sought to connect their expectations with Jewish ones, which centered on the hoped for appearance of the Jewish Messiah first in 1648, and then in 1666, (based on Cabbalistic calculations). Various Christian theologians scoured Jewish texts in order to find out exactly what was supposed to happen when Jesus would arrive as the political Messiah ruler. The Jews had been and still were expecting a political Messiah, so they should know. Similarly the Christians sought to find out from the Jews what the Temple had actually looked like so they could understand every portion of it when it would be rebuilt. (The Temple was supposed to be microcosm of the universe.)

Some of the Protestants who had returned to studying the messages of the Old Testament were accused by their opponents of being Judaizers. Sometimes the accusation was made because of their beliefs, and sometimes because of their adoption of certain Jewish practices. And many New Christians sought forms of Judaism within Christianity, or sought ways in which unacceptable doctrines of Christianity, such as that of the divinity of Jesus, or the doctrine of the Trinity, could be modified or restated so that they might be found compatible with a Jewish orientation.

Many scholars over the last few decades have turned up more and more material concerning these kinds of developments in different European countries and their colonies during the period from 1450–1800, indicating a variety of ways in which Jews and Christians took part in joint ventures, adopted some of each others beliefs and practices, and fused elements of each other's religious beliefs. These ranged from a transfer of learning, or a different interpretation of a portion of Scripture to the actual adoption by a Christian community in Hungarian Transylvania of Talmudic Judaism, (which was kept up into the 20th century). This development grew out of the anti-Trinitarianism that was then current in eastern Europe. Doubts about Trinitarianism led to researching the Jewish perspective, and then to adopting it. In fact it was a problem for many Christian groups to delineate what portions of Judaism had been overcome or superseded by the development of Christianity. Depending on what was decided on this matter, various portions of Jewish belief and practice might still be viable or even necessary as part of the true religious life.

The present volume is a collective venture by a group of scholars who have been working for a decade or more on various aspects of the interrelationships of Judaism and Christianity from the period of the Renaissance and the Reformation up to that of the Enlightenment. The undertaking began as a two day conference at the William Andrews Clark Library of the University of California at Los Angeles in April of 1992 on Jewish Christians and Christian Jews. The speakers and the audience had very lively formal and informal discussions (in the imposing lecture room and in the lovely gardens of the library) concerning many different aspects of the subject. We, and some of our fellow scholars who were not there, but are equally concerned with the subject, gathered our results together in the papers that appear here.

We are all interested and intrigued by the ways in which Judaism and Christianity interacted in the period 1450–1800, and in the ways in which various Jews and Christians adopted and adapted ideas and practices of the other group. We do not always agree about why these developments occurred or what they actually amounted to. We do however agree about the need to explore these developments, and to recognize them not as simply bizarre events, but as part of the special character of the religious and intellectual history of the period. Further, some of the episodes or theories that we discuss in this volume play a significant role in the later history of the relations of Jews and Christians even up to the present day.

The first four papers presented here by Bernard McGinn, Jerome Friedman, Richard Popkin and Allison Coudert deal with some of the basic forms of Jewish Christianity or Christian Judaism. McGinn analyzes Judaized Christianity that was presented by two of the great Christian Cabbalists, Pico della Mirandola and Guillaume Postel. Pico, in his attempt to recover the *prisca theologia*, studied the Cabbala, learned Hebrew from rabbis and New Christian scholars, and incorporated some of his Cabbalistic views in his grandiose project in his *Oration on the Dignity of Man*. Postel not only studied the Cabbala, and translated the *Zohar* into Latin, but also in a sense lived it. In his attempt to bring into being the true restoration of Christianity, he proposed a thoroughly Jewish Christianity.

Friedman examines the activities of many of the Christian Hebraists and Christian Cabbalists in the 16th century, and those of their Jewish and New Christian associates. He looks at some of the uses Jewish learning was put to by Christians, both Catholic and Protestant, by Jews working with Christians, and by New Christians trying to fit into a Christian world. Several New Christians became important professors of Hebrew at major European universities, and trained the future generations of Christian Hebrew scholars and professors. Friedman also indicates the part played by Jewish learning in the Reformation rejection of Scholastic version of Christianity, and in the early formulations of anti-Trinitarianism, especially that of Miguel Servetus, and the Spanish Erasmian, Juan de Valdes, who had fled to Italy.

Popkin takes the subject into the 17th century, and discusses the forms of Jewish Christianity and Christian Judaism that develop, chiefly out of the Millenarian and Messianic expectations of the time. English and Dutch Millenarians who were anxiously expecting the onset of the Millennium became involved with some Amsterdam Jewish intellectuals in editing needed Jewish texts, in constructing an exact model of the Temple, and in other matters. They sought evidence that the American Indians were Jews, and were perhaps the Lost Tribes of Israel. And later on they also became involved in the actual Jewish Messianic movement of Sabbatai Zevi. Some became Jewish Christians. On the other hand, some of the Jews who worked with them and got involved in their projects adopted more favorable attitudes towards parts of Christianity, and some may have actually become Christian Jews. Sabbatai Zevi was in fact labeled a "Quaker Jew". And Baruch Spinoza's own positive but non-divine view of Jesus may be an outgrowth of a form of Christian Judaism expressed in Amsterdam by a visiting rabbi from Jerusalem.

Allison Coudert's paper deals with the important late chapter in Christian Cabbalism, the preparation of Latin translations of a collection of medieval and Lurianic Cabbalistic writings done by Knorr von Rosenroth and Francis Mercurius Van Helmont and associates. This grand work was published in 1677–78 in Sulzbach, Germany, and became the main way that many non-Jewish European intellectuals gained knowledge of the Cabbala. Newton, Leibniz, Locke, Schelling and many others studied and often used these Latin texts. Coudert's paper examines the Millenarian reasons for the work of Knorr von Rosenroth and Van Helmont, and for their unusual philo-semitism. She shows how this affected the status of actual Jews living in Sulzbach. And she raises the possibility that by both personal contact and through their writings, these late 17th century Christian Cabbalists may have had a serious influence on the modern age that was to follow.

The papers of Arthur Williamson, David S. Katz, and James Force present intriguing case histories from Scotland and England in the 16th and 17th centuries. Reformation Scotland presumably had no Jews. Nonetheless one of its leaders, George Buchanan, was accused by the Portuguese Inquisition of Judaizing, and specifically of engaging in a Jewish practice while he was teaching at the Collège de Guyenne in Bordeaux. John Knox saw Israel as the model for understanding Scotland's special role in 16th century Christianity, in contrast to Buchanan who appealed to Roman models.

Katz takes up a specific and peculiarly English case of accepting an Old Testament view that had been dropped out of general Christian practice, namely that of celebrating the Saturday Sabbath, instead of the Lord's Day (Sunday). In England this may have looked at first as a crankish kind of reform, but it soon generated a great deal of polemical literature, a movement of Seventh Day observers who were constantly being hounded and punished, and finally led to one of views that developed into modern day Fundamentalism.

Force deals with the Jewish theology of one of the giant figures of modern times, Isaac Newton. He argues that Newton's strange, even heretical version of Christianity, (which appears mainly in his still unpublished theological papers) flows from his acceptance of the Jewish conception of the Godhead. Force indicates some of the Jewish literature that Newton probably studied.

And it is this Jewish conception which is all important in Newton's famous general scholium in *Principia Mathematica*, placing the Jewish God at the center of his theory of the physical universe, as the Lord God of Dominion who is continuously acting on the physical and the human universe.

Dagmar Barnouw's paper takes us to the end of the development of Jewish-Christian involvements from the Renaissance and Reformation to the Enlightenment. In Germany the Jewish philosopher Moses Mendelssohn and his followers expressed their Judaism in Enlightenment terms, and came close to the almost secular moral views of their Christian contemporaries like Lessing, (whose *Nathan the Wise* was a plea for tolerance and acceptance of Jews in a "Christian" secular society). In the decade after Mendelssohn several Jews and Jewesses became important figures in the German intellectual world. One of the stages on which this world performed was the salons of leading Jewish women, including Mendelssohn's own daughters. The initial acceptance of Jews in a Christian milieu soon created tensions about whether, even in a secular world, Jews could exist as different from Christians. The political developments in Germany in the face of the French Revolution and the Napoleonic invasions produced fervid German nationalism which saw Judaism as its enemy. The Jewish intellectuals felt enormous pressure from within and without to be accepted as Germans. Barnouw offers an analysis of the famous case of the greatest of the salon Jewesses, Rahel Levin Varnhagen, who converted just as she married an aristocrat German, and who finally committed suicide.

The situation lived through by the first generation of Enlightenment Jews involved what was to be called "the Jewish Question", could Jews persevre as Jews in a post-Christian Enlightenment world.

Finally, Gordon Weiner examines how the negative, anti-Semitic views of 16th and 17th Christians are mirrored in the emerging free Jewish world of Western Europe and of the European colonies. Starting first in The Netherlands, then in England, and in some of the colonies in the New World, the Spanish and Portuguese Jews treated Jews from Germany and Eastern Europe as inferior peoples, and developed a religious and social structure to keep them in their place. Specific regulations were drawn up to make Ashkenazi Jews second class Jews in terms of economic and social activities, and in terms of religious participation in the community. The Sephardic Jews of Amsterdam and London kept sending or encouraging the departure of Eastern European Jews to the new frontiers – Ireland and the colonies in the New World. In quite a few of the New World Jewish settlements the same anti-Ashkenazi regulations were adopted, especially to keep the Eastern Jews from taking over even where they were in the majority. Weiner also discusses the few places where there was equality between the two Jewish groups, and offers possible reasons for this difference.

We hope that this collection of essays will add to the understanding of the ways in which Judaism and Christianity, and Jews and Christians, interacted in the period 1450–1800. We hope that we have thrown some light on the ways in which Christians appropriated some aspects of Judaism and vice-versa, and on the ways these appropriations played a role in the history of the period. We are well aware that only a small fragment of world Jewry played any role in what we are discussing, since there were so few Jews in Western Europe. But, nonetheless, their activities and involvements with Christian scholars, theologians and Millenarian theorists was of great importance in the events of the time. And lastly we hope that what we are offering will encourage others to explore further into what we have raised, and to find many other places in which Jewish Christianity and Christian Judaism arose, and played a part in those histories.

RICHARD H. POPKIN
Pacific Palisades, California
May 1993

BERNARD MCGINN

2.   CABALISTS AND CHRISTIANS:

REFLECTIONS ON CABALA IN MEDIEVAL

AND RENAISSANCE THOUGHT*

> Se than I saye what we have to conferme those
> thynges that be taught us by the chyrche. Fyrst
> the prophetes that were instructed by the father
> almyghty god, and also theyr Cabala, that is to
> saye theyr secrete erudycyons not wryten in the
> byble.
>
> St. John Fisher[1]

This endorsement of Cabala by St. John Fisher, a conservative and notably prudent man (he lost his head over only one issue), should give pause to those who would dismiss Christian Cabala as a phenomenon of little importance, an intellectual dead end.[2] To demonstrate the importance of Cabala, however, would be the work of volumes rather than a brief essay.[3] My intention here is to advance some tentative observations on what the phenomenon of Cabala has to tell us about Jewish-Christian relations in the late Middle Ages and the Renaissance.

Even such a modest task is not without difficulties. Kabbalah in its many Jewish forms is fraught with puzzles and problems, especially to the outsider.[4] I take comfort in the words of Chaim Wirszubski who said, "Kabbalah, being a mystical discipline, has never been plain sailing; to be baffled and confused by it is no reproach to anyone."[5] Even Christian Cabala, a less complex phenomenon than Kabbalah itself, is devious, perplexing and not sufficiently studied.

John Fisher's quotation represents a view held in a number of circles in the early sixteenth century, one that can be fleshed out by turning to a passage in Luigi Ricchieri's *Lectionum antiquarum* which appeared in 1517. Ricchieri, who depended largely on Giovanni Pico della Mirandola for his information, distinguished three forms of Jewish thought: talmudic Judaism which is heretical; philosophical Judaism which is late and therefore can be discounted; and cabalistic Judaism, which is "the oldest of all, and true more than any other, because established opinion is that it was made known to Moses by the best and greatest God."[6] The development of this distinction

R.H. Popkin and G.M. Weiner (eds): Jewish Christians and Christian Jews, 11–34.
© 1994 *Kluwer Academic Publishers. Printed in the Netherlands.*

between three forms of Judaism has much to tell us about the origins of Cabala and Jewish-Christian relations in the later Middle Ages.

I. BACKGROUND

Christian attitudes toward the Jews underwent significant changes around the year 1100, though the extent of these and the history of their effects is still subject to debate.[7] The new militancy expressed in the First Crusade (1095–99) has often been thought to mark a major turning point, though this has recently been disputed.[8] The intellectual shift in Christian perceptions of the Jews in the twelfth century suggests that more weight should be given to the figure of the converted Jew Petrus Alfonsi than most students of Jewish-Christian relations have hitherto allowed.[9] Baptized in 1106, Petrus wrote his *Dialogi contra Judaeos* in 1110. As John Tolan has shown, "...the *Dialogues* were the best-known and most influential anti-Jewish text in the Middle Ages."[10] The text is found in 79 manuscripts (63 in its entirety, 16 in excerpts), as well in precis form in the more than 200 manuscripts of Vincent of Beauvais' *Speculum historiale* (see book 25). Petrus is best known as the first author to attack the Talmud for its failure to conform to reason and therefore its inferiority to Christianity.[11] While it is true that Petrus does not *specifically* describe Rabbinic Judaism as a heresy,[12] nor does he use that claim as a basis for a call to persecution or elimination of the Jews, it is evident that the approach that led to the condemnation of the Talmud in 1240 and the view found throughout the late Middle Ages and Renaissance that talmudic Judaism was a heresy has a prototype in his widely disseminated work.[13]

Less noticed has been Petrus's attitude toward the other types of Judaism, philosophical and mystical, that Pico, Ricchieri and others later distinguished in explicit fashion. The defense of Christianity that occupies *Dialogi* VI–XII describes two kinds of Christian teachings: those that can be proved by reason, primarily creation and the Trinity (!); and the Christological teachings that reason can show are possible but that depend on the *auctoritas* of Scripture.[14] Petrus's discussion of the rationality of belief in creation uses elements from Saadia Gaon's *Book of Beliefs and Opinions*,[15] thus showing a willingness to make use of Jewish philosophical materials that presages the broader encounter between Scholasticism and Jewish philosophy that marked the period c. 1150–1325.[16] The discussion of the rational grounds for belief in the Trinity shows an even more remarkable encounter, one that I take to be the first between medieval Jewish mysticism and Christian thought.

In demonstrating the three persons of the Trinity in dialogue VI, Petrus appears to criticize Saadia and philosophical Judaism and to uncover a proof for the Trinity in mystical, esoteric (should we say "proto-kabbalistic") Judaism. Saadia had attacked the Christian identification of three persons in one God as expressed through the triad of "essence", "knowledge" and "life".[17] Petrus "proves" that God must be a trinity of *substantia-sapientia-voluntas*,[18] and then goes on to provide a confirmation of this from Jewish esoteric speculation on the Tetragrammaton. Citing a work he calls the *Secreta secretorum*,[19] he claims that the Tetragrammaton written as IEVE in a triangular diagram illustrates both the unity of substance (the one name of IEVE) and the trinity of persons (i.e., IE, EV and VE, with the repeating E connoting the single divine nature).[20] [See diagram below.]

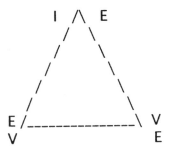

This form of speculation on the Divine Name may be related to that found in a noted source of Kabbalah, the *Sefer Yesirah*;[21] but there are important differences that cast doubt on claims that Petrus had direct knowledge of it.[22] The converted Jew uncovers further proofs for the Trinity in a variety of Old Testament texts: the three knots in the fringes commanded in Numbers 19; the form of blessing used by Jewish priests when they praise the Divine Name (the fingers of each hand segmented in three); and finally, the triple "Holy, holy, holy" of Isaiah 6:3.[23]

There were, to be sure, earlier contacts between Christianity and Jewish mysticism. As far back as the third century, Origen had displayed considerable acquaintance with Jewish esotericism, especially in his *Commentary on the Song of Songs*. Despite the literature that has been devoted to this issue,[24] no adequate study of Origen's relation to Jewish mystical traditions exists. It is also true that the Carolingian scholar Agobard of Lyons showed knowledge of the Jewish mystical ideas concerning the dimensions of the divine body, like those found in the *Shi'ur Qomah*,[25] but this notice appears to have had little effect on subsequent Jewish-Christian relations. Petrus Alphonsi's contact with medieval Jewish mysticism, on the other hand, began the tradition which culminated in the creation of Cabala.

François Secret in his *Les Kabbalistes chrétiens de la Renaissance* was the first who suggested that the history of Cabala, at least in its larval stage, should begin with Petrus Alfonsi.[26] What has not been noted before is that Petrus expresses, at least implicitly, a reaction to *three strands* of *contemporary* Judaism – the talmudic, the philosophical and the mystical. This is a departure from the standard patristic and early medieval judgment on "fossilized" Judaism as nothing more than unchanged adherence to the Old Testament. Petrus appears to be the first Latin author who knew something about all three strands of Judaism, though the triple distinction only became explicit at the end of the fifteenth century. I would suggest that this distinction, even when only implicitly present, provides a helpful way of thinking about Christian attitudes to Judaism beginning in the twelfth century.

Petrus Alfonsi's *Dialoghi* were widely influential – most Christians who wrote about the Jews in the later Middle Ages were aware of his work; many cite him explicitly. For example, in the mid-twelfth century he was the source of Peter the Venerable's attack on talmudic Judaism,[27] and towards the end of the century he was also mined by Alan of Lille whose *Contra haereticos* contains a summary of parts of his attack on the Talmud, ending with the ominous statement, "These are the many heresies of the faithless Jews" (Hec sunt hereses et quamplures perfidorum iudeorum).[28]

At the same time that Alan was picking up on Petrus's condemnation of talmudic Judaism, others, like Peter of Blois in his *Contra perfidiam Judaeorum*, were citing his use of esoteric Jewish interpretations of the Tetragrammaton as proofs for revelation of the Trinity in the Old Testament.[29] An even more important appearance is found in Joachim of Fiore who incorporated it into one of the most ambitious and challenging Trinitarian theologies of the late twelfth century.[30] Joachim, whose brief treatise *Adversus Judaeos* is one of the more tolerant medieval examples of the genre, mentions "hebreus quidam petrus" explicitly in his discussion of the Tetragrammaton in his *Expositio in Apocalypsim*.[31] Joachim's famous Trinitarian vision of the "ten-stringed psaltery" which he received at Casamari on Pentecost in 1183 may have predated his reading of Petrus Alfonsi, but the converted Jew's *Dialogi* were definitely a factor in the way in which he subsequently worked out his theology of the Trinity's action in history, as he explained it in both his *Expositio* and in two of the major "figures" from his *Liber figurarum*.[32] Joachim's speculations on the inner secrets of the IEVE are among the most important forerunners of Cabala in their witness to the desire of some medieval and Renaissance Christians to find inner consonance between esoteric Judaism and Christian belief.

There is also evidence for Christian knowledge of Jewish esoteric speculations about both the divine name and the opening verses of Genesis (traditional loci of mystical knowledge) that are independent of the influence of Petrus

Alphonsi. The *Ysagoge in Theologiam*, a text from the school of Abelard written about the middle of the twelfth century, held that "the testimonies [of the Old Testament] more evidently express the mystery of the Incarnation of the Word and the Trinity of persons in the unity of the divine essence in that language [i.e., Hebrew] than with Greeks or Latins."[33] Among the Trinitarian proofs alluded to is the threefold way of writing the divine name, that is, as Adonai, as the Tetragrammaton, and as three yods in a triangular form.[34] More detailed, and more clearly related to Jewish mystical speculation, is Alexander Neckham's exegesis of the coherence between the opening verse of Genesis in Hebrew and the first verse of John's Gospel found in his *De naturis rerum* of c. 1205.[35]

It would be beyond the scope of this essay to sketch even the broad lines of Christian attitudes toward the three strands of Judaism in the period between c. 1200 and 1486 when Pico della Mirandola first made "explicit" appeal to Cabala. The story of Christian reactions to talmudic Judaism has lately attracted a number of studies. Christian encounters with philosophical Judaism, especially with the thought of Solomon ibn Gabirol and Maimonides, have also been much studied. My theme is Christian reaction to the third strand of Judaism – the esoteric/kabbalist dimension – a less studied, but no less interesting phenomenon.

The works of Gershom Scholem and François Secret have dispelled the notion that Christian Cabala was born, full-grown like Athena, from Pico's noble brow in 1486. From the other direction, Scholem also suggested the possibility of Christian influence, particularly of the thought of John Scottus Eriugena, on early Kabbalah both in Provence and in Gerona,[36] though this is far more questionable.[37] Yehudah Liebes has studied Christian influences on the *Zohar*.[38] It is clear that the complete history of the contacts between Jewish and Christian mysticism that led up to the creation of Cabala still remains to be told.

A number of late medieval converts from Judaism form an important part of the story of these contacts. There is no need here to review what can be read in Scholem and Secret about figures like Abulafia's mysterious disciples at Capua in the 1280s, Abner (Alphonsus) of Burgos (c. 1320), and Pedro de la Caballeria and Paul de Heredia in fifteenth-century Spain.[39] It is worth noting, as well, that esoteric/kabbalist Judaism continued to exert an influence on some born Christians during the centuries between Joachim and Pico. While a cabalist treatise once ascribed to Ramon Llull (1232–1316) is now known to be pseudonymous, Moshe Idel has argued that the Catalan thinker's *ars combinatoria* may be related to texts of ecstatic Kabbalah.[40] Perhaps the most notable case is the Catalan physician, polymath and apocalypticist, Arnold of Vilanova (d. 1311), whose *Allocutio super Tetragrammaton* used both Petrus

Alfonsi and Joachim but went beyond each in trying to detect the Christian Trinity in esoteric Jewish speculation about the Divine Name.[41]

It would, of course, be a mistake to push the explicit origin of Cabala as a distinctive complex of ideas back into the twelfth century, or even into the thirteenth. Nevertheless, even the summary information given here indicates that an important trajectory in Christian polemics began in the twelfth century, one that found its full voice in the writings of Pico della Mirandola and his successors, the *true* Christian cabalists. The implicit recognition of three strands in *contemporary* Judaism that we can discern in Petrus Alfonsi made it possible for some Christian thinkers to rethink Jewish-Christian relations by finding in esoteric Judaism demonstrations of the truth of Christianity.

II. CABALA AND CHRISTIAN TRUTH IN THE RENAISSANCE

The second part of this essay will look at two major Christian cabalists, Giovanni Pico della Mirandola (1463–94) and Guillaume Postel (1510–81). There are important differences between them, both linguistically in terms of their knowledge of Hebrew and command of kabbalist sources and intellectually in how far they were willing to use Cabala in their plans for the reform of Christianity. However, they share at least one essential principle: the belief that the "real" Judaism to be found in Kabbalah demonstrated the truth of the fundamental Christian mysteries of the Trinity and the Incarnation.

In transforming Jewish Kabbalah into missionary Christian Cabala, of course, Pico and Postel were forced to make fundamental changes in its structure and dynamics.[42] From the viewpoint of Kabbalah itself, Moshe Idel has argued that "the basic change that the theosophical Kabbalah underwent in the Christian presentation is the obliteration of the theurgical nature of this mystical lore."[43] (Even Pico's well-known yoking of "practical Cabala" with natural magic is more contemplative and speculative than properly theurgical.) From the viewpoint of Cabala, that is, how the new lore functioned within the context of Christian belief and practice, however, two other shifts are equally revealing: first, Cabala's taking on the role of a key element in the Renaissance program of religious universalization; and, closely allied to this, Cabala's move from esoteric to exoteric teaching. Both these shifts are evident in Pico and expanded upon in Postel.

Pico's interest in Kabbalah represents a distinctive coming together of the fitful contacts between Jewish mysticism and Christianity that go back to Petrus Alphonsi combined with a distinctively Renaissance search for the unity of all religious truth. Nicholas of Cusa's *De pace fidei* written late in 1453 in the shadow of the Fall of Constantinople was designed to show "...how, by the expert knowledge of a few men wise in all the differences found in the religions of the world a certain easy concord might be discovered and, through it, lasting peace might be established by a fitting and true means."[44] Marsilio Ficino's *De religione christiana* (c. 1474), close in spirit to Cusa, argues that all religions have some share in divine revelation. Ficino not only was one of the first to investigate how the *prisca theologia* of the ancient Gentile theologians revealed Christian truth, but he also attempted to confirm such Christian teachings as the Trinity, the Incarnation, the Passion and original sin from a melange of undigested Jewish sources, rabbinic, philosophical and mystical.[45] Pico went beyond his teacher both in his knowledge of Jewish mystical sources and also in the clarity with which he argued that it was esoteric mystical Judaism, *not* other forms of Judaism, which revealed the truth of Christianity.

Pico's relation to Judaism must be seen as a part of the broad program by which he sought to achieve what Charles Trinkaus termed "a retrospective reconciliation of Christians, Jews and Gentiles."[46] The young prince was not novel in seeking the inner harmony of all religions in the hidden revelation of the essential truths of Christianity in non-Christian religious and philosophical sources, but rather in the more learned and comprehensive way he went about this task. From the perspective of the history of Jewish-Christian relations, Pico's significance resides in the fact that he made Cabala the essential mediating link in the universalizing and harmonizing agenda of the Renaissance ecumenists.

First, a word about Pico's Jewish contacts.[47] The young polymath's first Jewish teacher was Elijah del Medigo whom he knew from his student days at Padua (1480–82). The crucial figure in the prince's knowledge of kabbalist literature, as C. Wirszubski's study has shown, was the pugnacious pederast and convert to Catholicism born in Sicily as Samuel ben Nissim Abulfaraj, but better known under the inflated pen-name of Flavius Mithridates (Guglielmo Raimondo Moncada in Italian).[48] Mithridates was a figure of typically Renaissance contrasts, who combined a number of odious personal traits with real skills as a kabbalist and translator. His *Sermo de Passione Domini* preached before the pope in 1481, as well as the Christianizing interpolations in the kabbalist translations he made for Pico in 1485, show that he "was in a sense Pico's forerunner as regards the latter's notion that the esoteric tradition of the Jews confirmed Christianity."[49] Nevertheless, Mithridates was not the Prince of Mirandola's only source of knowledge of Kabbalah. In his *Oratio* Pico mentions another Jewish convert, one "Dactylus Hebraeus," skilled in Kabbalah, who testified that Kabbalah revealed the Trinity.[50] We also know that Pico met with Johanen Alemanno in 1488, and he may well have been in contact with him earlier.[51] Finally, Judah Abravanel (Leone Ebreo) had some contact with Pico between 1492 when Leone arrived in Naples as an exile from Spain and Pico's death in 1494. The extent of this acquaintance is difficult to determine,[52] but it may well have had an effect of Leone's masterwork, the *Dialoghi d'amore*, as will be suggested below. Thus, the Renaissance scholar's knowledge of Kabbalah was primarily of the Italian variety, best represented by Abraham Abulafia and Menachem Recanati,[53] which was less theurgical and more philosophically oriented than the Spanish Kabbalah as found in the *Zohar*.[54] This doubtless facilitated the philosophical-theological appropriation of Jewish esotericism engineered by the Count of Mirandola.

Pico's remarkable creation – the first true Christian Cabala – was produced during two years of fervid activity and controversy. Five or six months of study of Hebrew and reading of Mithridates' translations culminated in 1486 in the famous 900 *conclusiones* finished in November of that year and published in Rome by Silber on December 7.[55] The famous *Oratio*, intended as the introduction to the public disputation of the *conclusiones* was composed at the same time, as was the vernacular *Commento sopra una Canzona de Amore da Girolamo Benivieni* which also shows evidence of Pico's fascination with Cabala.[56] When Pope Innocent VIII and the Roman curia stepped in to prevent the public disputation and to initiate an investigation of the *conclusiones*, Pico defended them in his *Apologia* published in Spring of 1487.[57] This did not prevent the condemnation of the *conclusiones* in the papal brief "Etsi ex iniuncto nobis" of 4 August (not published until December of 1487).[58] After the count's brief flight to France and his arrest there, he returned to Florence, where he worked on his *Heptaplus*, or commentary on the beginning of Genesis, in 1488. This too shows evidence of his cabalist concerns.[59] It is only in his final works, the *De ente et uno* of 1492 and the subsequent *Disputationes in astrologiam* that there is less direct appeal to Cabala.

A glance at the contents of the ambitious 900 *conclusiones* (not *quaestiones* be it noted!)[60] shows how important Cabala was to the Count of Mirandola. It is well known that Pico devoted two of the 39 sections of his *conclusiones* to Cabala – 47 *conclusiones* according to the teaching of the kabbalists themselves, and no less than 71 *conclusiones* "according to his own view" (*secundum opinionem propriam*) that "especially support the Christian religion."[61] It is less well known that along with these 118 *conclusiones* there are over 20 more in other sections that clearly represent cabalist lore and that demonstrate how Pico made use of Jewish esoteric mysticism as a key element in his universalizing agenda.[62]

We can get some sense of what Pico got from Cabala by a look at some of the *conclusiones* along with passages in the *Oratio*, the *Commento*, and the *Apologia*. Perhaps the fundamental point to be grasped at the outset is that Cabala does not teach anything new – it rather reveals that the truths that Christians already hold, especially concerning the Trinity and the Incarnation, have always been known, especially to Jews but also to some Gentiles. This is one of Pico's major innovations that marks him as the real creator of Cabala: his insistence that it is the missing link between the "prisca theologia" of the Gentile theologians and full Christian revelation.[63]

Without getting into too many of the details of the cabalist conclusions (well investigated by Wirszubski), we can take a brief look at how Pico understood and used Cabala, both in the *conclusiones* and in the other works written between 1486 and 1488. The first of the *conclusiones cabalistice secundum opinionem propriam* divides Cabala into *scientia Sephiroth* and *scientia Semot*, "as into practical and speculative." The second subdivides speculative Cabala into four parts which Pico says correspond to his fourfold division of philosophy.[64] The third *conclusio* says that practical Cabala "practices the whole of formal metaphysics and lower theology." This practical Cabala is allied with "magia naturalis" in the famous ninth of the "conclusiones magicae secundum opinionem propriam," which reads "There is no science which gives greater proof of Christ's divinity than magic and Cabala."[65]

This, interestingly enough, was the only one of the conclusions involving Cabala to be included among the 13 condemned by the papal commission. In defending it in the "Quaestio quinta de magia naturali et cabala Hebreorum" in the *Apologia*, Pico introduced a distinction between the "prima et vera Cabala," that is, the revealed truth that God first gave to Moses, and "that part of Cabala which is a science and is not revealed theology," explaining that it was only the latter whose superiority he was asserting among the *human sciences* (and not over revelation).[66] Wirszubski is correct to point out that this distinction introduces a contradiction into Pico's basic understanding of Cabala which presupposes that Cabala is always divinely revealed knowledge.[67] This is clear from the treatments of Cabala both in the *Oratio* (repeated at the beginning of the *Apologia*),[68] as well as from the description of Cabala given in the *Commento* where it is said:

> This principle [that is, secrecy] was very religiously observed among the ancient Hebrews, and for this reason, their secret doctrine, which contains an explication of the abstruse mysteries of the law, is called *Cabala*, which means *Receiving*, because they receive it from each other, not through writings, but by oral transmission. It is a doctrine which is clearly divine, and worthy of being shared with only a few; it is a very important foundation of our faith.[69]

Pico not only had a much more complex sense of Cabala than any of his predecessors, but he also was more ambitious in the uses to which he put it. To be sure, the Count fits into the long, if sporadic tradition which sought to use Jewish esoteric traditions to demonstrate the truths of the faith, especially the Trinity (see *conclusiones cabalistice secundum opinionem propriam* #5,6,20,33,34,61) and those relating to the Incarnation of the Word and his messianic salvific activity (see #7,8,14,15,21–26,30,32,34,37–43,45–47,51– 52). He also found in Cabala confirmation of Christian teaching regarding the coming eschaton (#1,9,16,44). An important mystical element that Pico takes over from cabalistic texts (one, however, that originated in Maimonides and was "kabbalized" by Abulafia and Flavius Mithridates)[70] was that of the twofold mystical kiss by which the soul attains God – the "binsica" in which the soul briefly separates from the body in ecstasy, and the "mors osculi" (which sometimes follows from the "binsica"), that is, the ultimate attainment of God when the body leaves the soul in physical death.[71]

If Pico's missionary intent was not substantially different from that of his predecessors stretching back to Petrus Alphonsi, what is different, as Wirszubski has shown, is his twofold method of proving Christianity.[72] Not only does the Count provide a Christianized interpretation of the meaning of existing texts from the Old Testament, as well as from rabbinic and kabbalistic sources (e.g., *conclusiones cabalistice secundum opinionem propriam* #1, 21– 24), but he also applies the techniques of the Jewish kabbalists themselves, especially the *ars combinandi* and letter symbolism, to demonstrate Christian beliefs (e.g., #1, 59–61 for the former and #1,6,14–16 and 43 for the latter). This application of kabbalistic techniques, heretofore more adumbrated than employed, constitutes his greatest originality.

In his famous *Oratio*, Pico avered that on Sinai God had given Moses not only the Law, "but also the Law's true exposition with the manifestation of all the mysteries and secrets which are contained beneath the husk and rough face of the words of the Law."[73] As Wirszubski points out, the way in which the mysteries and secrets are hidden is twofold: either beneath the *meaning*, or beneath the *letters themselves* as elements of language.[74] In relation to the former aspect, Pico went beyond his predecessors in pointing to the homology between the traditional Christian four senses of Scripture and the four methods of kabbalistic interpretation he found in Bahya ben Asher's *Commentary on the Pentateuch*.[75] To the Renaissance Christian this would have served as another confirmation of the "Christianity" of Jewish esoteric speculation.[76] In terms of a concentration on the mysteries hidden under the letters themselves, Pico utilized a rich bag of the hermeneutical procedures that later cabalists, following Joseph Gikatilla, came to distinguish according to the triple formula of *gematria* (numerical equivalents), *notarikon* (acrostics) and *temurah* (transposition).[77] Thus, as Moshe Idel has pointed out, with Pico hermeneutics "became a leitmotiv of the entire Christian Kabbalah."[78]

The Count of Mirandola broke new ground in his employment of Cabala to create a link between Christianity, Judaism and other forms of wisdom, especially the *prisca theologia* of the Gentiles. This, of course, is based on a premiss almost as old as Christian thought itself, which claimed that all the wisdom of later ages had begun with the revelation to Moses. Pico suggests this theme when he says in his *Oratio*, "omnis sapientia a barbaris ad Graecos, a Graecis ad nos manavit."[79] Pico occasionally pointed to the convergence between Cabala and Plato, and even to that between Cabala and Peripatetic philosophy (as in the case of Themistius), but he primarily used speculative Cabala in conjunction with the ancient Gentile wisdom of Orpheus, Zoroaster, Hermes and Pythagoras. The connection is evident in the tenth of the "conclusiones cabalistice secundum opinionem propriam" which states: "That which the cabalists call Metatron is without doubt what that which Orpheus calls Pallas, Zoroaster the 'Maternal Mind,' Hermes the Son of God, Pythagoras Wisdom and Parmenides the Intelligible Sphere."[80] The Renaissance quest for the unity of the truth found in all religions, so well expressed in Cusa's *De pace fidei*, is clearly at work here. As Wirszubski has shown, Flavius Mithridates himself, the source of so much of Pico's knowledge of Kabbalah, was influenced by the Cardinal's conception of the *coincidentia oppositorum* and imported it into his kabbalistic translations.[81] Finally, we can note that Pico also showed originality on side of the practical Cabala (as Frances Yates and others have pointed out) with his controversial alliance between Cabala and natural magic as joint witnesses to the truth of Christianity.[82] But this has been well studied and need not delay us here.

One final point concerning Pico's creation of Cabala should be mentioned. Kabbalah in its Jewish form was ancient esoteric lore meant to be communicated orally and only written down in part for conventicles of the elect. This was all well and good in its time and place, as Pico always admitted. But Cabala as a Christian missionary tool was essentially exoteric – Pico intended to dispute his cabalistic conclusions publically and he was anxious to see them into print. In order to achieve its purpose, then, Cabala had to be what Christian Knorr von Rosenroth later so well termed it: *Kabbala Denudata*. This shift was to have repercussions on Kabbalah itself – it appears to be at least part of the reason why some Jews began to publish kabbalistic texts in the sixteenth century.[83] We can catch a glimpse of another effect from a glance at Judah Abravanel, another of Pico's Jewish friends.

Judah, or Leone Ebreo as he was known in the Renaissance, wrote his *Dialoghi d'amore* about 1500–1502, though they were not published until 1535, well after his death. The *Dialoghi* are among the most remarkable products of Renaissance thought, arguably the most systematic and penetrating account of that favorite Renaissance theme, the nature and role of love.[84] This is not the place for an analysis of what Leone actually has to say about love, but two aspects of his presentation deserve note here because of the light they cast on the new situation in which Kabbalah found itself due to the challenge presented by Cabala. First, the communication of a good deal of Kabbalah in a work probably written in the vernacular (and therefore accessible even to Gentiles) was surely unusual.[85] Second, and more important, Leone's mingling of Kabbalah with a wide range of other systems of thought – pagan, Christian and Jewish – is, as Moshe Idel has stressed, a new phenomenon among Jews at the end of the fifteenth century.[86] Shlomo Pines said that Leone transformed Plato into a kabbalist.[87] It is difficult not to think that the challenge represented by Pico's Cabala had something to do with this transformation. Leone's universalizing of Judaism (reminiscent of that later created by Elijah Benamozegh at the end of the nineteenth century)[88] was probably a factor in the legend of his conversion to Christianity.[89]

Giovanni Pico della Mirandola has appeared to many as a strange, even an exotic, figure. But even the *princeps concordiae* seems normal when compared with Guillaume Postel. Several monographs have been devoted to Postel's life and thought,[90] as well as numerous studies by François Secret concerning his relation to Cabala.[91] On the basis of these accounts, it is possible to make some general remarks about what Postel contributed to Christianity's encounter with esoteric Judaism, though this is by no means to plumb everything that went on in his richly furnished and oddly lit mind.

Pico was interested in mystical experience, as his animadversions on the "binsica" indicate; Postel based his system of thought on mystical experiences, especially that of his "immutation" of 1552.[92] Pico had more knowledge of Hebrew than the majority of contemporary Christian scholars; Postel was a linguist with real command over Hebrew, Arabic and Aramaic.[93] Finally, Pico's 900 *conclusiones* imply a reformist program for Christian learning based on Renaissance universalism; Postel's hopes for the restitution of all things, however, was a mystical-apocalyptic ideology so bizarre to contemporaries that its author was spared the stake only because the authorities were convinced that he was insane.

As a young orphan, Postel began his language studies at the College Sainte-Barbe in Paris. Here he later taught and was influenced by the reformist circle of Ignatius of Loyola. It is difficult to know exactly when he came into contact with the Joachite tradition, especially in its late medieval Francophile version, but the French prophet's combination of esoteric Jewish mysticism with Joachite expectations for a coming final age of perfection on earth was at the center of his unusual program characterized by the twin phrases *restitutio omnium* and *concordia mundi*.[94] It appears that it was not until 1536, during his first trip to the East, that he made acquaintance with Kabbalah.[95]

After some years in the circle of Francis I, Postel lost the king's favor in 1543 as the result of vision he had concerning Francis's duty to begin the work of universal restitution. The scholar fled to Rome where he was admitted to the Jesuits as a novice in March, 1544, and later ordained. In December of 1545, however, Ignatius gave him leave to depart because of his strange apocalyptic ideas (Postel had already come to identify himself with the long-awaited *papa angelicus* of Joachite tradition).[96] This was a turning point in Postel's career – the hopes that he had pinned on the Jesuits as the agents of apocalyptic reform (the Joachite *viri spirituales*) began to fade. In their place he plunged into studies of Jewish esoteric literature under the guidance of an Ethiopian priest who explained the books of Enoch to him, and other scholars, such as the Hebraists Johann Albert Widmanstadt and Andraeus Masius.[97]

The key element in Postel's emerging new ideas, however, came as a result of his departure for Venice in 1547, where he met an illiterate pious woman, Madre Zuana in Venetian dialect (the "Venetian Virgin" of his written works), who had founded a hospital for the sick and poor. At the time, he was already engaged on translating the *Zohar*, and he was amazed in his conversations with Madre Zuana (also referred to as Iohanna or Jehanne in French) by her ability to reveal the secrets of the *Zohar* and Kabbalah in general. As he put it in one passage:

> She suggested from her point of view certain doubts, the deepest in the world, to which I did not know how to reply. Then she said to me: "Oh, how little you know by your own understanding." After this I found in the text of the *Zohar* the same questions she had proposed, but in the manner of the ancients, that is, with a very obscure solution, or else with the advice "vehebenzeh," that is, "think well and understand this." When I wished to make the translation [It. *Parafrasi]*, it would have been absolutely impossible for me to have accomplished it had not she who holds all the teachings of the world and possesses the key of David unfolded and developed it for me first...In the Second Coming under the Maternal Form or Figure, she knew the whole secret doctrine which from Moses until the time of Christ had been preserved in the Cabala and which from Christ the Father had been as totally hidden and ignored among envious Jews as it was among Christians.[98]

Madre Zuana, as evidenced from her miraculous perceptions of the *Zohar* and other Jewish esoteric texts, was none other than the female Messiah, the necessary feminine complement to the masculine revelation made in Jesus Christ. She was the Second Coming under the Maternal Form. Given this conviction on Postel's part, we can agree with Marion Kuntz that, "The two years in Venice under the tutelage of the 'one who held the keys of David' were the turning point in Postel's outlook."[99] He even managed to find a

Joachite confirmation of her position, noting that she had identified herself with the figure of Mary in a carved nativity in San Marco that had supposedly been ordered by Joachim himself.[100]

In 1549 Postel went off to the East to buy Oriental books and perfect his Hebrew. When he got back to Venice in 1550 Madre Zuana was dead and he returned to Paris. It was here that the most dramatic event of his life took place, the extended mystical experience he called the "immutation" that culminated on January 6, 1552.[101] Postel was convinced that the Venetian Virgin had undergone such an immutation about 1540 which made her into the female complement to Jesus. His own immutation, fully dependent on her continued activity, "destroyed" (It. *disfatta*) his old matter and made him into a new creature who was at once "COMPREHENSORE & VIATORE," in the language of Christian mysticism, one who enjoys the vision of God and yet still remains in this life.[102]

Postel's descriptions of his immutation are typical examples of the movement among sixteenth-century Christian mystics toward intense autobiographical accounts of their experiences of God. Whether we judge him authentic or not, there is no question that the immutation set the stage for the final three decades of his life. His first account of it is found in the 1553 publication entitled *Les Tres Merveilleuses Victoires des Femmes*, a book whose claims led to his second exile from France. By the same year, he had completed his first translation of the *Zohar*, which he unsuccessfully sought to have published by Oporinus in Basel. Cabala was a key factor in the French savant's increasingly complex expectations for himself, for the French monarchy, and for the world.[103] The intense efforts he continued to make down to the end of his life to get his translations published show that he was convinced that the Church's opposition to his vision of the *restitutio omnium* might be corrected if the authorities could only see that everything that he had set forth, especially the necessity for a female redemptive figure, was already contained in the "Mosaic" revelation found in the Zoharic doctrine of the union of the male and female principles. The Preface to his second version of the *Zohar* made between 1562 and 1569 puts it with unaccustomed clarity: "My one aim was to demonstrate, whereever I was allowed to, Christ in each of his comings, the purpose of the Law."[104]

By late 1554 Postel was back in Venice after a brief teaching period in Vienna. It was here that his two major defenses of his immutation and of the Venetian Virgin, *Il libro della divina ordinatione* and *Le prime nove del altro mondo*, were published in 1555. In the same year, he was called up before the Inquisition and eventually declared dangerously mad rather than heretical on September 17. He was condemned to perpetual imprisonment. Postel spent the years 1555–1559 in the Ripetta prison in Rome, but he escaped during the riots following the death of Paul IV. He returned to France, but proved incapable of staying out of trouble. In 1564 he was confined to the monastery of Saint Martin des Champs where he lived under a rather benign house arrest until his death in 1581.[105]

Pico della Mirandola found in Cabala something that functioned like the Triborough Bridge does for New Yorkers – a convenient connection between three rather different worlds. Guillaume Postel went further. This is obvious from a glance at the Preface to his second translation of the *Zohar*, an interesting mingling of an account of the history and meaning of the Jewish mystical text with a defense of his doctrine of the dual coming of Christ, his own identity as *papa angelicus*, and his hopes for France as the "judaized" nation which will save the world. According to Postel, because the *Zohar* was nothing other than the oral law given to Moses on Sinai, its true author was the Holy Spirit, or Jesus Christ.[106] This revelation was kept hidden down to the time of Simeon the Just, the Last High Priest, who received Jesus into his arms (Lk. 2:25–28) and who was responsible for writing the message down. Simeon ben Yohai, who belonged to the secret followers of Jesus among the Jews (the "Nicodemites"), later redacted it into its present form. Postel, in his role as the "pope of this natural and Zoharine theology" (*hujus theologiae naturalis et Zoharinae Papa*)[107] the one who summarizes the work of all previous prophets (and is, of course, predicted in the *Zohar*), is now to reveal its full meaning in the dawning fourth age that has begun with his immutation.[108] Once again, the esoteric must become exoteric, though Postel gives this transformation an apocalyptic dimension lacking in Pico.

Postel agreed with Pico that the four senses of Scripture are to be found in the Cabala, though he went further in asserting that they were only imperfectly present up to now among the Christian doctors.[109] He also gave greater importance to particular cabalistic texts, especially the *Zohar*, a work known to Pico only by reputation. For Postel, the *Zohar* becomes a form of "revelation of revelation," or, in Joachite terms, the *intelligentia spiritualis* of the Scriptures. Although the French prophet was a part of a long tradition that attempted to find in esoteric Judaism a proof for Christianity, with him this trajectory took a new direction. When the Venetian Virgin explained the *Zohar* to him and he in turn utilized Zoharic male-female symbolism to prove that true redemption, that is, the *restitutio omnium*, required the action of female as well as male incarnations in a new age of history, radical possibilities were opened up for Cabala that had not been available in Pico.[110] These implications are best seen in Postel's insistence that the universal religion of the dawning fourth age of history is best termed "Christian Judaism." [111]

Though Postel continued to think of himself as a good Catholic and was generally negative to the mainline Reformers (though not to the Spiritual wing of the Reformation), his insistence that true Christianity was actually Christian *Judaism* marks something of a revolution in the encounter between Christianity and esoteric Judaism. "We are Christian Jews," as he put it, "much more truly than those literal Jews of long ago, and we are Israelites as it were, because we accept and adore the King of the Jews and King of Israel, Jesus, true God, Angel of the Great Council and true man."[112] As early as 1547 in the Hebrew edition of the *Candelabri typici in Mosis tabernaculo...interpretatio*, he could describe himself as "a man from Kefar Sekania, by the name of Eliahu kol maskaliah, who has converted to Judaism through love of Israel."[113] This did not mean, however, that he had abandoned Christianity. Rather, Postel saw himself as returning to the one true religion which had been abandoned by those Jews who rejected Christ and which had also been increasingly forgotten by so-called Christians. "All the capital and primary truths" of this religion "were written in the *Zohar* just as they were in the Gospel."[114] This religion, which he later came to call Sabbathism, would triumph in the coming apocalyptic era. Hence Israel was crucial to the destiny of the world – "...and I say it was necessary *de jure* that God created the world for the sake of Israel according to final intention."[115]

Looked at from the perspective of Christian encounters with Jewish esotericism and the creation of Cabala, Postel's Sabbathism is a novel development, not least in its apocalyptic dimensions. This is why in the long run I cannot agree with William Bouwsma's judgment that Postel's cabalism was a "conservative adaptation."[116] Though it did share many assumptions with earlier uses of Jewish esotericism, it passes beyond all of them in its conviction that conversion was equally necessary (or unnecessary for the enlightened) on both sides.[117] All that was needed was the Christological reading of the *Zohar*, the exoteric dissemination of what Jewish Kabbalah had kept well hidden.

NOTES

* This essay has profited from suggestions made by participants of the 1992 Conference on Jewish Christians and Christian Jews at the Clark Memorial Library, as well as from comments from Michael Fishbane and Moshe Idel.

1. John Fisher, *The English Works* (London: EETS XVII, 1876), 335–36.
2. This tendency unfortunately marked the pioneering book in the field, Joseph Leon Blau, *The Christian Interpretation of Cabala in the Renaissance* (N.Y.: Columbia, 1944), e.g., vii and 99. In this paper, I will distinguish between authentically Jewish Kabbalah and its Christian counterpart expressed by the term Cabala.
3. According to Blau, 88, n.42: "It is questionable whether in one lifetime any scholar could trace all the excesses of those who cut cabala to suit their interpretations." For a brief overview, see Gershom Scholem, *Kabbalah* (New York: Quadrangle, 1974), 196–201.

4. Like most outsiders, my knowledge is largely based on the pioneering works of Gershom Scholem, and, more recently, on the writings of Moshe Idel.

5. Chaim Wirszubski, *Pico della Mirandola's Encounter with Jewish Mysticism* (Cambridge, MA: Harvard, 1989), 151.

6. See *Ludovicii Caelii Rhodigini Lectionum Antiquarum Libri XVI* (Basle: Froben, 1517), Bk. VI, cap. 1 (p. 251), and Blau, 100–01. For this threefold Christian understanding of Judaism in Pico, see François Secret, *Les Kabbalistes chrétiens de la Renaissance* (Paris: Dunod, 1964), 4.

7. Two recent summaries are Gilbert Dahan, *les intellectuals chrétiens et les juifs au moyen âge* (Paris: Editions du Cerf, 1990), and Heinz Schreckenberg, *Die christlichen Adversus-Judaeos-Texte (11.–13. Jh.)* (Frankfurt: Peter Lang, 1991, 2nd ed.). See also the still useful work of A. Lukyn Williams, *Adversus Judaeos: A Bird's-Eye View of Christian Apologiae until the Renaissance* (Cambridge: Cambridge University, 1935). Other helpful studies include Amos Funkenstein, "Basic Types of Christian Anti-Jewish Polemics in the Later Middle Ages," *Viator* 2(1971):373–82; Jeremy Cohen, *The Friars and the Jews. The Evolution of Medieval Anti-Judaism* (Ithaca: Cornell, 1982); and the same author's "Scholarship and Intolerance in the Medieval Academy: The Study and Evaluation of Judaism in European Christendom," in *Essential Papers on Judaism and Christianity in Conflict. From Late Reformation to the Reformation*, ed. by Jeremy Cohen (N.Y.: New York University, 1991), 310–41.

8. See Robert Chazan, *European Jewry and the First Crusade* (Berkeley: University of California, 1987); and the review of Irving Marcus in *Speculum* 64(1989):685–88. Cf. B. McGinn, "Violence and Spirituality: The Enigma of the First Crusade," *Journal of Religion* 69(1989):375–79, for the wider context.

9. On Petrus, see Schreckenberg, 69–85. Both Funkenstein, "Basic Types," 378–79; and Cohen, *Friars and the Jews*, 23–31, recognize the innovations in Petrus's views, but I believe that they do not go far enough. My evaluation of Peter's importance has been helpfully clarified by the dissertation of John Victor Tolan, *"To Slay with your own Sword." Petrus Alfonsi and his Place in the History of Medieval Thought* (University of Chicago Dissertation, 1990).

10. Tolan, 249. This dissertation discusses the transmission of the text on 182–93 and 204–52. The mss. are listed on 308–56.

11. Petrus's *Dialogi* appear in an inferior edition in J.-P. Migne, *Patrologia Latina* (hereafter PL) 157:507–605. There is a better edition (used by Tolan) in the unpublished 1982 Berlin dissertation of Klaus-Peter Mieth. The material on the Talmud can be found mostly in cc. 541–51 and 602–50. Petrus's major attack centers on the irrationality of aggadic statements that imply corporeality to God (see, e.g., cc. 541, 543, 550–51). He also appears to have some knowledge of the traditions concerning the dimensions of the divine body found in the *Shi'ur Qomah*. Michael Fishbane argues that in one place at least Petrus preserves a more original reading than that found in the preserved Talmudic texts; see his "The Holy One Sits and Roars: mythopoesis and the Midrashic Imagination, " *Journal of Jewish Thought and Philosophy* 1(1991):10–12.

12. His attitude can be conveyed by the following summary statement: Judaeos de tota lege Moysi nichil nisi parum observare et illud parum deo non placere (PL 157:593).

13. Cohen, *Friars and the Jews*, 29, admits: "...Peter may almost have arrived at the conclusion that for medieval Jewry the Talmud had supplanted the Bible as the basis for religious life and teaching – as did those who officially condemned and burned the Talmud in the thirteenth century."

14. On this distinction, see Tolan, 63.

15. See Tolan, 65–68.
16. The key figures from the Jewish side are Solomon ibn Gabirol and later Maimonides. On the former, see B. McGinn, "Ibn Gabirol: The Sage among the Schoolmen," in *Neoplatonism and Jewish Thought*, ed. by Lenn E. Goodman (Albany: SUNY, 1992), 77–109.
17. See Daniel J. Lasker, *Jewish Philosophical Polemics against Christianity in the Middle Ages* (N.Y.: Ktav, 1977), 55–57.
18. *Dialogi* VI (PL 157:606–07). On the anti-Saadia element, see Tolan, 69 n.112.
19. Despite much speculation, the *Secreta secretorum* remains unidentified and its relation to the traditions that subsequently coalesced into Kabbalah therefore conjectural at best. Alfred Buchler, "A Twelfth-Century Physician's Desk Book: The *Secreta Secretorum* of Petrus Alfonsi Quondam Moses Sephardi," *Journal of Jewish Studies* 37(1986):206–12, suggests that the work was a compilation involving three elements: (1) a magical work known as the *Sefer ha-Razim*; (2) the famous esoteric text (probably 2nd–6th cent CE) known as the *Sefer Yesira*; and (3) an alchemical text. According to this hypothesis, it was the version of the *Sefer Yesirah* found in the *Secreta secretorum* which was the source of Petrus's speculations on the Tetragrammaton.
20. I give here the whole of the key passage in *Dialogi* VI as found in the Mieth edition and cited by Tolan (pp. 71–72 n. 119): Trinitas quidem subtile quid est et ineffabile et ad explanandum difficile, de qua prophete non nisi occulte loquuti sunt et sub velamine, quoadusque venit Christus, qui de tribus una personis, fidelium illam mentibus pro eorum revelavit capacitate. Si tamen attendas subtilius et illud dei nomen, quod in Secretis secretorum explanatum invenitur, inspicias, nomen, inquam, trium litterarum quamvis quatuor figuris, una namque de illis geminata bis scribitur, si, inquam, illud inspicias, videbis, quia idem nomen et unum sit et tria. Sed quod unum, ad unitatem substantie, quod vero tria, ad trinitatem respicit personarum. Constat autem nomen illud his quatuor figuris "i" et "e" et "v" et "e," quarum si primam tantum coniunxeris et secundum, "i" scilicet et "e," erit sane nomen unum. Item si secundam et terciam, "e" scilicet et "v," iam habebis alteram. Similiter si terciam tantum copulaveris atque quartam, "v" scilicet et "e," invenies et terciam. Rursus si omnes simul in ordinem conexeris, non erit nisi nomen unum, sicut in ista patet geometrica figura. (The figure given in the edition in PL 157:611 is a circular one based on Joachim of Fiore's subsequent elaborations. All the mss. of the *Dialogi* have a triangular figure.)
21. On the *Sefer Yesirah*, see Gershom Scholem, *Origins of Kabbalah*, ed. by R. J. Zwi Werblowsky (Princeton: Princeton University, 1987), 24–35.
22. For example, Michael Fishbane informs me that the permutations of the "Great Name" YHW in the *Sefer Yesirah* involve three letters rather than two – YHW, HWY and WYH.
23. The use of the "trisagion" of Is. 6:3 as a proof of the Trinity appears in some "proto-cabalists," such as the convert Pedro de la Caballeria whose *Zelus Christi* was written about 1450. See Secret, *Les Kabbalistes chretiens*, 16–17; and Gershom Scholem, "Considerations sur l'histoire des débuts de la Kabbale chrétienne," in *Kabbalistes chrétiens* (Paris: Albin Michel, 1979), 17–46, esp. 31. (This paper first appeared in German in 1954 in *Essays presented to Leo Baeck*, but I will cite the augmented and corrected French version.) For a survey of Christian attempts to show Jewish knowledge of the Trinity, see Dahan, *les intellectuals chrétiens et les juifs*, 488–94.
24. On Origen and the Jews, see, for example, Ephraim E. Urbach, "The Homiletical Interpretation of the Sages and the Expositions of Origen on Canticles, and the Jewish-Christian Disputation," *Scripta Hierosolymitana* 22(1971): 247–75; Nicholas de Lange, *Origen and the Jews* (Cambridge: Cambridge University Press, 1976); and Reuven Kimelman,

"Rabbi Yohanan and Origen on the Song of Songs: A Third-Century Jewish-Christian Disputation," *Harvard Theological Review* 73(1980):567–95.

25. E.g., Agobard of Lyon, *De Judaicis superstitionibus* (PL 104:86–87).

26. Secret, *Les Kabbalistes chrétiens*, 8–9.

27. Peter the Venerable, *Tractatus adversus Judaeorum inveteratam duritiam* (PL 189:507–650).

28. Alan of Lille, *Contra haereticos* in Ms. Charleville, Bibliothèque Municipale 113, f. 237r, as edited in Tolan, *"To Slay you with Your Own Sword"*, 349.

29. Peter of Blois, *Contra perfidiam Judaeorum*, cap. 5, "Testimonia legis ac prophetarum de Trinitate" (PL 207:833).

30. For Joachim's views on the Trinity, see B. McGinn, *The Calabrian Abbot. Joachim of Fiore in the History of Western Thought* (N.Y.: Macmillan, 1985), chap. 6, "The Trinity in History" (pp. 161–203).

31. Joachim of Fiore, *Expositio in Apocalypsim* (Venice, 1527; reprint Frankfurt: Minerva, 1964), f. 36vb. See the whole discussion on ff. 35va–37ra. Other considerations of the IEVE, e.g., *Psalterium decem chordarum* (ibid.), ff. 257r-v, 277ra-va, do not mention Petrus by name, though the latter text interestingly includes a reference to Is. 6:3.

32. See Tolan, *"To Slay You with Your Own Sword"*, 209–10; and McGinn, *Calabrian Abbot*, 170–71 (but correct the mistake that mentions Petrus's *Disciplina Clericalis* rather than the *Dialogi*). It is clear that both the "Psaltery" figure and the "Three Circles" figure of what became the *Liber figurarum* were developed with the help of Petrus's understanding of the Tetragrammaton.

33. *Ysagoge in theologiam*, Liber II, prologus, in *Ecrits théologiques de l'école d'Abélard. Textes inédits*, ed. Arthur Landgraf (Louvain: Spiclegium Sacrum Lovaniense, 1934), 127.

34. Ibid., 281–82.

35. Alexander Neckham, *De naturis rerum. Libri duo*, ed. Thomas Wright (Rolls Series, vol. 34), 3–11. See Raphael Loewe, "Alexander Neckham's Knowledge of Hebrew," *Mediaeval and Renaissance Studies* 4(1958), 19–22; and for the connection with Jewish mysticism, Yehudah Liebes, "Christian Influences in the Zohar," *Immanuel* 17(1983–84), 56–59.

36. Gershom Scholem, "Jüdische Mystik in West-Europa im 12. und 13. Jahrhundert," *Miscellanea Mediaevalia. Band 4. Judentum im Mittelalter* (Berlin: Walter De Gruyter, 1966), 50–54; and *Origins of the Kabbalah*, 314, 375. See also Gabrielle Sed-Rajna, "L'influence de Jean Scot sur la doctrine du kabbaliste Azriel de Gerone," *Jean Scot Erigène et l'histoire de la philosophie* (Paris: CNRS, 1977), 453–63.

37. There were certainly important Neoplatonic influences on early Kabbalah, but more likely from the Arabic tradition. See Moshe Idel, "Jewish Kabbalah and Platonism in the Middle Ages and Renaissance," *Neoplatonism and Jewish Thought*, 319–51.

38. See Liebes, "Christian Influences," 43–67.

39. See Secret, *Les Kabbalistes chrétiens*, chap. II; and Scholem, "Des débuts," 26–38.

40. Moshe Idel, "Ramon Lull and Ecstatic Kabbalah. A Preliminary Observation," *Journal of the Warburg and Courtauld Institutes* 51(1988),170–74.

41. See the edition of Joaquin Carreras Artau, "La 'Allocutio super Tetragrammaton' de Arnaldo de Vilanova," *Sefarad* 9(1949):75–105; and the discussion of Eusebio Colomer, "La interpretación del Tetragrama bíblico en Ramon Martí y Arnau de Vilanova," *Miscellanea Mediaevalia* 13.2(1981):937–45. C. Wirszubski, *Pico della Mirandola's Encounter*, 166–67, notes that Arnold "foreshadowed Pico's Christianizing interpretation of the symbolism of letters," though he denies there is any proper Kabbalah in

the *Allocutio*. Ramon Marti also cites Petrus's interpretation of the Tetragrammaton in his *Pugio fidei*, tertia pars, distinctio iii, cap. iv. See *Pugio fidei* (Leipzig, 1687; reprint Farnborough, 1967), 685. On Marti's place in Jewish-Christian confrontation, see Cohen, *Friars and the Jews*, chap. 6; and Robert Chazan, *Daggers of Faith* (Berkeley: University of California, 1989), 115–36.

42. On this issue, see especially the unpublished paper by Moshe Idel, "Jewish Kabbalah in a Christian Garb: Some Phenomenological Remarks." My thanks to Prof. Idel for allowing me to cite this.

43. Idel, 11. See also M. Idel, *Kabbalah. New Perspectives* (New Haven: Yale University Press, 1988), 262–64.

44. Nicholas of Cusa, *De Pace Fidei*, ch. 1, in *Nicolai de Cusa. Opera Omnia. Vol. VII. De Pace Fidei*, edited by Raymond Klibansky and Hildebrand Bascour (Heidelberg: Meiner, 1959), 4. It is interesting to note that the role that the Jew plays in ch. 9 is as a witness to the Trinity after the Word has shown how the three Persons do not imply plurality but only "productive simplicity."

45. Marsilio Ficino, *De religione christiana*, caps. xxx–xxxiv in *Opera omnia* (Basel, 1576) Vol. 1, ff.90r–113r. On this treatise, see Charles Trinkaus, *"In our Image and Likeness". Humanity and Divinity in Italian Humanist Thought* (Chicago: University of Chicago, 1970) 2:734–53.

46. Trinkaus, *"In our Image and Likeness"* 2:722.

47. On Pico's Jewish contacts in general, see David Ruderman, *The World of a Renaissance Jew* (Cincinnati: Hebrew Union College Press, 1981), chap. 4.

48. See F. Secret, "Nouvel précisions sur Flavius Mithridates maître de Pic de la Mirandole et traducteur de commentaires de kabbale," *L'Opera e il Pensiero di Giovanni Pico della Mirandola nella Storia dell'Umanesimo* (Florence: Istituto Nazionale di Studi sul Rinascimento, 1965) 2:169–87.

49. Wirszubski, 69. For a detailed study of Mithridates' kabbalist translations as the source of Pico's *Conclusiones*, see Wirszubski, Part Two.

50. See G. Pico della Mirandola, *De Hominis Dignitate. Heptaplus. De Ente et Uno*, ed. Eugenio Garin (Florence: Vallecchi, 1942), 160 (hereafter Garin). There is no secure identity for this "Dactylus" (It. Dattilo). For a discussion, see Scholem, "Des débuts," 20–22.

51. On the connection between Pico and Alemanno's views of Kabbalah, see Moshe Idel, "The Magical and Neoplatonic Interpretations of the Kabbalah in the Renaissance," in *Jewish Thought in the Sixteenth Century*, ed. Bernard Dov Cooperman (Cambridge, MA: Harvard University Press, 1983):186–242, esp. 190, 200–03.

52. See Heinz Pflaum, "Leone Ebreo und Pico della Mirandola," *Monatsschrift für Geschichte und Wissenschaft des Judentums* 72(1928):344–50.

53. See Wirszubski, 59–64, for a summary of the kabbalist sources of Pico's two lists of cabalist theses in his *Conclusiones*.

54. See Idel, "The Magical and Neoplatonic Interpretations of Kabbalah," 88–91, for the character of Italian Kabbalah.

55. I will make use of the modern edition of Bohdan Kieszkowski, *Giovanni Pico della Mirandola. Conclusiones sive Theses DCCCC* (Geneva: Droz, 1973).

56. I will use the editions of these two works found in Garin.

57. The only full editions are to be found in the early printings. I will use the *Opera omnia* published at Venice in 1557.

58. The text of the papal brief may be found in the *Bullarium Romanum* (Turin ed.) 5:327–29. The brief condemns the whole of the *conclusiones* because of an unspecified number

of dangerous and heretical items; the documents relating to the *processus* conducted at Rome between Feb. 20 and July 31 discuss only 13 of the 900. See the edition in Léon Dorez and Louis Thuasne, *Pic de la Mirandole en France (1485–1488)* (Paris: Leroux, 1897), 114–46. For an overview of the events, see Dorez and Thuasne, 51–70. Pico was absolved of all charges by Pope Alexander VI in 1493.

59. The *Heptaplus* concludes with a cabalistic commentary on "beresit" (Garin, 374–83). For the place of this in the history of Renaissance Cabala, see F. Secret, "Beresithias ou l'interprétation du premier mot de la Genèse chez les Kabbalistes chrétiens," *IN PRINCI-PIO. Interprétations des premiers versets de la Genèse* (Paris: Etudes Augustiniennes, 1973), 235–43.

60. On the genre of Pico's *conclusiones*, see Kieszkowski, 8–9.

61. These two groups are found in Kieszkowski's edition, pp. 50–54 and 83.

62. Though there is bound to be some disagreement in this area, I count 23 other *conclusiones* that involve Cabalist teaching. See #2 "secundum Themistium" (p. 40); #55 and 71 "secundum opinionem propriam nova in philosophia dogmata inducentes" (pp. 64–65); #132 "secundum propriam opinionem...in doctrinam Platonis" (p. 70); and #11 and 67 of "conclusiones de mathematicis secundum opinionem propriam" (pp. 74, 76). Especially important are the numerous references to Cabala in the "conclusiones...secundum propriam opinionem de intelligencia dictorum Zoroastris et expositorum eius Chaldeorum" (no less than 5 of 15 – 6,7,13–15 on pp. 77–78), the 6 references out of 26 to Cabala in the "conclusiones magicae secundum propriam opinionem" (#6,7,9,15,25,26 on pp. 79–80), and finally the 6 references of 31 in the "conclusiones de modo intelligendi hymnos Orphei" (#4,5,10,13,15,21 on pp. 80–82). Thus, in sheer numbers the Cabala acounts for almost one-sixth of the *conclusiones* – far more than any other single source.

63. See Wirszubski, 187–97.

64. Prima est scientia, quam ego voco alphabetarie reuolucionis, correspondentem parti philosophie, quam ego philosophiam catholicam voco. Secunda, tercia et quarta pars est triplex merchiaua [i.e., the kabbalist "work of the Chariot," or *ma'aseh merkavah*], correspondentes triplici philosophie particularis, de divinis, de mediis, et sensibilibus naturis (ed. p. 83). On these divisions and their sources, see Wirszubski, ch. 12.

65. Nulla est sciencia, que nos magis certificet de diuinitate Christi, quam magia et cabala (ed. p. 79).

66. See the *Apologia* (Venice ed.), ff. 24v–28r. Key texts are cited in Wirszubski, 123–25. This distinction is already reflected in his defense of the conclusion before the papal commission on March 2, 1487; see Dorez and Thuasne, 125.

67. Wirszubski, 144–45.

68. *Oratio* (Garin, 154–60). This well-known text is available in several translations.

69. *Commento* III.ix, st.9 (Garin, 580–81). I make use of the translation of Sears Jayne, *Commentary on a Canzone of Benivieni by Giovanni Pico della Mirandola* (New York: Peter Lang, 1984), 169. On the relation of Cabala to the "mysteries of the Law," see #72 of the "conclusiones cabalistice secundum opinionem propriam."

70. See Wirszubski, ch. 13.

71. See "conclusiones cabalistice" #11 and 13; and *Commento* III.8, st.4 (Garin, 557–58).

72. Wirszubski, 162–69.

73. *Oratio* (Garin, 156).

74. Wirszubski, 173–75.

75. See the text in the *Apologia* (Venice ed.), f. 27r: Sicut enim apud nos est quadruplex modus exponendi Bibliam, literalis, mysticus sive allegoricus, tropologicus et anagogicus, ita est et apud Hebraeos. Litteralis apud eos dicitur Pesat...Allegoricus

Midras...Tropologicus dicitur Sechel.... Anagogicus dicitur Cabala, et hoc quia illa expositio quae dicitur ore Dei tradita Moysi, et accepta per successionem, modo praedicto, quasi semper sensum sequitur Anagogicum. On the source in Bahya ben Asher, see Wirszubski, 262–63.

76. Pico may well have been on to more than he knew here, since Gershom Scholem has argued that the fourfold interpretation developed by some thirteenth-century kabbalists probably depends on the Christian four senses. See "The Meaning of Torah in Jewish Mysticism," in *On the Kabbalah and its Symbolism* (New York: Schocken, 1960), 52–62. M. Idel agrees in *Language, Torah, and Hermeneutics in Abraham Abulafia* (Albany: SUNY, 1989), 82.

77. For some representative texts on this threefold pattern, see Blau, *Christian Cabala*, 8–9, 16, 32, 57, 105–06.

78. Idel, *Kabbalah*, 263. On the key role of hermeneutics, see also Idel's "Jewish Kabbalah in a Christian Garb," 7–9.

79. *Oratio* (Garin, 142). The same text is repeated in the introduction to the *Apologia*. Pico may have known the witness to this theme by Porphyry, as cited in Eusebius, *Praeparatio evangelica* XIV.10.

80. Illud quod apud Cabalistas dicitur Metatron, illud est sine dubio quod ab Orpheo Pallas, a Zoroastre materna mens, a Mercurio Dei filium, a Pythagora sapiencia, a Parmenide sphera intelligibilis nominatur (ed., p. 84). On Metatron rather than Hohkma as the correct reading, see Wirszubski, 199–200.

81. Wirszubski, 103–05, 238, 251.

82. See Frances Yates, *Giordano Bruno and the Hermetic Tradition* (Chicago: University of Chicago Press, 1964), Chap. V. See also Idel, "Magical and Neo-Platonic Interpretations"; and Wirszubski, ch. 12.

83. See Idel, *Kabbalah*, 256–57; and "Jewish Kabbalah in Christian Garb," 13.

84. Though influenced by both Ficino and Pico, the *Dialoghi* go far beyond any mere imitation. Anyone who reads them will agree with the remark attributed to Tullia d'Aragona, the greatest Renaissance female writer on the topic, who said, "Nei casi d'amore penso che si possa dire forse molto più e certo con più leggiadro stile, ma meglio, ch'io creda, no." Cited by Giuseppe Saitta, "La Filosofia di Leone Ebreo," *Giornale critico della Filosofia Italiana* 5(1924), 19 n.2.

85. The original language of the *Dialoghi* is a topic of controversy. Arthur M. Lesley argues that they were first written in Hebrew as an expression of a mediating Jewish humanism which sought to make Platonism serve Judaism. See his "The Place of the *Dialoghi d'amore* in Contemporaneous Jewish Thought," *Ficino and Renaissance Neoplatonism*, edited by K. Eisenbichler and O.Z. Pugliese (Ottowa: Dovehouse Editions, 1986), 69–86. In the same volume, however, Riccardo Scrivano argues that they were written "in Latin, or better yet, in the vernacular." See his "Platonic and Cabalistic Elements in the Hebrew Culture of Renaissance Italy: Leone Ebreo and his *Dialoghi d'amore*," 129.

86. Idel, "Magical and Neoplatonic Conceptions of Kabbalah," 190. Idel notes that Alemanno preceded Leone in this line.

87. S. Pines, "Medieval Doctrines in Renaissance Garb? Some Jewish and Arabic Sources of Leone Ebreo's Doctrines," *Jewish Thought in the Sixteenth Century*, 369.

88. Elijah Benamozegh in his posthumous work *Israel et l'humanité*, first published in 1900, says: "For ultimately, the Kabbalah alone is capable of restoring harmony between Hebraism and the Gentile world" (Part 1, ch. 1, from the forthcoming translation of Maxwell Luria in the Classics of Western Spirituality Series).

89. This legend seems to have begun with the Venice edition of 1541 and was furthered by Christianizing interpolations into the text. See G. Saitta, "La Filosofia di Leone Ebreo," 16–18.

90. See especially William Bouwsma, *Concordia Mundi: The Career and Thought of Guillaume Postel (1510–1581)* (Cambridge, MA: Harvard, 1957); and Marion L. Kuntz, *Guillaume Postel. Prophet of the Restitution of All Things. His Life and Thought* (The Hague: M. Nijhoff, 1981)

91. For a brief summary, see Secret, *Les kabbalistes chrétiens*, 171–86. Secret's many contributions include both editions of texts and interpretive essays. In addition, see the essay of William Bouwsma, "Postel and the Significance of Renaissance Cabalism," first published in 1954 and available in Paul O. Kristeller and Philip P. Wiener, eds., *Renaissance Essays* (New York: Harper and Row, 1968), 252–66.

92. The role of mystical experience in Postel's program deserves special emphasis, as shown in the unpublished paper of William V. Hudon, "Mystical Experience in the Life and Thought of Guillaume Postel."

93. Joseph Scaliger, however, made the snide remark that Postel was "linguarum non ignarus, sed nullius ad unguem peritus." See Kuntz, 35.

94. On Postel's place in the Joachite tradition, see Marjorie Reeves, *The Influence of Prophecy in the Later Middle Ages. A Study in Joachimism* (Oxford: Clarendon Press, 1969), esp. 287–89, 381–84, 479–81. Cf. F. Secret, "Guillaume Postel et les courants prophetiques," *Studi Francesi* 3(1957):375–95.

95. Kuntz, 25.

96. For an overview of the development, see B. McGinn, "Angel Pope and Papal Antichrist," *Church History* 47(1978):155–73.

97. Kuntz, 65–68.

98. From the *Prime nove del altro mondo, cioe l'admirabile historia...intitulata La Vergine Venetiana* (Appreso del Auttore, 1555. Unpaged; British Museum copy). I have adopted in part the English translation of H. A. Milne Home made from the French of M. Morard, *First News of the Other World* (London, 1922), 42–43. A similar passage testifying to the Venetian Virgin's ability to interpret the *Zohar* can be found in Postel's other major work describing Madre Zuana's activity, entitled *Les tres merveilleuses victoires des femmes* (Paris: Iehan Gueullart, 1553), ff. 11–12.

99. Kuntz, 89.

100. This peculiar claim reflects the old view that Joachim had ordered portrayals of the coming *viri spirituales* for the mosaics of San Marco, pictures which proved to illustrate the Franciscans and Dominicans. See Reeves, *Prophecy*, 96–100.

101. On the immutation, see the texts and discussion in Kuntz, 101–08.

102. See *Prime nove del altro mondo*, the section beginning "La Historia della Immutatione del Primogenito" (trans., 38–41). Just as Christ is the necessary New Adam and the Venetian Virgin the New Eve, Postel is the New Cain, the Messianic Child born from their union who will begin the restitution of all things.

103. Postel translated the *Zohar* twice, and also made translations of the *Sefer Yesirah*, the *Bahir*, and other Jewish mystical texts. On Postel's translations of the *Zohar*, see F. Secret, *Le Zohar chez les kabbalistes chrétiens de le renaissance* (Paris: Durlacher, 1958), 51–78, which includes a transcription of the preface to his first translation 104–14; and Secret, "L'hermeneutique de Guillaume Postel," *Archivio di Filosofia. Umanesimo e Ermeneutica* No. 3(1963):91–145, which edits the prefaces to the second version. Antonio Rotondo in his *Studi e richerche di storia ereticale italiana del cinquecento* (Turin: Giappichelli, 1974), 119–59, has further important particulars and corrections to

Secret's presentation. For general remarks on the role of the *Zohar* in Postel, see Kuntz, 110–14, 136–38, 168, 235.

104. "Praefatio in Zoaris versionem," in Secret, "L'hermeneutique," 133: Unicus meus scopus fuit Christum ubique quatenus mihi licuit in alterutro adventu suo demonstrare, finis enim Legis est.

105. Postel continued to publish tracts and to have both freedom of movement and some influence during this last period, See Kuntz, Part III (pp. 144–77).

106. Secret ed., 124.

107. Secret ed., 134.

108. This is a summary of the central message to be found in the Secret ed., 124–34.

109. See the text from the ms. found in Paris, Bibliothèque nationale, Fonds fran. 2113, f. 994, quoted in Secret, "L'hermeneutique," 112.

110. For a brief summary, see the comment from British Museum, Sloane ms. 1410, f. 381: Et veni vide Sechina est inferius (Domina mundi Jesus) et Sechina superior (masculinitas Christi et majestas), as cited in Secret, "L'hermeneutique," 102.

111. On Postel's view of Christian Judaism, see Kuntz, 129–38.

112. A text from Paris, Bibl. nat., fonds latins 3401, f. 67, as cited in Kuntz, p. 130 n.422.

113. See F. Secret, *Guillaume Postel 1510–1581 et son interpretation du Candelabre de Moyse* (Nieuwkoop: De Graaf, 1966), 13.

114. From the "Praefatio," in Secret ed., 128: ...eas omnes veritates, et maxime capitales et primarias, quas Christus de seipso voluit intelligi, et in Novi Testamenti scriptis poni, esse verissime citatas...affirmari de se esse scriptas, sit inquam cuivis demonstrabile, illas easdem in *Zohare*, sicut in Thargumis fere omnibus, et in Midrassim et Rabboth de Christo intelligi a Mosis usque temporibus sic solitas, ita ut verum consonet sic vero, necesse est de ea re, et duce Spiritu sancto, esse in *Zohare* sicut et in Evangelio scriptas.

115. "Praefatio," ed. Secret, 135: Licet enim Scriptura dicat propter Adamum, Chavam, et Cainam, eorumque posteros, de facto fuisse creatum mundum, tamen de jure est omnino necessarium, ut ille Deus, qui verissimus Israelita incarnandus ex Israelis semine volebat, quum voluntate omnino immutabili elegerit Israelem ut regnum eius iam a satanae invidia destructum restituetur et duraret in aeternum, est inquam de jure necessarium ut propter Israelem condiderit finali intentione mundum. Postel often insists that in the Maternal Coming which initiates the final age we are "judaified and israelified" (*judaificemur et israelificemur*; see Secret, 132, 136).

116. Bouwsma, "Postel and Renaissance Cabalism," 266, who goes on to explain: "It aimed at absorbing new materials into a scheme dominated by the assumptions and purposes of the past: the systematic unity of all things, the expansion of Christianity, the apocalyptic end of history."

117. See Rotondo, "Guillaume e Basilea," 133, on this aspect.

JEROME FRIEDMAN

3. THE MYTH OF JEWISH ANTIQUITY:

NEW CHRISTIANS AND CHRISTIAN-HEBRAICA

IN EARLY MODERN EUROPE

Christian Hebraica, the Christian use of Hebrew, rabbinic, or Cabbalistic sources for Christian religious purposes found new expression in fifteenth- and sixteenth-century Europe.[1] This interest in Jewish opinion must seem curious, considering that Jews were traditionally conceived as the very essence of religious blindness. Yet, several factors account for this change. The Protestant search for accurate translations of the Old Testament certainly made knowledge of Hebrew imperative. But even before the Reformation, the Italian Renaissance witnessed a nostalgic interest in classical modes of thought, including a mythical view of ancient Greek and Roman learning and, additionally, a corresponding myth of Jewish antiquity. Christian scholars did more than use Hebrew to translate the Old Testament, however, or glorify some Old Testament personalities as *prototypical Protestants*. Christian Hebraica became controversial because rabbinic sources were also used to interpret the New Testament, and most surprising of all, to examine historically central Christian doctrines. Paradoxically, these efforts all entailed close Christian cooperation with Jewish scholars and the creation of a fantastic mythology of Jewish antiquity, despite the traditional intellectual enmity separating these two religious communities. This article will describe this search for a mythical Jewish antiquity and the prominent role played by *New Christians*, recent Iberian Jewish converts to Christianity, in propagating this myth.[2]

The nostalgic Renaissance interest in the classical past provided a fundamentally positive cultural milieu for all aspects of ancient learning. Fourteenth-century humanists believed that the Christian Middle Ages experienced a deterioration of ancient learning and a loss of the cultural appreciation and insight that was fundamental to the pre-Christian world.[3] The result was a new classicism which affected virtually every aspect of fourteenth and fifteenth centuries culture from political theory to rhetoric, from painting and literature to sculpture. Even major political and religious institutions were affected by the new learning. Powerful new governments in France and Italy found Roman law far more congenial to centralized rule than was medieval feudal law.[4] The papacy even found classic pagan themes beneficial

R.H. Popkin and G.M. Weiner (eds): Jewish Christians and Christian Jews, 35–55.

to the Christian spirit and commissioned Michaelangelo to adorn St. Peter's Cathedral, specifically designed to reflect the new mood of a revived church, with aesthetic motifs drawn from the ancient pagan world. Renewed classicism was not confined to modes of public expression; another dimension to this fascination with antiquity was the *ancient theology*, the systematic use of esoteric non-Christian sources to create an incredible myth of universal intellectual development.[5]

The *ancient theology* taught that Plato and Pythagoras studied the wisdom literature of Hermes Tresmegistus at the school of the priests while traveling in Egypt. They then brought these teachings to Greece and subsequently passed them to the rest of the world. It was obvious that Hermes, who, it was believed, lived in Egypt long before the time of Moses, had additional influence. His account of creation was strikingly similar to the description in Genesis and his ideas of a *celestial ministrant* ran parallel to messianic ideas in the New Testament.[6] The best educated opinion of cultured Europeans postulated that a unilineal chain of intellectual development reached from Hermes to Moses, to Pythagoras, Plato, to Jesus, and then into the Arab and Christian worlds. Hermes was the original fount from which all philosophy, wisdom and truth spread to the rest of the world.

The myth of Hermes Tresmegistus fostered by Marsilius Ficino was discredited in the seventeenth-century. In fact, Hermes was a second or third century Egyptian syncretist who borrowed from, rather than influenced, these other schools of thought. But for almost two centuries, the Hermetic myth served the needs of an intellectually thirsty medieval Europe hoping to account for the intellectual lineage of classical ideas they, as Europeans, had somehow lost and now miraculously found again. When this spurious development was given a religious foundation, as was the case when the Christian Cabbalah was added to this amalgam, this new and amplified ancient theology proved culturally and religiously explosive.

Pico della Mirandola and Johannes Reuchlin sensitized several generations of scholars to the idea that there existed a secret, oral, Jewish-Cabbalist tradition of wisdom which predated even Hermes and stretched back over the centuries to Adam in the Garden of Eden. As a result of their efforts, generations of Christian Cabbalists believed that God gave Adam, either through Adam's initial creation or as a result of his partaking of the Tree of Wisdom, an understanding of the verbal mechanisms, codes and formulae through which creation had been effected. Through the agency of this wisdom, Adam named all the animals and plants in the Garden of Eden. In turn, this same secret oral wisdom was given to Moses on Mount Sinai along with the written law. Reuchlin explained, "Cabbalah means the perception of God's word by hearing. It is said [in Scripture] *Moshe kibbel*, which means, Moses heard, and perceived the oral law from Sinai."[7]

The key to this secret wisdom was predicated upon the mathematical evaluation of words in the Old Testament since Hebrew letters and numbers are the same. Hence, much as the Old Testament contained words with a verbal grammar, it also constituted a numerical code with its own rules of a mathematical grammar. This numerical grammar consisted of formulae such as *gematria* and *notarikon* through which letters and words of the Old Testament might be transposed and even substituted for each other and thereby give new meaning to the verbal text. By moving from the verbal to the mathematical text and back again, a scholar could force the Bible to yield its most esoteric secrets. Even more, this elucidation would provide the key to the very process of divine creation and Reuchlin spent thousands of hours attempting to discover the "wonder-working Word" through which he believed Jesus, who was the "Word," had performed his miracles.[8] In all this, Hebrew numerology provided the key and Reuchlin became ecstatic when he considered the power contained in the proper use of that language. He wrote, "When reading Hebrew I seem to see God Himself speaking," and "God wished His secrets to be known to man through Hebrew."[9] Through an understanding of Cabbalah, Reuchlin believed "that we ourselves became producers of marvelous works, above human power. And although we are at the same time constituted in nature, we hold dominion over it and work wonders, portents and miracles which are signs of the divinity–by the one name I have been eager to explain to you."[10]

According to devotees of the Christian Cabbalah, Hermes came to know of these Cabbalistic secrets and after systematizing them, passed them on to subsequent generations, including Pythagoras and Plato. The Jewish Cabbalah alone, however, without subsequent Hermetic flourishes, represented a purer and earlier form of this wisdom, totally free of the taint of medieval development so distrusted during the Renaissance. In a word, the Hermetic and neoplatonic interpretation of Christianity, so popular in Renaissance Italy, represented the very best Egyptian and Greek classical traditions while also reflecting a divine Hebrew truth as old as mankind. These culturally diverse strains of thought later merged with heterodox ante-Nicene Christian sources such as Pseudo-Dionysius. The resulting amalgam was an eclectic form of middle and neo Platonic Christianity which Reuchlin, like Ficino, was convinced went back to the first apostles and to wise Jews before that. As Reuchlin explained, "There is nothing in our philosophy that did not belong to the Jews before."[11] If this composite did not look like medieval Catholicism, so much the worse for the latter.

Judaism did in fact teach the concept of an *oral law* existing along side a written law, but not as a mystical construct. It was ironic that this concept was derived from a rather mundane rabbinic *post hoc ergo propter hoc* justification of the post-Scriptural Talmud as a legitimate method through which the Old Testament might be interpreted. More than any other corpus of Jewish writings, this body of work was considered to be inimical to Christian truth. Moreover , *Moshe kibbel* does not mean, as both Pico and Reuchlin claimed, that *Moses heard* but only that Moses received, and no oral tradition is mentioned in Scripture. It is not difficult to account for Pico's peculiar understanding of this *oral tradition* for he learned it from his major source of Cabbalistic idea, Flavius Mithridates, a highly gifted thinker and New Christian polemicist.[12] Unknown to Pico was the fact that for over a century this new version of an oral law was a stock in trade concept of New Christian converts who used Cabbalistic mysticism to explain how Judaism led into Christianity and hence, why they themselves justifiably converted to that religion. In effect, more than any other single individual, Flavius Mithridates molded two centuries of subsequent Christian Cabbalistic thought with an argument predicated upon New Christian conversionary needs. Pico, unfortunately, knew almost no Hebrew at all and very little Jewish mysticism other than what Mithridates taught him and translated for him at the rate of forty pages a day. But Mithridates was not alone. We read about similar New Christian voices from Jewish religious authorities. In 1512 Rabbi Abraham Farissol, author of the anti-Christian polemic, *Magen Avraham* [the shield of Abraham], was aware of, and regretted, the rapprochement taking place between certain former Jews and Christians. He wrote about converts "employing the idiom of the [cabbalistic] *Zohar*, the *Bereshit Rabba*, and midrashic compilations in which they proclaimed the incarnation of God, his nativity, glorification, and resurrection."[13]

It is amazing that European intellectuals became enthralled with the basic myth that lay at the heart of Christian Cabbalah for it assumed that the same people who had waged a fifteen-hundred year campaign against Christ actually possessed the essence of religious wisdom. It is doubly amazing when one considers that this notion of an oral law was, in fact, a perversion of the rather mundane rabbinic rationale for the Talmud. In any event, it was irrelevant to Christian needs if rabbinic Jews wished to believe that the Talmud was of divine origin, and was whispered into Adam's ear thousands of years before Moses even considered the possibility of burning bushes. It was equally irrelevant to Christian needs if New Christians borrowed this idea of an altered *oral law* to explain to those Jews who had not yet converted how Jewish mysticism, and not Talmudic argument was the essence of truth and might prepare the way for Christianity. But it was utterly fantastic that Christians, who possessed grace, might learn from Jews, who denied its existence. Most outrageous of all, the result was that Reuchlin proudly boasted that he, like Jesus, would be able to perform miracles when for over a thousand years Jewish anti-Christian polemicists had castigated Jesus as little more than, of all things, a magician. But then, Renaissance scholars wished to circumvent a thousand years of decayed religious development by substituting views untainted by that age and no ideas were more foreign to this medieval development than were those of Cabbalistic Judaism.

Renaissance humanists, however, were not alone in building a myth of Jewish antiquity with materials drawn from New Christian conversionary ideas. There was yet another, more orthodox, Protestant dimension to this myth.

Compared to the fantasy of Cabbalistic mythology, Protestant Hebraica would seem to be the heart of reason and in keeping with legitimate Christian ends. Hebrew was fundamentally important if proper religion would rest upon the shoulders of God's word.[14] Indeed, Protestants criticized the Roman Catholic Church for departing from Scripture and justifying these innovations through use of a method of Scriptural exposition known as the four-fold method of interpretation.[15] According to this method, a word of the Bible could be interpreted literally, allegorically, tropologically and anagogically. In other words, every single word of the Bible could have a literal meaning indicating one thing and a spiritual meaning indicating its very opposite. In an attempt to understand what Scripture actually said rather than what it could be made to indicate, Protestant authorities condemned anything but a literal/historical interpretation of God's word. In 1532 Luther recalled how "when I was a monk I was a master in the use of allegories and I allegorized everything...even a chamber pot, but afterwards I reflected on the histories...I recognized that allegories are nothing."[16] Now, however, he could write, "This is my last and best art: to translate Scripture in their plain sense. The literal sense does it...the other is tomfoolery, however brilliant the impression it makes."[17] Other Protestant scholars were equally emphatic. Capito of Strasbourg wrote, "Unless the historical interpretation...has faithfully laid the foundation, whatever reflection is built upon them will collapse in ruins, wandering about in unsure passages, making a laughing stock with its allegories."[18] The issue was simple, as the Spanish theologian Michael Servetus explained: "The Hebrew tongue, when translated into any other tongue, is defective and the spirit is almost lost."[19] But, if translation was the intent of these different scholars, they might have easily used the extensive variety of Hebrew dictionaries, lexicons and grammars prepared by earlier Christian Hebraists such as Agricola, Reuchlin, all of which were readily available. In almost all cases prominent Christian scholars bypassed the grammatical studies prepared by Christians in favor of a variety of medieval rabbinic writings. The Swiss reformer Oecolampadius was quite direct when he noted that "without the ability to read Hebrew and consult the commentaries of the Hebrews, I would not have dared to undertake Scriptural study."[20] Martin Bucer was even more effusive about rabbinic sources. When commenting about his own work, he wrote "I have strained all the powers of my nature to this end; that I should expound the individual points truly and above all according to the history."[21] To accomplish this end, Bucer used a variety of rabbinic sources including David Kimchi, Ibn Ezra and even Rabbi Solomon, though the latter troubled him. In one location he noted about them, "Amongst them there are two others, Abraham son of Ezra and David Kimchi, who have with great endeavor pursued the true significance of the words and natural word order...They interpret scarcely anything without the warrant of parallel texts which they cite with great attention to the proper sense well beyond the practice of others. I confess to the glory of God who gives all things useful, that I have been greatly aided in the commentary of the Psalms by these men, as I have indicated throughout the work."[22] Even the New Testament, though written in Greek and not in Hebrew, benefited from Hebraica. As a reluctant Luther was forced to concede "without Hebrew there can be no understanding of the Scriptures of the New Testament. Although it is written in Greek, it is full of Hebraisms."[23] In part, Protestant use of Hebrew materials reflected careful linguistic scholarship and the desire to use all good available materials. But another dimension to Protestant Christian Hebraica involved their own particular myth of Jewish antiquity.

Protestant interest in Jewish scriptural scholarship seemed more reasonable than the fantastic Cabbalistic myth of a secret oral tradition, and they rejected the fantastic Hermetic bubble, both with and without its Cabbalistic codicil. But Protestants did not reject the idea that earlier times knew truth to an extent which eluded contemporary Christianity or that Christianity must restore this truth and was able to do so. Indeed, according to Protestant systematics, the problems associated with contemporary Catholicism originated directly from its removal from Gospel truth and Apostolic Christianity. Scholars may have disagreed about the specific date of *the fall of the church*, but all agreed that the church had fallen.[24] Servetus believed the church fell in 325 when the doctrine of the trinity was accepted at the Council of Nicea and when Constantine pressed the Apostolic Christianity into service for the imperial state. Others, such as Luther, believed that the break with Apostolic faith came as late as the ninth century. Others gave no specific date but, like Erasmus, believed there had been a slow and gradual erosion of truth. Whatever their differences, all Protestant reformers wished to circumvent centuries of Christian tradition to return to, as Servetus put it, "what the first Christians believed." For these restitutionists, no less than for Christian Cabbalists, medieval Catholic tradition was perceived as erroneous and corrupted. But however seemingly reasonable the notion that Christian roots might be restored by a return to Scripture, the application of this idea proved no more useful than the seemingly fantastic Christian Cabbalah. Even more, one finds that the most strident call for Apostolic restitutionism, like the call for a Christian Cabbalah, had strong New Christian roots.

If one group of Spanish New Christians in Italy used Cabbalah as an entry path into a Christianity stripped of its medieval and therefore, Christian heritage, another, entirely different set of Spanish New Christians, for whom Cabbalah meant little, believed it was possible to tie together their ancient Jewish roots with Protestant thought.[25] Moreover, it was also in Italy that Jewish converts to Protestantism created a new rendition of what they considered a return to Ebionite Jewish-Christianity. Ebionite Christianity, perhaps the oldest Jewish-oriented Christian heresy, was firmly anchored upon the bedrock of the Epistle of James and the common sense idea that Jesus preached repentance to his own people in the tradition of Amos, Jeremiah, and other prophets. In *The Shield of Abraham*, Abraham Farissol noted that some Jewish converts to Christianity maintained precisely such views. Farrisol wrote: "One of their sages described their faith in the following manner...to observe all the practical precepts [of the Law] and at the same time to remember the Christian concept of God."[26]

From the perspective of the sixteenth century, this neo-Ebionite halfway house between Pharisaic Judaism and Apostolic Christianity came to represent a viable pathway into Christianity for former Jews [who did not share in the traditions of medieval Catholicism] much as it was also a pathway back to the Old Testament for certain evangelical Restitutionist Christians who wished to eliminate much of medieval Catholic tradition. George Williams has astutely detected these two movements in Italian Unitarianism: "that of Italian dissenters moving towards Judaism but that also of Jewish Catholics (Marranos) moving into radical Protestantism."[27] The latter group, largely associated with Juan de Valdez and Michael Servetus, would play an important role in developing the ideological foundation of Christian Hebraica as a tool to create a restored Apostolic/Ebionite Christianity.

Though Valdez may be perceived as both a Protestant as well as an evangelical Catholic, many of Valdez's contemporary New Christian followers were Nicodemites and sought to define Christianity along far more radical lines.[28] These individuals, the group Farissol called *Ebionite* converts, Williams has termed *Josephite* Anti-Trinitarian and he had argued that they were less concerned with proving the theological unity of the Godhead [which they already assumed as former Jews] than with asserting that Jesus, whose biological father was Joseph, was fully human. According to Williams, the Josephites "pressed for a complete humanization of Jesus, even to the elimination of the first and second chapter of Matthew and part of the third chapter of Luke as prejudicial to Joseph's paternity."[29] This led to a Christianity in which Jesus could be accepted, along with James or Hillel and other moralists of the Pharisaic tradition, as the greatest of moral teachers but was not in himself subject to worship and veneration. In the 1530's the Franciscan Jerome Galeato propagated this form of Judeo-Christianity. In the 1540's Jerome, Matthew, and Bruno Busale of Padua were also associated with this tendency along with John de Villafrancha, and the Neapolitan Cistercians Lawrence Tizzano and John Laurento di Buongiorno—all of whom were Josephite or Ebionite Christians.[30]

Whether this Judaizing tendency is best described as Ebionite, Josephite, or New Christian Restitutionist, it was first apparent in Naples, the Italian port of entry for many Spanish New Christians. Eventually, Padua, the home of so many non-conformist ideas and a center for Servetus' popularity in Italy, would also become a center of Judaizing New Christian activity.[31] By mid-century, this New Christian impact could be measured when Ebionites assembled in January of 1550 at the Padua home of Jerome Busale, the leader of the Paduan Anti-Trinitarians. They assembled once again that same year in Venice where they created something of an Ebionite catechism which pointedly rejected Christ's divinity.[32]

Those assembled in Venice concluded that Jesus was one of several children born to Mary and Joseph and was not God but a natural man of exceptional spiritual quality. Since Jesus was totally human, all forms of vicarious atonement were unacceptable. Christ's sole soteriological benefit for humanity lay in the simplicity of his moral teachings and the exemplary path of suffering he chose for himself. Former Jews could easily accept such views as well as the battery of supporting New Christian ideas which included a rejection of angels and devils. Additionally, the souls of the wicked died with their bodies. There was no hell but the grave. Naturally, the implications of these views were quite radical; without a divine Christ even prayer directed to Jesus might prove difficult to justify. Indeed, this early-modern form of Ethical Culture could appeal to almost anyone intent upon removing doctrine, dogma and ecclesiastical tradition from consideration while retaining some vague belief about faith, good works and the godhead. These views led an unhappy Bullinger to write to John Calvin that "the horrible heresy of Ebion teems again, that Jesus Christ was born of the corruptible seed of Joseph. In order to affirm this they must deny a good part of the gospels."[33] We might consider that rejecting large parts of the Gospels may have troubled orthodox Christians more than it troubled Restitutionist New Christians. Even more, New Christians found it just as convenient to cut away much of the medieval Catholic intellectual tradition they did not share and embrace Jesus and Mary as they would other significant mortals such as Moses and Miriam, Samson or Deborah.

New Christians carried Ebionite views along with their Hebrew skills into the Christian community. Many New Christians were employed as Hebrew typesetters and editors in the Italian printing industry.[34] Bomberg, Aldine, and other Christian presses published many Old Testament Hebrew texts for Christian use and thereby aided the spread of Christian Humanism and Reformation Scripturalism. These texts were largely produced through the efforts of such sincere New Christians as Cornelius Adelkind. Similarly, many, possibly most, teachers of Hebrew at German and other north European universities during the early decades of the 16th century were in fact recent converts. Matthew Adrian, Werner Einhorn of Bacharach, and other Hebrew teachers Luther brought to Wittenberg and about whose judaization he continually complained, were New Christians. Indeed, so many New Christians became Protestants that John Emmanuel Tremelius, the distinguished Calvinist translator and Paul Fagius' successor at Cambridge in 1549, translated Calvin's Catechism into Hebrew in 1555. Tremelius was in a position to understand the spiritual needs of New Christians and why they might be drawn to a Christian denomination which still valued the old covenant, since he had been born to Jewish parents in Ferrara in 1510.[35] Calvin, however, was already well aware of Restitutionist New Christian thought; when he read the works of Michael Servetus he encountered a full course in New Christian apologetics.

Michael Servetus rejected the trinity, and with it all Christian soteriological tradition, because that concept of the Godhead was not mentioned in the New Testament and could not be reconciled with Old Testament Jewish monotheism. Moreover, it was not apparent to logic and even the earliest ante-Nicene Church Fathers did not discuss this theory of the Godhead. All these objections to the trinity mentioned by Servetus were generally conceded by serious theologians. Yet, Christianity found the trinity a necessary, if cumbersome theological construct. Both Scripture and the early Church Fathers refer to a hidden Father, a Son who was revealed in both spirit and matter, and a paraclete coming after Jesus' death. Somehow, all three expressions of divinity must be part of the same Godhead. If each was totally separate, however, Christianity might indeed court polytheism, as Servetus argued. If they were just three different names for the same being, this construct could not provide for both a material Jesus as well as a hidden Father as part of the same Godhead. Moreover, there were important soteriological reasons why only a mortal Jesus could atone for mankind and only a divine Father could forgive them. Orthodox trinitarian formulae, for these reasons, tried to walk a delicate line between various unacceptable positions.

For Servetus the origin of the trinitarian conundrum was the direct product of rejecting Jewish monotheism. Servetus explained that the apostles, as Jews, "did not hold the trinity or three persons in the divine being but that men in later times added this."[36] Indeed, Servetus' Jewish sources even indicated when this addition to pure apostolic teaching took place, "The Hebrews affirm that there was a change in the Christian religion at the time of Constantine," Servetus explained, "and [Rabbi] Ibn Ezra affirmed this [when commenting] upon Genesis 27 where he makes mention of Constantine and [Pope] Sylvester."[37] The origin of the problem was cultural in nature and "because of the poverty of Greek names in divine names, the apostles could not express this matter [of the Godhead] to the Greeks...nor should they have caused us so much trouble had the Greeks learned Hebrew."[38] As a result, over time, the proper Hebrew view of God was lost in favor of a new and incorrect Greek view. The remedy was to recall that John and the other apostles were Jewish and he noted that "The matter will turn far easier if we do not overlook the Hebraisms here, seeing that John was a Hebrew."[39] Servetus continued, "This is a clear issue for the Hebrews: what we call person, they call image. Reader, examine from the point of original causes what the first Christians understood by the term person."[40]

Unlike Greek Christianity, Pharisaic Judaism understood the Godhead as an indwelling of emanations rather than as separate persons. Servetus noted: "The rabbis call divinity *shechina* from the verb, *shachan*, to inhabit, which signifies inhabitation. Therefore, the divinity of Christ is an inhabitation within God."[41] Servetus believed that even contemporary Jews, like the Spanish exegete Rabbi Isaac Arama, had a better understanding of the Godhead than Christianity. When discussing New Testament notions of the messiah, Servetus observed: "The Hebrews said in this sense, the messiah is from the beginning, not because of some sophistical trinity but because His person and visible form subsisted in God. Thus Rabbi [Isaac] Arama said in Genesis, that before the creation of the sun, the name of their messiah was already seated on the throne of God."[42] Servetus was not very concerned that his system was so heavily dependent upon sources seemingly inimical to Christianity. "More reliance is to be given to one truth which an enemy confesses," he argued, "than to a hundred lies on our side."[43] And, even more, were the Jews enemies?

Servetus also accommodated Jewish opinion regarding Old Testament prophecies of Christ. When treating Psalms 2.7 "Thou art my son; this day have I begotten thee" Servetus noted: "I can not refrain here from sighing when I see the replies that Rabbi Kimchi made against the Christians on this point. I find the reasons with which they sought to convince him so obscure that I cannot but weep. They argue against him that the literal meaning did not refer to David."[44] But if David did not refer to Christ, what of Isaiah,

Jeremiah or other Old Testament prophecies of Christ? Servetus went to an extreme and argued that there was no such thing as prophecy at all. He wrote, "each of the prophets pursued, according to the letter, their history, as the course of their history led them."[45] Servetus proceeded to interpret all of the Old Testament prophets along historical, non-spiritual lines of argument. Isaiah, Jeremiah and others referred not to Christ but to Cyrus, Hezekiah, Zerubabel or other contemporary heroes of the times.

Servetus' ideas were more than nominally influenced by Rabbi David Kimchi.[46] Advanced Christian students of Hebrew studied Ibn Ezra and Rashi, Rabbi Solomon, but boasted of their familiarity with David Kimchi's excellent but difficult work. David Kimchi, medieval Jewry's most prominent grammarian, exegete, and its most accomplished anti-Christian polemicist emphasized that the Old Testament text should be explained within the cultural climate producing it. On the premise that the text must have made sense to contemporaries, it could not have been referring to an individual, such as Christ, who would come only many centuries later. Christianity, on the other hand, found Jesus *prefigured* in the Old testament, even if this meant that Old Testament authors did not appreciate what they were truly writing about. In this case, David's Psalms provided a point of argument and Servetus simply accepted the totality of Kimchi's premises and views. In short, Servetus sacrificed almost all of what he considered an erroneous Christian tradition in favor of a more hostile Jewish tradition which he identified with the apostles. However extreme these positions, these ideas fell upon fertile ground in Poland, Lithuania and especially Hungarian Transylvania where Jocobus Paleologus, Symon Budny, Vehe-Glirius, Frances David and others created a highly Judaized form of Unitarianism and where the Jewish-Christian sect *Shomrei Shabbat* began their three century history.[47]

The idea, pregnant but radical, that Pharisaic Judaism was essentially the same *as what first Christians believed*, was also evident among thoroughly orthodox Protestant scholars. Indeed, however hostile they may have been to Servetian radicalism, almost all competent orthodox Christian Hebraists accepted the same logic regarding Jewish antiquity.

Sebastian Münster, professor of Hebrew and theology at the University of Basle from 1528 to 1553 was the most prolific Christian Hebraist of the sixteenth-century.[48] By the end of the century no fewer than one hundred thousand copies of his many volumes, which included grammars, dictionaries, and other linguistic aids, had been published. Münster created the first Protestant translation of the Old Testament Hebrew Bible and published many of Kimchi's works as well as other rabbinical writings. Indeed, it was Münster's editions of Kimchi's grammars and his Old Testament glosses that other Christian Hebraists used. Münster also published the excellent work by

Elias Levita, the most competent and original Jewish Hebraist since Kimchi. Though Münster was at home in Greek as he was in Hebrew, he made use of rabbinic sources for interpreting the New Testament because he assumed that Jesus was a good Jew and that his parables and ideas were best understood in terms of the Jewish culture of Judea and Samaria. Moreover, Münster assumed that Jesus spoke Hebrew, not Greek, and yet the New Testament writings were transmitted in Greek and not the language of the apostles. To place the historical Jesus into a more Jewish cultural frame of reference Münster translated the Gospel of Matthew back into Hebrew and provided the text with a cultural, demographic, and historical gloss drawn from Josephus, the Yossiphon, and other early Jewish and Christian sources.[49]

Münster's *ethnographic* approach emphasized the importance of local ethnic concerns in attempting to extract the cultural meaning of New Testament religious concepts. An ethnographic overlay could also provide the New Testament with the color, depth, and perspective that the objective language of the text might not convey. This was an extremely innovative and daring approach to Scripture for it also assumed that religious truth was as much the product of a cultural milieu as it was an expression of God's revealed truth.

The writings of Paul Fagius, certainly one of the most gifted orthodox Hebraists of his day, provide an excellent example of reformed use of rabbinic literature to explain, elucidate, if not define, Christian New Testament concepts.[50] Paul Fagius was even more extreme than Münster for he assumed that even the essence of Pharisaic Judaism could contribute to Protestant Christianity. Like Münster, Fagius was a well considered scholar and he published much Hebraica at his press in the city of Isny where he also cooperated with Elias Levita. After serving as a minister in Isny in Germany, Fagius was invited to fill Capito's position as professor of Hebrew at Strasbourg. He was also invited to fill a similar position at the University of Constance and the Landgrave of Hesse offered him the chair of theology at Marburg. in fact, Fagius went to Constance where he remained for two years, then went to Strasbourg and eventually accepted a position at Heidelberg at the invitation of Frederick II, the Elector of the Palatinate. When Strasbourg returned to the Catholic Church during the Smalkaldic wars of religion, Fagius accompanied Bucer to England, where he died in 1549.

No work more clearly typified the nature of Fagius' interest in Hebraica than his small treatise entitled *Hebrew Prayers*.[51] This was not a translation of the Old Testament and not even a discussion of New Testament *Hebraisms* but a short volume describing contemporary Jewish blessings over wine, bread and fruits and also the Jewish long grace recited after meals. Far from wishing to provide simple ethnographic information, as Münster might have done in a similar effort, Fagius had other ideas. At the time of publication, Catholics and Lutherans were deeply divided over the meaning and celebration of the Lord's Supper. Within Protestant ranks, Lutherans and Calvinists were equally at odds about the meaning of this ritual. While Christians argued by attempting to explain the words of the New Testament in various ways, Fagius pointed out what other Christians ignored: these rituals predated Christ by several centuries and, even more, that "such customs of blessings from that time have still endured among the Jews."[52] Fagius explained that "you have here, Christian reader, the customary table blessings of the Jewish people, which are used to this very time on festive and celebration days...and which Luke the evangelist describes when he makes mention of the cup both before and after the Lord's Supper."[53] Fagius described how the head of the family blessed the wine and the bread and how they were divided among all the participants at the table. Fagius' explanation of the Jewish long grace also had meaning for Christians. He wrote, "this is the cup which Christ commended to His disciples at His meal, along with the mysteries of his blood."[54] In the remainder of the volume Fagius examined other Jewish blessings and presented them in a Christian context as well. Clearly, Fagius believed that if one wished to know what the first Christians believed, one might investigate the rituals of contemporary Jews, rituals which Jesus would have recognized long after his death.

This same pro-Pharisaic approach characterized many other of Fagius' publications such as his translation of the apocryphal *Book of Tobit*, and the minor Talmud treatise *The Ethics of the Fathers*.[55] Each of these publications dealt with another aspect of Jesus' pharisaic religious culture which Fagius believed has application to Protestantism. The story of Tobit told about a man living during the Assyrian conquest of Israel in 722 BC. At that time, the populations of ten of Israel's twelve tribes were carried away in captivity. While all of those about him assimilated into Assyrian culture, Tobit refuses to do so and practiced whatever rituals were possible. Tobit especially participated in rituals involving the preparation of bodies for burial, for which he could hope for no compensation. Fagius argued that Tobit remained a good Jew because he was able to practice some few rituals but primarily because of his abiding faith in the Hebrew God. In this sense, Tobit the Pharisee was actually a good Protestant.

Fagius' very favorable assessment of rabbinic culture also pervades his translation from Aramaic of *The Ethics of the Fathers*, which concerned Pharisaic social ethics and personal morality. Fagius' treatment of this work was unique for he was able to extract Christian notions of piety and grace from a pharisaic work usually considered anathema by Christian authorities. Yet, over and again Fagius demonstrated how the content of this treatise was Christian in nature. On almost every page we read "This sentence clearly agrees with the sayings of Christ."[56] Over and again Fagius concluded, "This sentence makes clear to what extent the *Ethics* agrees with the doctrines of the apostles of Christianity."[57] Fagius was not troubled that in all these many pages the rabbis demonstrated religious wisdom but lacked an appreciation of Christ. This was the great difference between Judaism and Christianity, all the more unfortunate considering how close the religions were in other respects.

These similarities were again emphasized in Fagius' translation and critical edition of the *Wisdom of ben Sira*, a book of Jewish moral maxims and aphorisms written in Aramaic dating from the second century before Christ.[58] Regarding the moral value of these maxims, Fagius observed that "the ancient wisdom of the ancient Jewish people, who more than other ancient people of the earth, had precepts known to them from God."[59] Despite the Pharisaic nature of these admonitions to righteousness and good works, Fagius believed they were of great value "for the cultivation of piety, the formation of morals in an institutional life, which certainly must be the proper goal of all our studies."[60]

While Münster and Fagius were both totally orthodox Protestants, their writings provoked a great storm of criticism from more conservative scholars for whom the differences between Judaism and Christianity were more clear cut. Luther, especially, was upset that Jesus seemed to look more and more Jewish. There was, after all, a huge difference between Judaism and Christianity and Luther advised that great care must be exercised lest the Hebrew context dictate the meaning of the Christian message itself as merely a variant of contemporary Jewish thought. Additionally, Lutherans were distressed by this creative Christian use of an Old Testament-based Pharisaic culture since so much of Lutheranism is predicated upon the Pauline dichotomy of Law and Gospel which envisioned the Pharisee as the essence of everything Christianity opposed. For Lutherans, use of Hebrew was acceptable but only if nothing Jewish went along with it.[61]

While Calvinism accepted the continuing validity of the old covenant and, as a result, the Old Testament and the value of Jewish studies, it did not encourage overt reliance upon Jewish sources. Too many theological radicals made dangerous use of the Old Testament social ethics for advancing a revolutionary social/economic agenda. Some peasant insurrectionists, for instance, believed that the Old Testament concept of a fifty year jubilee, when all land returned to its original owners, justified the forceful confiscation of land from wealthy feudal landlords.[62] Then too, Calvin believed he saw the worst effects of excessive rabbinic authority in the Restitutionist opinions of those who believed that the Apostolic or Jewish Christian idiom should be restored. In his encounter with Michael Servetus' writings and then with the Spanish theologian himself, Calvin was horrified that rabbinic authorities might be used to validate the authenticity and acceptability of Christian dogma. It was this body of work which led to Servetus' execution in Geneva at Calvin's hands. Curiously, it was Michael Servetus who sent Calvin copies of his writings, believing that he and the French reformer shared a common notion of Jewish antiquity. It would seem he was wrong.

At no time did either Münster or Fagius accept Servetus' radicalism, which they detested. But at not time did they diverge from the same mythical view of Jewish antiquity which made Servetus' radicalism possible.

Neither Münster, nor Fagius nor Servetus ever questioned the single lynch-pin of their religious argument, the equation of Judaism and Christianity. How could Servetus equate ancient Christianity with Pharisaic Judaism when the latter clearly rejected the former? Hence, in assuming that ancient Judaism provided a sure foundation for early Christianity, Servetus essentially rejected all those beliefs and ideas entertained by Greek and Latin Church Fathers, which set Christianity apart from Judaism. Yet, the ancient Judaism Servetus envisioned existed only within his own sixteenth-century Spanish imagination and was not much more realistic than the myth of Jewish antiquity motivating Christian Cabbalists. They also imagined, through their sixteenth-century European eyes, that they could see the reflection of their own views in ancient waters.

The more orthodox Münster and Fagius found Hermes and cabbalah laughable. Still, both Münster and Fagius, and other orthodox scholars believed that one could hop-scotch backwards in time, pick up Jesus' Jewish roots and then **re**discover and **re**establish the original Gospel idiom as if the intervening years and developments were just so much dirty clothes to be changed and discarded. Despite the differences between Pico, Servetus, Münster and Fagius, for all these scholars ancient Judaism and early Christianity were more alike than were ancient and medieval Christianity. In all cases, a Renaissance inspired dislike for all things medieval Catholic led to the ennoblement of the ancient Pharisaic Jew as a proto-Protestant, as a knowing magus or as an Ebionite. In all cases, New Christians helped mold these visions of the past because they enabled the religious integration of Jewish converts without their having to accepts miles of medieval inconvenience.

In the end, all of these desires to return to an apostolic antiquity remained merely fond wishes because that age, like Eden, never really existed. Both sets of myths assumed that Jesus and the apostles were Cabbalistic [alternative: Ebionite] Jews sorely misunderstood by the subsequent Greek and Latin culture which incorrectly transmitted this mystical Cabbalistic [Ebionite] spiritual message to medieval Christianity which, in turn, further corrupted even this already faulted message.

Other historical obstacles also made myths of the past irrelevant. By the middle of the sixteenth century, Protestantism, like the medieval Catholicism it hoped to replace, became mired in sectarian doctrinal conflict, embedded in the political problems involving rulers and princes that afflicted medieval Christianity, and was flayed upon the same superstitious popular belief surrounding saints and miracles that had become medieval religion. In short, however strenuously some innovative thinkers might have opposed historical Christianity, the search for an ideal and truthful Christian past was no more intellectually viable than Pico's return to Hermetic truth or to the garden of Eden and no more apt to be accepted by powerful rulers, common people attuned to shrines, pilgrimages and prodigies than by the Catholic Church itself. As a result, the myth of Jewish antiquity left few permanent developments.

By 1553 Servetus had been executed for heresy in Geneva, Fagius and Münster were both dead and no new generation of outstanding Christian Hebraists took their place. Even Transylvanian Unitarianism ultimately found Ebionite Restitutionism too Jewish. By the end of the seventeenth century, Hermes was proven to be a second or third century Egyptian syncretist rather than the fount of all wisdom, and the myth of Egyptian wisdom as well as that of a Christian and Jewish antiquity collapsed. The New Christian scholars that had played an important role in the molding of both myths were now assimilated into Christian circles and no longer needed these conceptual bridges reaching from the Jewish to the Christian communities. As a result, visions of the glorious past faded and were replaced with visions of the glorious future in which the coming progress of mankind would lead into some utopia strikingly similar to the condition devoted followers of ancient theology and Christian Cabbalah thought they had discovered in the Garden of Eden. Jews wishing to assimilate into a new enlightened, rationalist and progressive cultural milieu would, once again, play a leading role in building this new mythology predicated upon future expectations much as they played an important role in explicating cultural interpretations of a noble antiquity. Whether forward or backward looking, New Christians of the early period as well as assimilated rationalist Jews of the modern period, created ideologies that were merely an expedient tool to facilitate their assimilation while deluding themselves with the possibilities of social change. They, like Servetus, were wrong.

NOTES

1. Christian Hebraica, here distinguished from Christian Cabbalah, has an extensive bibliography. See Jerome Friedman, *The Most Ancient Testimony, Sixteenth-Century Christian*

Hebraica in the Age of Renaissance Nostalgia, (Athens, 1983); J. Perles, *Beitrage zur Geschichte der Hebräischen Studien* (Munich, 1884); Ludwig Geoger, *Das Studium der Hebräische Sprache in Deutschland nom Ende des 15 bis zum mitte des 16 Jahrhunderts* (Breslau, 1870); H. Hailpern, *Rashi and the Christian Scholars* (Pittsburgh, 1963). Standard literature on the Christian Cabbalah includes: Gershom Scholem, "Zur Geschichte der Anfänge der Christlichen Kabbalah,"*Essays Presented to Leo Beack* (London, 1954); Joseph L. Blau, *The Christian Interpretation of the Cabala in the Renaissance* (New York, 1944); François Secret, *Le Zohar chez le Kabbalistes chrétiens de la Renaissance* (Paris, 1958), and *Les Kabbalistes chrétiens de la Renaissance* (Paris, 1964); Catherine Swietlicki, *Spanish Christian Cabala: The Works of Luis de León, Santa Teresa de Jesus and Juan de la Cruz* (Columbia, 1980); Frances A. Yates, *The Occult Philosophy in the Elizabethan Age* (London, 1979); E. Benz, *Die Christliche Kabbala: Ein Steifkind der Theologie* (Zurich, 1958); L. Gorny, *La Kabbale: Kabbale juive et Cabale chrétiennes* (Paris, 1977); and Jerome Friedman, *op. cit.*.

2. Historians disagree concerning the extent to which New Christians were actually Marranos, or secret Jews. This problem is discussed by the following: Cecil Roth, *This History of the Marranos* (1932. New York, 1974) is generally considered a romantic exaggeration. More persuasive is Perez Zagorin's *Ways of Lying: Dissimulation, Persecution and Conformity in Early Modern Europe* (Cambridge, 1990); from a different point of view, see Jerome Friedman "Jewish Conversion, the Spanish Pure Blood Laws and the Reformation: A Revisionist View of Racial Antisemitism," *Sixteenth Century Journal*, 18 (1987): 3–29; Benjamin Netanyahu, *The Marranos of Spain from the Late XIVth to the Early XVIth Century According to Contemporary Jewish Sources* (New York, 1966) and his *Don Isaac Abravanel, Statesman and Philosopher*, (Philadelphia, 1953); Yosef H. Yerushalmi, *From Spanish Court to Italian Ghetto: Isaac Cordoso, A Study in Seventeenth Century Marranism and Jewish Apologetics* (New York, 1971) and *The Reeducation of Marranos in the Seventeenth-Century* (Cincinnati, 1980) and *Assimilation and Racial Antisemitism* (New York, 1982); Antonio D. Ortiz, *Los Judeoconversos en Espanya y America* (Madrid, 1971); Israel S. Revah, "Les Marranes," *Revue des études juives* 117 (1959): 29–77; Juan Blazquez Miguel, *Inquisition y Cripto judaismo* (Madrid, 1988); Angela S. Selke,*The Conversos of Majorca: Life and Death in a Crypto-Jewish Community in XVII Century Spain* (Jerusalem, 1986); Luis Coronas Tejeda, *Conversos and Inquisition in Jaén* (Jerusalem, 1988); Yosef Kaplan, *From Christianity to Judaism: The Story of Isaac Orobio de Castro*, trans. by Raphael Loewe (Oxford, 1989); and, Antonio J. Saraiva, *Inquisição e critãos-Novos* (Porto, 1969).

3. See, Roberto Weiss, *The Renaissance Discovery of Classical Antiquity* 2nd. ed. (Oxford, 1988); Michael Mooney, ed., *Renaissance Thought and Its Sources* (The writings of Paul O. Kristeller) (New York, 1979); Albert Rabil, Jr., ed., *Renaissance Humanism: Foundations, Forms, and Legacy*, 3 vols. (Philadelphia, 1988).

4. See, for instance, Myron P. Gilmore, *Argument from Roman Law in Political Thought, 1200–1600* (New York, 1967); Paul Vinogrodoff, *Roman Law in Medieval Europe*, 2nd. ed., (oxford, 1972); Lauro Martinez, *Lawyers and Statecraft in Renaissance Florence* (Princeton, 1978); and for the papacy, John F.D'Amico, *Renaissance Humanism in Papal Rome* (Baltimore, 1983).

5. For the ancient theology, see the following: D.P. Walker, *The Ancient Theology* (London, 1972); *idem, Spiritual and Demonic Magic from Ficino to Campanella* (London, 1958); Frances A. Yates, *op. cit.*; *idem, The French Academies of the Sixteenth Century* (London, 1947, reprint 1967); *idem, The Theatre of the World* (London, 1969); *idem, The Rosicrucian Enlightenment* (London, 1972); J.N. Hillgarth, *Ramon Lull and Lullism and*

Fourteenth-Century France (Oxford, 1971); Charles G. Nauert, *Agrippa and the Crisis of Renaissance Thought* (Urbana, 1965); Brian Copenhaver, *Symphorien Champier and the Reception of the Occult Tradition in Renaissance France* (The Hague, 1978).

6. Concerning Hermes, see Frances A. Yates, *Giordano Bruno and the Hermetic Tradition* (London, 1964); A.J. Festugiere, *La revelation d'Hermes Tresmegistus* (Paris, 1944-45); Conrad Eisenbichler, *et al.*, ed.s, *Ficino and Renaissance Neoplatonism* (Ottawa, 1986).

7. Johannes Reuchlin, *De Arte Cabbalistica*, (1517) p. 23.

8. Johannes Reuchlin, *De Verbo Mirifico* (Basel, 1494) f. A2^r· Concerning Reuchlin, see: Ludwig Geiger, *Johannes Reuchlin: Sein leben und Seine Werks*(Leipzig, 1871); Max Brod, *Johann Reuchlin, Sein Leben und sein Kampf* (Stuttgart, 1965); and, Guido Kisch, *Zasius und Reuchlin* (Constance, 1961).

9. Johannes Reuchlin, *Briefwechsel*, edited by L. Geiger (Tübingen, 1875). Letter of October 11, 1508, no. 102, p. 105.

10. J. Reuchlin, *De Verbo Mirifico* (Basel, 1494) f. B4^r, *et al.*

11. J. Reuchlin, *De Arte Cabbalistica* (1517) p. 23.

12. Chaim Wirszubshi's, *Pico della Mirandola's Encounter with Jewish Mysticism* (Cambridge, 1989) provides an exceptional description of Pico's reliance upon Flavius Mithridates.

13. Samuel D. Lowinger, "Selections from the Magen Avraham of Abraham Farissol," in *Hazofe le-Hochmat Yisrael*, ed. S.D. Lowinger (Budapest, 1928) pp. 277-297; see also his "Recherches sur l'oevre Apologistique d' Abraham Farissol," *Revue des etudes juives*, 105 (1939):24. See note 55 below.

14. For a discussion of Hebraica within Protestant circles, see the following by Jerome Friedman: "Michael Servetus: The Case for Jewish Christianity," *Sixteenth Century Journal*, 4 (April, 1973): 87-110; "Sebastion Münster, the Jewish Mission, and Protestant Antisemitism," *Archive for Reformation History*, 70 (1979): 238-259; "Sixteenth-Century Christian Hebraica: Scripture and the Renaissance Myth of the Past," *Sixteenth Century Journal*, 11 (1980): 65-85; "Luther, Forster, and the Curious Nature of Wittenberg Hebraica," *Bibliotheque D'Humanisme et Renaissance*, 42 (1980): 611-619; "Protestants, Jews and Jewish Sources," *Piety, Politics, and Ethics*, ed. Carter Lindberg (Kirksville, 1984): 139-156; "Unitarians and New Christians in Sixteenth Century Europe," *Archive for Reformation History*, 81 (1990): 216-238; and, "Alienated Cousins: Jews and Unitarians in Sixteenth-Century Europe," *The Proceedings of the Unitarian Universalist Historical Society*, vol. XXII, part 1 (1990-91): 63-76.

15. On this subject, see: Henri De Lubac, *Exegede Médiéval: Les Quatre Sens de l'Ecriture*, 4 volumes (Paris, 1959); C. Spicq, *Esquisse d'une histoire de l'exégèse latine au moyen age*, (Paris, 1944); Beryl Smalley, *The Study of the Bible in the Middle Ages*, 2nd ed., (London, 1952).

16. Cited in Friedman, *The Most Ancient Testimony*, p. 127. Concerning Luther's approach to Scripture, see J.S. Preus, *From Shadow to Promise* (Cambridge, MA, 1969); Heinrich Bornkamm, *Luther and the Old Testament* (Philadelphia, 1969).

17. Friedman, *The Most Ancient Testimony*, p. 128.

18. Wolfgang Capito, *In Habakuk Prophetam...* (Strasbourg, 1526) f.5^r· Concerning Capito, see James Kittelson, *Wolfgang Capito: From Humanist to Reformer* (Leiden, 1975).

19. Michael Servetus, *Biblia Sacra ex Santis Pagnini Tralatione...* (Lyon, 1542) Introduction. Roland Bainton's biography *Michael Servetus: The Hunted Heretic* (Boston, 1953) remains the best introduction to Servetus' life and views. For an in-depth analysis of Servetus' views with particular reference to his use of Jewish sources and exegesis, see my *Michael Servetus: A Case Study in Total Heresy* (Geneva, 1978). On Servetus' radical

exegetical method, see my "Servetus and the Psalms: The Exegesis of Heresy," *Histoire de l'exegese au XVIe siecle*, ed. Olivier Fatio (Geneva, 1978), 164–178.

20. J. Oecolampadius, *In Iesaiam Prophetam Hypomnematon* (Basel, 1525) f. a3vo.

21. Martin Bucer, *Sacrorum Psalmorum Libri Quinque* (Basel, 1547). Sig. 5^{b}·23. See J. Müller, *Martin Bucers Hermeneutik* (Gütersloch, 1965).

22. ibid., In the *Ratio Explanationis*, following the two introductory prefaces.

23. P. Smith, "Conversations with Luther," *Table Talk* (Boston, 1915) pp. 181–2.

24. For the concept of the fall of the church, see Franklin Littel, *The Origins of Sectarian Protestantism* (Formerly, *The Anabaptist View of the Church*) (New York, 1964) pp. 46–78. Also, George Williams, *The Radical Reformation*, 3rd. rev. ed. (Kirksville, 1992).

25. The religious tendencies of New Christians rarely receive adequate investigation. Both Christian and Jewish scholars generally assume all New Christians were really secret Jews, if for different reasons. Unfortunately, this view is incorrect. On the subject of New Christian religious tendencies, see the following by Jerome Friedman: "New Christian Religious Alternatives," *1492 and After*, forthcoming; "Jews and New Christians in Reformation Europe," *Reformation Europe: A Guide to Research*, ed. William Maltby (St. Louis, 1992): 129–158; "Jewish Conversion and the Spanish Pure Blood Laws: A Revisionist View of Racial Antisemitism," *Sixteenth Century Journal*, 18 (1987): 4–29.

26. Abraham Farissol, *Magen Avraham (The Shield of Abraham)*, cited in Samuel Lowinger, "Additional Citations from Rabbi Abraham Farissol's The Shield of Abraham," *Revue des etudes juives*, n.s. 5(1940): 43. On Farissol, see Hayim Hillel Ben-Sasson, "The Reformation in Contemporary Jewish Eyes," *Proceedings of the Israeli Academy of Sciences and Humanities*, 4 (Jerusalem, 1969–70) 239–326. I present a different view of Jewish attitudes in my "The Reformation in Alien Eyes: Jewish Perceptions of Christian Troubles," *Sixteenth Century Journal* 14 (1983): 23–40. See note 12.

27. George H. Williams, "The Two Social Strands in Italian Anabaptism, ca. 1526–1565," *The Social History of the Reformation*, L.P. Buck and J.W. Zophy, eds. (Columbus, 1972) pp. 161 f.

28. See Marcel Bataillon, "Juan de Valdés nicodémite?" *Aspects du libertinisme au xvie - siecle* (Paris, 1947); Jose Nieto, *Juan de Valdes and the Origins of the Spanish and Italian Reformation* (Geneva, 1970); Edmondo Cione, *Juan de Valdés: La suo pensiero religioso*, 2nd. ed. (Naples, 1963); and, A. Gordon Kinder, *Spanish Protestants and Reformers in the Sixteenth Century* (London, 1983).

29. Williams, "The Two Social Strands," p. 161f.

30. ibid., pp. 176–181.

31. For Italian restitutionism, see Delio Cantimori, *Eretici Italiani del Cinquecento Ricerche Storiche* (Florence, 1939) and *Per la Storia degli Eretici Italiani del Seculo XVI in Europe* (Rome, 1937); Aldo Stella, *Dall' Anabattismo al Socianismo nel Cinquecento: Ricerche Storiche* (Padua, 1967) and *Anabattismo e Antitrinianismo in Italia nel XVI Seculo: Nuove ricerche storiche* (Padua, 1969).

32. See Williams, "The Two Social Strands," p. 180f.; Stella, *Anabattismo e Antitrinarianismo*, pp. 64–72; and, Emilo Combra, "Un sinodo Anabattista a Venezia, anno 1550," *Revista Cristiana* 13 (1885): 21–24, 83–87.

33. Cited by Williams, "The Two Social Strands," p. 177.

34. For a discussion of the relationship between Jewish converts to Christianity and early Christian printers, see J. Friedman, *The Most Ancient Testimony*, p. 36; David Amram, *The Makers of Hebrew Books in Italy* (Philadelphia, 1909); and, H.F. Brown, *The Venetian Printing Press* (New York, 1891).

35. On Tremelius, see *The Dictionary of National Biography*, ed. Leslie Stephen (Oxford, 1917) 19:1112. The title of Tremelius' Hebrew translation of Calvin's catechism is *Sefer Chinuch B'Chirei Yah [Catechism of the Elect]* (London, 1554). On Tremelius' importance for Christian Hebraica, see Friedman, *The Most Ancient Testimony*, p. 250.

36. Michael Servetus, *Restitutio Christianismi* (Vienna, 1553) pp. 399–400; *De Erroribus Trinitatis, libri Septem*, f. 42b–43a.

37. Servetus, *Restitutio Christianismi*, pp. 399–400.

38. Servetus, *De Erroribus Trinitatis, libri Septem*, f. 15b.

39. *ibid.*, f. 117a.

40. Servetus, *Restitutio Christianismi*, p. 108.

41. *ibid.*, p. 38.

42. *ibid.*, p. 134. Rabbi Isaac ben Moses Arama (1420–1494) author and popular preacher, exerted an important influence upon late fifteenth-century Spanish Jews. He was exiled from Spain in 1492 and settled in Naples where he died two years later. His important work, *Akedath Yitzchak* which provided an interpretation of the five books of Moses, was not generally known among Christian scholars. See B. Heller Willenski, *Rabbi Yizhac Arama u-Mishnato* (in Hebrew) (Jerusalem, 1958).

43. Servetus, *De Erroribus Trinitatis, libri Septem*, f. 43a.

44. Michael Servetus, *De Erroribus Trinitatis, libri Septem* (Hagenua, 1531) f. 56b.

45. Michael Servetus, *Biblia Sacra ex Santis Pagnini Tralatione...* (Lyon, 1542). Introduction.

46. Concerning Kimchi, the reader might consult the following: Frank Talmage, *David Kimchi* (Cambridge, MA, 1976); also by Talmage, "David Kimchi as Polemicist," *Hebrew Union College Annual*, vol. 38 (1967); and, "David Kimchi and the Rationalist Tradition," in volume 34 of that same journal. While many Old Testament books were important for both Jewish and Christian messianic arguments, the Psalms were particularly important because David's autobiographical language, if applied to Christ, would have God speaking about the messiah in the first person in language that could have little meaning for David. This would mean, from the Jewish point of view, that David had little real idea of what he was saying. See J. Baker and E.W. Nicholson, *The Commentary of Rabbi David Kimchi on Psalms CXX–CL* (Cambridge, 1973); R.G. Hobbs, "Martin Bucer on Psalm 22: A Study in the Application of Rabbinic Exegesis by a Christian Hebraist," *Historie de l'exégèse au XVIe siècle*, ed. O. Fatio (Geneva, 1978); E.G. Kraeling, *The Old Testament Since the Reformation* (London, 1955); and, Jerome Friedman, "Servetus on Psalms," *Histoire de l'exégèse au XVIe siecle*, ed. O. Fastio (Geneva, 1978).

47. Concerning the role of Judaization in the Lithuanian and Transylvanian Unitarian movements in the second half of the century, see Jerome Friedman, "Unitarians and New Christians in Sixteenth-Century Europe," *Archive for Reformation History*, 81 (1990); George H. Williams, "The Christological Issues Between Frances David and Faustus Socinus During the Disputation of the Invocation of Christ, 1578–1579," *Antitrinitarianism in the Second Half od the 16th Century*, eds. R. Dan and A. Pirnat (Leiden, 1982):287–321. Concerning Jewish Christian sects finding their origin during these years, see *The Encyclopedia Judaica* 15:140; Antal Pirnat, *Die Ideologie der Siebenbürger Antitrinitarier* (Budapest, 1961). The following studies about individual Judaizers will also prove useful: For Paleologus, Karl Landsteiner, "Jacobus Paleologus," in *XXIII Jahres-bericht über das K.K. Josefstädter Ober-Gymnasium für das Schuljahr 1873* (Vienna, 1873); Antal Pirnat, "Jacobus Paleologus," in *Studia nad arianizmem pod redakcja Ludwika Chmaj* (Warsaw, 1959); Stanislas Kot, "Jacque Paleologue, defenseur de Servet," in *Autour de Michel Servet et de Sebastien Castellion*, ed. B. Becker (Haarlem, 1953): 104–106. For Symon Budny, see Stanislas Kot, "Szymon Budny: Der grösste Häretiker Litauens im 16 Jahrhunderts,"

in *Studien zur Älteren Geschichte Osteuropas*, 1(Graz, 1956):63–118; Earl M. Wilbur, *A History of Unitarianism in Transylvania*, 349, 368–371; Williams, *Radical Reformation*, index S.V. Budny. For Vehe-Glirius, a neglected but talented Judaizing theologian see Robert Dan, *Matthia Vehe-Glirius, Life and Work of a Radical Antitrinitarian and His Collected Writings* (Leiden, 1982).

48. For the most recent discussion of Münster's views, see Friedman, *The Most Ancient Testimony*. The standard studies of Münster are: K.H. Burmeister, *Sebastion Münster: Versuch eines biographischen Gesamtbildes* (Basel, 1963); and, *Eine Bibliographie mit 22 Abbildungen* (Weisbaden, 1964); also, Victor Hantzsch, *Sebastion Münster, Leben, Werk, Wissenschaftliche Beduntung* (Leipzig, 1898).

49. Sebastion Münster, *Evangelium Secundum Mattaeum in Lingua Hebraica...* (Basilae, 1537).

50. Paul Fagius' interest in rabbinics and an analysis of the Jewish sources he used for exegetical purposes is presented in Friedman, *The Most Ancient Testimony*. The best biography of Fagius is R. Raubenheimer, *Paul Fagius aus Rheinzabern* (Grunstadt, 1957).

51. Paul Fagius, *Precationes Hebraicae quibus in Solemnioribus Festis Iudaei...* (Isny, 1542).

52. Prefatory letter to the above.

53. *ibid.*

54. *ibid.*, f.A3.

55. Pal Fagius, *Tobias Hebraice...* (Isny, 1542); *Sententiae Vere Elegentes Piae...* (Isny, 1541).

56. See Friedman, *The Most Ancient Testimony*, pp. 113–114, for Fagius' many approving statements of the *Ethics*.

57. Fagius, *Tobias Hebraice...*, p. 4, and Friedman above.

58. Paul Fagius, *Ben Syrae, Vetustissimi authoris Hebraei* (Isny, 1542).

59. *ibid.*, f. A1.

60. *ibid.*

61. Luther's much favored Hebraist, Johannes Forster, had novel ideas. Forster's Hebraica was of an interesting sort because its only value lay in expurgating anything *Jewish* from study of that language. Forster believed, for instance, that Aramaic was a Jewish invention created to fool Christians, as did Luther, and that Hebrew three letter verb structure was predicated upon the persons of the trinity. For a complete discussion of this unusual linguist, see my *The Most Ancient Testimony*, pp. 165–176; and Friedman, "Luther, Forster, and the Curious Nature of Wittenberg Hebraica," *Bibliotheque D'Humanisme et Renaissance*, 42 (1980): 611–619.

62. See Hans J. Hillerbrand, "The German Reformation and the Peasant's War," *The Social History of the Reformation*, eds. L.P. Buck and J.W. Zophy (Columbus, 1072), pp. 106–136; Michael Baylor, "Thomas Müntzer's *Prague Manifesto*," *Mennonite Quarterly Review*, 63 (1989): 30–57; R.R. Betts, "The Social Revolution in Bohemia and Moravia in the Later Middle Ages," *Past and Present* 2 (November, 1952): 24–31; Peter Blickle, *Die Revolution von 1525*, 2nd. ed. (Munich, 1987). For a good listing of current work on the subject of the Peasant's War, see George H. Williams, *The Radical Reformation*, 3rd. rev. ed., (Kirksville, 1992) p. 139, note 2.

RICHARD H. POPKIN

4.   CHRISTIAN JEWS AND JEWISH CHRISTIANS

IN THE 17TH CENTURY

Christian Jews are not just Jews who have Christmas trees in the house in late December each year, and Jewish Christians are not just Christians who like pastrami and gefilte fish. Nor are they just the Jews for Jesus, or the occasional Christian convert to Judaism, nor are they people who convert from Judaism to Christianity and become total Christians, nor are they *conversos*, forced converts to Christianity from Judaism, who reverted to Judaism.

What I want to explore here is a phenomena, and I think an important one, that occurred in 17th century Europe, when members of each religious community were drawn close together because of their common conviction that the end of days, the culmination of Providential history, was about to take place. In theory, and to some extent in practice, they developed theologies and theodicies that fused Judaism and Christianity. The various kinds of Jewish Christianity and Christian Judaism provided powerful vital force for the Messianic and Millenarian movements of the time. The traditional central issue which divided Jews and Christians from ancient times onward was whether the Messiah had arrived in the beginning of the first century of the common era in the person of Jesus of Nazareth. In the 17th century more important was the shared expectation that the Messiah would appear or reappear in the very near future, and usher in the Millenium, the Messianic Age, that Jews and Christians had been awaiting for sixteen hundred years. As we shall see, an actual proposal was made to stop arguing about what happened in Palestine around the years 1–32, and instead start planning for what would happen around 1656–1666, when the fulfillment of the expectations of both groups would take place.

What gave emphasis to the phenomena I will deal with is the emergence of very strong convictions on the part of both Jewish and Christian thinkers that the finale of human history was taking place before their very eyes, that they were actual living *at the end of days*, described in *Daniel* and in *The Book of Revelation*. I think at the end of the 15th century this type of phenomena aroused among Spanish Jews and Millenarian Christians, who saw in the very events taking place, the forced conversion of the Jews in Spain, the conquest of the infidel Moors in Granada, and the Explusion of the Jews in 1492, overwhelming evidence that God was acting in history. As a result a remarkable number of Jewish Christian and Christian Jewish views emerged

R.H. Popkin and G.M. Weiner (eds): Jewish Christians and Christian Jews,   57–72.
© 1994 *Kluwer Academic Publishers.   Printed in the Netherlands.*

that played an important role in the events leading up to 1492 and in the next couple of decades until the Spanish Inquisition clamped down on the Millenarian fervor, and on any signs of Judaizing amongst the Christians.[1] I think, and have offered my evidence elsewhere, that Columbus's vision of what he was doing, and the role his undertaking had in Spain at the time, can only be understood in these terms.[2]

The Spanish expectation was not fulfilled. Jesus did not return in glory in Spain, the Messiah did not save the Spanish Jews when they were expelled, Jerusalem was not liberated and rebuilt. Instead the Catholic Church found itself attacked from within Christendom, and found itself cast in the role of the church of the Anti-Christ. The military might of Spain, the greatest power in the world at the time, was defeated by two upstart Protestant groups, the sailors of England and the inhabitants of the Lowlands, the Dutch. The defeat of the Spanish Armada, the success of the Dutch Rebellion, the union of the Two Crowns of Scotland and England, the defeat of the Catholic armies by Gustavus Adolphus, the success of the Reformation, were overwelming signs again that God was acting in history, at least from the Protestant perspective.

There was an outpouring of Millenarian works by theologians in England, Scotland, The Netherlands, Sweden, and Germany, that the end of history was at hand. In the first decades of the 17th century theologians began to decipher God's plan by relating the scenarios in *Daniel* regarding the fall of four mighty empires, and in *Revelation* about the destruction of Anti-Christ, the conversion of the Jews, the reappearance of the Lost Tribes, and the rebuilding of Jerusalem, to the very events of the time. They figured out that the climactic events would occur 1260 years after the fall of the Roman Empire, By 1640, this had come to be dated at 1655–56.[3] As the time drew near, there was great excitement about what had to be done. At the beginning of the Puritan Revolution, John Dury, Samuel Hartlib and Jan Amos Comenius met in London to set down all the preparatory things that needed to be accomplished, and to divide up the work.[4] Part of what they saw as necessary was bringing Jews and Christians together for many crucial reasons. The Biblical prophecies indicated that the Jews and Christians would be joined when the Messiah appeared or reappeared, that the Messiah to come would be the political Messiah awaited by the Jews, and that He [or She[5]] would bring the Jews, converted or unconverted back to Palestine. Further, the Temple and the Holy City would be rebuilt according to its original divine architecture, that the Lost Tribes would reveal themselves, and lead the return to Zion.

To prepare for all of these great developments it would be desirable, if not necessary, to become involved in actual current Jewish affairs. Also some Christians suspected that the Jews had secret access to divine hints or clues in their mysterious Kabbalistic works. Unlike the situation in Spain in the late 15th century, there were no legal or avowed practicing Jews in England. They had been expelled in 1290. There were Jews in The Netherlands, mainly people who had escaped from Spain and Portugal and began creating a Jewish community at the end of the 16th century. The people who gravitated to The Netherlands had all been Christians in Iberia, and when they got to Holland and reverted to Judaism, were thus Christian Jews in a meaningful sense. Their religious training had been in Catholicism. They had the same life-style as other Spaniards and Portugese, and most of them read the Bible in Spanish and/or Latin, not in Hebrew. Because this group was more cosmopolitan than the ghetto Jews of Central and Eastern Europe, it was easier for the Protestant Millenarians to make contact and converse with them. In The Netherlands, from the 1620's onward Christian scholars were learning Hebrew and were discussing religious points with Jews. Christians were also attending Jewish religious services. Two rabbis became quite involved with Christians in projects of joint concern. Rabbi Judah Leon and the leader of the Collegiants, Adam Boreel, joined forces to construct an exact accurate model of Solomon's Temple. Boreel financed the project to the point of having rabbi Judah Leon living in his house for some years. The Temple model became one of the glories of Amsterdam, was on display in rabbi Judah Leon's garden for years until he took it to England to give to Charles II, after which it has still not been traced.[6] They also joined forces in a project, which lasted at least thirty years, on editing the *Mishna* in Hebrew with vowel points, notes, and translations of the text into Spanish and Latin.[7]

The other rabbi who became important, and much more important, in Christian circles, was Menasseh ben Israel, who was born in La Rochelle, France, was raised in Lisbon, and then turned up in Amsterdam in his teens, and became a teacher of Hebrew. It is not known where he received his education, but Menasseh by the 1620's exhibited a broad knowledge of Jewish and Christian literature.[8]

One possibility that has not been fully explored is that Menasseh, as well as rabbi Isaac Aboab de Fonseca, was a student of a most remarkable figure in early Amsterdam, Abraham Cohen Herrera, probably the most learned person in Holland of the time. Herrera, born Alonso Nunez Herrera, in Florence, Italy, where his father was the financial agent of the Duke of Tuscany, was given an education in Jewish, Christian and Moslem philosophy, in Florentine Neo-Platonism, and in Jewish religious materials. The family was New Christian, that is converts from Judaism. Apparently his grandfather was the last chief rabbi of Cordova before 1492. The family in Florence were New Christians, which enabled the father to hold high office with the Duke of Tuscany. The son, Alonso Nunez Herrera, with his great combination of Jewish, Christian and Moslem learning, then studied the Cabbala at Dubrovnik under Israel Sarug, the first disciple of Isaac Luria to bring the new rendering of the Cabbalistic materials to Europe. Herrera as a man of learning also had to be a man of affairs. He became the business agent of the Sultan of Morocco. It was just his luck that he was in Cadiz on the Sultan's business the day that the Earl of Essex raided the city and took forty hostages back to England. Herrera was one of them. and for four years he protested vehemently that he was not a Spaniard and should not be held. Finally through the influence of the Sultan of Morocco on Queen Elizabeth he was released. He moved to Holland and was one of the founding members of the Jewish community in Amsterdam. With all of his wealth and learning he seems to have played practically no role in the general world of the time, and to have passed on his knowledge only to Menasseh and Isaac Aboab. He wrote his masterpiece *Puerto del Cielo* in Amsterdam, the most important statement of Kabbalistic philosophy for the general European world.[9]

We find in the late 1620's that Menasseh was teaching Christians Hebrew and that they were consulting him on various subjects. He became the first Hebrew printer in The Netherlands, and was an important bookseller, obtaining Hebrew books for Jewish and Christian scholars from Poland, Italy and the Levant. In 1632 he published his *Conciliador* in Spanish, showing how various troublesome passages in Scripture could be explained. The work was a great success and was translated into Latin by one of the sons of the renowned professor, Gerard Vossius. From then on one finds Menasseh in contact with all sorts of learned Christians, people coming from various countries to hear him preach and to confer with him. The Portuguese Jesuit, Antonio de Vieria came from Brazil to talk to him. He became friendly with John Dury, the Scottish Millenarian who was preacher for Princess Mary. He was in contact with the leading mystical Millenarians, and apparently shared their expectation that the Messiah would soon be on the scene.[10]

As I have shown elsewhere, one of Dury's (and Samuel Hartlib' s) plans once the Puritan Revolution had begun was to establish a College of Jewish Studies in London. It would make Jewish learning available to Christians through publication of clasical Jewish texts, and public lectures, and "to make Christianity less offensive to Jews" by showing that Christianity was just an extension of Judaism. In the brochure for the proposed College Dury made clear that part of it was to help in converting the Jews to Christianity.[11] In the Hartlib papers, a very large collection that was deposited at the University of Sheffield after World War II, and in Dury's papers that are at the Staatsarchiv in Zurich, there is a lot of discussion about the plans for the college. Its faculty was to consist of Adam Boreel, a German Hebraist, J.S. Rittangel, and

Menasseh ben Israel (this at a time when no Jews were allowed in England.) The College never came into being,[12] but Dury and his friends kept in contact with Menasseh, and Boreel started the publication project with his work with rabbi Templo on the Hebrew text of the *Mishna*, (finally published in 1646 by Menasseh, and paid for by Dutch Millenarians). Menasseh's name was listed as editor instead of Boreel, because as Boreel explained the Jews would not buy the edition if a Christian was the editor.[13] One of the reasons for the *Mishna* project is that the texts include the most exact descriptions of the Temple and the ceremonies held therein. This would be crucial information if Jerusalem was about to be restored.

A crucial development, with many ramifications discussed below, occurred when Dury and his friends began to suspect that the American Indians were the Lost Tribes of Israel. Reports from New England, led a Norfolk preacher, Thomas Thorowgood, to publish *Jewes in America, or the Probability that the Indians are of that Race*, with a preface by Dury.[14] Dury consulted Menasseh about it, and also regarding a report he had had from Menasseh earlier concerning a Portuguese explorer, Montesinos, who claimed to have encountered an Indian group in the Andes Mountains having a Friday evening *Jewish* service. Dury's remarks indicate that he saw the news about the Jewish Indians as clear evidence that the end of days was at hand. He and others wanted Menasseh's opinion as well as his explanation of what the Jewish view was concerning the reemergence of the Lost Tribes.[15] After answering a few questions, Menasseh finally wrote his own work on the subject, *Esperanca de Israel*, which was immediately translated into English by a wild Millenarian friend of John Milton and Hartlib, Moses Wall, with a dedication to the Parliament of England (actually written by Dury rather than Menasseh). The work also appeared in Latin and Dutch, and became a proof-text for those expecting the imminent end of the world. The work came out three times in England in 1650, 1651 and 1652.[16] The Dutch version appeared in 1666, A Spanish version was published in Smyrna just before the Sabbatai Zevi movement began.[17]

Menasseh, who was called *the* Jewish philosopher, confirmed the expectations of the Scottish and English Millenarians. He wrote under Dury's influence a humble address to Cromwell telling the Lord Protector that almost all of the prophecies foretelling the end of the world had already been fulfilled, and one crucial non-fulfilled prophecy was that the Jews be spread to the four corners of the world. One corner was missing, namely the British Isles.[18] Immediately, important English diplomats were sent to discuss with Menasseh the conditions under which he would come to England to negotiate with Cromwell over the re-admission of the Jews.[19]

A most important Portuguese Jesuit, Antonio de Vieria, came to Amsterdam from Brazil where he was converting Indians, to confer with Menasseh about the signs of the coming of the Messiah. Vieira hoped to bring the Jews back to Portugal to await the coming of Jesus who would first come there, and then lead the Portuguese Jews to Palestine.[20]

At the end of 1654 Menasseh went to Belgium to see the recently abdicated Queen Christina.[21] While he was there he apparently became aware of an amazing work, *Du Rappel des Juifs*, by Isaac La Peyrère, and probably met its author who was living next door to Christina. La Peyrère was, in terms of this paper, a Jewish Christian, and maybe a Christian Jew. He seems to have been from a Portuguese converso family residing in Bordeaux. He became the secretary of the Prince of Condé in 1640, and soon wrote *Du Rappel des Juifs*, in which he claimed that the long expected Jewish Messiah would soon arrive and join forces with the King of France, who would lead the Jews to Palestine, take part in the rebuilding of Jerusalem, and then rule the world with the Jewish Messiah and his Jewish court. In developing this French oriented Messianic scenario, La Peyrère said that a Messiah had arrived in the first century who was the Messiah for the Gentiles. Now there would be a second Messianic episode for the Jews. The first was Jesus in the spirit, the second would be Jesus in the flesh, the Jews expected political Messiah. To prepare for his coming, La Peyrère urged that the Jews be recalled to France, that anti-semitism be made illegal, that the Jews be Christianized to the extent that they would have a Jewish Christian church (to which only Jews could belong) that would have no doctrines or practices that were offensive to the Jews. The fuller statement of La Peyrère's theory appeared in his *PraeAdamitae*, which existed in manuscript until published in Amsterdam in 1655 at Christina's expense. This work, which caused a sensation in Europe, and was banned and burned everywhere, was dedicated to all the Jews and all the synagogues of the world by one who wishes he were one of them. La Peyrère was born and raised a Calvinist. After being arrested for publishing his book on the pre-Adamites, he converted to Catholicism and apologized personally to the Pope in order to win his freedom.[22]

Right after learning about La Peyrère's *Du Rappel des Juifs*, Menasseh returned to Amsterdam and told a gathering of Dutch Millenarians at the home of Peter Serrarius that the coming of the Messiah was imminent. Based on this a Czech Millenarian, Paul Felgenhauer, wrote and quickly published *Good News for the Jews*,[23] dedicated to Menasseh, the Good News being that the *Jewish* Messiah was about to arrive. Menasseh added to the volume a list of the people he knew who knew that the arrival of the Messiah was imminent. This list contained a couple of English Millenarians, Abraham Von Frankenburg, the leading Boehmist of the period, Mochinger, a Silesian mystic, and the author of *Du Rappel des Juifs* not named. Shortly thereafter

Menasseh wrote his most Messianic work, *Piedra gloriosa*, about Daniel's dream, (with magnificent illustrations by Rembrandt), and arranged to go to England. Before he left he made met La Peyrère in Amsterdam, and he and Felgenhauer tried to arrange a debate with him about the pre-Adamite theory.[24]

Menasseh's conviction that the coming of the Messiah was imminent coincided with the Millenarian view that it would happen in 1655–56. Dury and Hartlib published von Frankenburg's *Clavis Apolyptica* which predicted the conversion of the Jews in 1655. Some like the Baptist minister Henry Jessey learned Hebrew and used it as their daily language in preparation for the Messianic age. London seems to have been in a frenzy of expectation in the late summer of 1655.[25] In this frenzy various manifestations of Jewish Christianity occurred, The founder of the Quakers George Fox had made his slogan, "to be a Jew externally is nothing; to be a Jew internally is everything."[26] Margaret Fell tried to get Menasseh to join the Quakers, and bring his brethren into the fold as well.[27] Puritan theologians proclaimed that England was the New Israel. They, and Cromwell as well, insisted that only the English Protestants were pure enough of spirit to make the Jews realize that Christianity (English style) was the fulfillment of Judaism.[28]

When Menasseh came to London in September 1655 he was wined and dined by leading English Millenarians. Robert Boyle's sister, Lady Ranlegh had dinner parties for him. Adam Boreel, the leader of the Dutch Collegiants, came to London and held a dinner for him with Boyle and Henry Oldenburg. After the negotiations for the re-admisssion of the Jews broke down, Menasseh went to Oxford and Cambridge where he was well received, and even stayed at the home of the Arabist, Pocock.[29]

Menasseh's stay in England did not lead either to Jews being officially re-admitted or to the conversion of the Jews. In the one work Menasseh wrote and published in England, *Vindicae Judaeorum*, believed to have been written at the request of Robert Boyle, the author answered various charges brought against Jews, and then proposed his own and La Peyrère's solution to the apparent conflict between Judaism and Christianity. "For, as a most learned Christian of our time hath written, in a French book, which he calleth the *Rappel of the Iewes* (in which he makes the King of *France* to be their leader, when they shall return to their country), the Iewes, saith he, shall be saved, for yet we expect a *second* coming of the same Messiah, and the *Iewes* believe that that coming is the *first* and not the second, and by that faith shall be saved; for the difference consists only in the circumstance of time."[30] This proposed peace treaty would allow, and even justify, Jews and Christians having different views about what happened in the first century, but would join their expectations about the future. They would hence be Jewish-Christians or Christian-Jews about the imminent Messianic occurence.

Shortly after Menasseh wrote this a great Messianic episode did in fact occur in England. One of the leaders of the Quakers, James Nayler, announced that Jesus was in him, and he was Jesus, He replicated Jesus's entry into Jerusalem by riding into Bristol on the back on an ass, with his followers singing Hosanna in the highest, and proclaiming him the King of the Jews. Wild expectations took place, and Nayler was soon arrested, and was tried for blasphemy by the House of Parliament, where Cromwell defended him. He was convicted. He only answered questions by repeating direct quotations from what Jesus said in the Gospels. He was severely and brutally punished and jailed. He seems to have caused such a furor that the Quakers quickly disowned him, and tried to eradicate traces of his teachings and writings.[31] His followers fled, some going to Holland, and some to far corners of the trading world of the Quakers. A decade later people were referring to Quaker Jews and Jewish Quakers, and these may included the Naylerites.

We have no information about whether Menasseh and Nayler and his followers ever intersected in England. At the beginning of 1657 Nayler went to prison. Later in the year Menasseh left England, his mission having failed. And as various Millenarians sadly pointed out, 1655 and 1656 came and went without the Jews converting or the Messiah appearing.

In 1657 Dury received a letter from Serrarius reporting what he took to be the amazing philochristian views of one rabbi Nathan Shapira of Jerusalem. The rabbi was a fund-raiser, who went regular to Europe to collect monies from the Jewish communities in Poland to help their destitute brethern in Jerusalem. Because of the Swedish invasion of Poland he was unable to go there, and so went to Germany and Amsterdam. He had written to Menasseh about the terrible condition of the Jews in the Holy Land, and Menasseh actually presented this letter to Cromwell as a reason for readmitting the Jews to England. When rabbi Shapira asked the Spanish-Portuguese Synagogue in Amsterdam for contributions they told him they only gave money to Sefardim, Spanish Jews, not to Askenasim, German and eastern Jews. When he left in despair he ran into some Christian Millenarians, and this encounter had dramatic effects, and quickly became part of the evidence for the Christians that God was acting in history, preparing for the conversion of the Jews, to be followed by Jesus's return to reign on Earth. Thus the end was near.[32]

All of the information we have about rabbi Shapira's visit comes from the Christian Millenarians. Peter Serrarius sent a letter about it to Dury, who quickly published a pamphlet entitled *An Information Concerning the Present State of the Jewish Nation in Europe and Judea. Wherein the Footsteps of Providence preparing a way for their Conversion to Christ, and for their Deliverance from Captivity are Discovered.*[33] The rabbi had told the

Millenarians how terrible were the conditions of the Jews in Palestine and Poland. Dury saw this as indicating that the worse their misery, the sooner their deliverance, so soon the Jews would be restored, when their minds will become enlightened so that they will acknowledge the true Messiah, Jesus. But more exciting than what was happening to the Jews were the views rabbi Shapira was reported to have offered about Christianity, views which were taken by the Millenarians as indicating that the rabbi was a real Christian Jew. [At this point I should add a word of caution. All we know about this is what the Millenarians said. I have been told for the last nine and a half years, since I first gave a talk about rabbi Shapira in Israel, that in some unpublished sermon[s] the rabbi was quite anti-Christian. The date of the sermon[s] has not been established, and no text has been forthcoming].[34]

The rabbi was asked what he made of the proof text *Isaiah* 53, concerning the Messiah. In response rabbi Shapira offered his view that there have been many, many instantiations of the Messiah. Each time he comes, he finds mankind too wicked, so he goes away. In the rabbi's list of instantiations, he included Jesus of Nazareth, and said that "our Forefathers wrongfully put [him] to death and that Sin lies upon us unto this day."[35] When Serrarius heard this, he wrote Dury that "When I heard these things, my bowels were inwardly stirred within me, and it seemed to me that I did not hear a Jew, but a Christian of no mean understanding, who did relish he things of the Spirit, and was admitted to the inward mysteries of our Religion."[36] On another occasion the rabbi was asked what he thought of the Sermon on the Mount, and replied that he thought it was the fount of all wisdom, and indicated that he thought it was the teachings of the most pure and ancient rabbis. And when rabbi Shapira watched the Millenarians praying, he declared that if were but ten men so holy praying in Jerusalem for the coming of the Messiah, the Messiah would quickly come.

On the basis of this and other surprising observations of the rabbi, Serrarius said to Dury, "Is it to be believed that Christ is far distant from a soul so constituted? or that any such thing can be formed without Christ in a man?...I see Christ in his Spirit, and cannot but love him, and those that are like him, of which he saith many are at Jerusalem."[37] In fact the Millenarians so loved rabbi Shapira that they took on his fund-raising, and in the first known case, Christians were raising substantial sums for the Jews in Jerusalem. This has led some to say that the rabbi was insincere and just wanted to get money from the Gentiles. I do not kow whether this was the case, but when the rabbi got back to Jerusalem, he was condemned for taking money from Gentiles, and it took years for him to be exonerated.[38] The Millenarians found in rabbi Shapira a striking case of a Christian Jew. He avowed Christian sentiments. He had Jesus in his Pantheon of Messiah appearances, and held Jesus's views in the highest regard. The rabbi was still a Jew nonetheless because he was still waiting for the Jewish Messiah. The Millenarians saw the rabbi as on the verge of conversion, and got him to take a copy of the New Testament back to Palestine to have it properly rendered into Hebrew.

What may be a spinoff from rabbi Shapira's expression of a Christian Judaism is the discussion about Christ that appears in Spinoza's *Tractatus*, which has always puzzled Jewish commentators, and made some Christian ones think Spinoza had just about converted. Spinoza was expelled from the Jewish community of Amsterdam in the summer of 1656, then went to live with the Dutch Collegiants, who were led by the Millenarian, Adam Boreel. Serrarius was Spinoza's patron, who introduced him to the Quaker leader, and to other radical Protestants of the time. (Serrarius also became Spinoza's contact with the world outside of The Netherlands. He received his mail, and transmitted answers.[39]) So, Spinoza was in contact with the very people who were meeting and talking with rabbi Shapira. He may, for all we know, have been present at some of the episodes described by the Millenarians.

In the *Tractatus*, which started out as a response to the Jewish community that had expelled him, and grew into a most important statement of the Bible criticism and liberal politcal philosophy, Spinoza stated that Jesus was the human being who was closest to God. Later on, Spinoza told Oldenburg that he believed all the facts about Jesus in the Gospels except the claim that he was resurrected. Spinoza asserted that the message of the Sermon on the Mount was the central Divine Message in the Bible. "to love God above all things and one's neighbor as one's self...This is the cornerstone of religion, without which the whole fabric would fall headlong to the ground."[40] When Spinoza described what he took to be the positive content of religion. "He who firmly believes that God, out of the mercy and grace with which He directs all things, forgives the sins of men, and who feels his love of God kindled thereby, he, I say, does really know Christ according to the Spirit, and Christ is in him."[41] Spinoza did not make Jesus into a supernatural, or even superhuman, being. But he made Christ the spirit that provided the basis for moral-religious life. We know from later accounts that Spinoza never joined any Christian group, though he spent the rest of his life with Christians, mainly Millenarian ones. He did not keep up any Jewish customs or practices, and saw the positive part of both Judaism and Christianity as moral living, not what he called ceremonial activities.

Spinoza and rabbi Shapira expressed what I have called Christian Judaism. A more full blown version appears in an undated unpublished discussion of John Dury in answer to a question posed to him, He received a letter apparently from Germany asking if it was possible to be a true and believing Christian and a faithful follower of the Law of Moses. The unidentified letter writer indicated that he and some friends were trying to do both, be Christians and Jews. Dury's answer, which only exists in manuscript,[42] explores the question at length, and slowly comes to a positive answer, "Yes. But if you are going to do it, do it in Amsterdam, not in Germany."

On the other side, one finds Christians accepting Jewish dietary rules and other Jewish practices.[43] In the late 1650's and 1660's one reads of Quaker Jews and Jewish Quakers. The Quakers, seeing themselves as internal Jews, became very involved with Jews in Holland, Germany, Italy, in the Levant, the Caribbean, and in Rhode Island.[44] From the outset the Quakers were denounced as non-Christians, refusing to accept the doctrine of the Trinity, or the Divinity of Jesus. The discussions of these matters in Quaker theologians like William Penn bring out the ahistorical aspect of Quakerism. They were not concerned about what happened in the first century. They were and are concerned about the Spirit and how it operates on people, They saw the Jews, as the first to feel the power of the Spirit, the Light, as the clearest potential Quaker members. A lot of Quaker pamphlets were written, an enormous number, to make Jews see the light. In Penn's "Visitation to the Jews", he explained that the Second Coming was in fact the appearance of the Quakers in the 1650's, people filled with the Spirit of God.[45] Actual Jews were superstitious, engaged in a lot of idolatrous ceremonies, but had the Spirit, the Light, within, if they could be brought to realize this. Hence, in Margaret Fell's pamphlets to the Jews, she stressed passages in the Old Testament that should make the Jews become Quakers.[46]

A most interesting figure in the Quaker movement, almost a Jewish Quaker, was Samuel Fisher, an Oxford graduate who became a Quaker in 1654. He decided to witness his faith in Rome and Constantinople to convert the Pope and the Sultan. En route, he was with the Quaker mission in Amsterdam around 1657. He attended Synagogue services, and tried to make them into Quaker meetings, He agreed to be quiet during the services if members of the congregation would talk with him afterwards. He happily reports he spent three to four hours after services in the houses of Jews He worked with Spinoza in translating two of Margaret Fell's pamphlets into Hebrew. And he worked out, maybe with Spinoza, his radical Bible criticism, which he published in 1660, containing all the points Spinoza was later to make famous.[47] Fisher left Amsterdam for Rome, and went from one Jewish community to another. We have a handful of his letters, in which he says that he stayed for days, for weeks, with various Jewish communities in Germany and Italy, living with them, and talking with them. This would indicate he was living a Jewish life, and that the Jews in these various communities accepted him.[48] He finally returned to England, not having converted either Pope or Sultan, but very rich from sources unknown. His chief convert was not a Jew, but William

Penn![49]

David Katz and I have long suspected that there was an intimate conection between the Quaker Messianic movement of James Nayler and the Jewish one that began in 1665 with when a Turkish Jew, Sabbatai Zevi, announced that he was the long awaited Messiah and that he was commencing the Messiah Age on Jewish New Year's Day, 1665. Without going into our evidence here, let me just mention a few points – Sabbatai Zevi's father worked for Quaker merchants in Turkey. There is a German woodcut of 1666 showing the two great imposters facing each other – James Nayler and Sabbatai Zevi.[50] The British Library, a couple of years ago acquired some Polish pamphlets about Sabbatai Zevi from 1666. One calls him a Quaker Jew, and one is purported to be from the Quakers in Bristol inquiring about whether Sabbatai Zevi is the real Messiah.[51]

The dramatic news reaching Europe in late 1665 and early 1666 that the Jewish Messiah had arrived or appeared in the person of Sabbatai Zevi set off tremendous waves amongst the Millenarian Christians. They had been waiting for the reappearance of Jesus, waiting in 1655 and 1656. They saw hope again in 1657 with the activities of rabbi Shapira. But, then nothing more. Suddenly the news from the Levant about Sabbatai Zevi, which created much Jewish Christian activity and thought. What was one to make of this? Serrarius, who became the leading Christian Sabbatian, put out pamphlets about the wondrous events signalling the arrival of the Messiah. We were told that the Lost Tribes had reappeared and were beseiging Mecca; that a ship had sailed into Aberdeen harbor with white and blue silk sails and flags in Hebrew letters, and many other such amazing signs. Serrarius wrote to Dury in Switzerland to alert im to the great news. The English Millenarian, Nathaniel Homes recalled that Menasseh ben Israel had told them that there would be two Messiahs, so there was no great surprise that a Messiah other than Jesus had turned up. Dury first tried to minimize the news, and interpret Sabbatai Zevi as a local Ottoman potentate, the King of the Jews in Turkey. Then he saw that he would have to put Sabbatai Zevi into a Providential scheme. Both he and Jean de Labadie offered the interpretation that God was rewarding the Jews by having their Messianic moment occur, and punishing Christians (because they were not pure enough) by delaying the Christian Millenium.

The brief Messianic career of Sabbatai Zevi, who actually converted to Islam, involved quite a few important Christians, who in various ways became through this Jewish Christians. Serrarius became a complete follower, and died en route to meet to the Turkish Messiah. Others like Henry Oldenburg, Labadie, Increase Mather in New England, and maybe Dury, and even Jan Amos Comenius, saw that the climax of Christian expectations had to come out of the developments of living Jewish history.

There is a magnificent collection, made in the 1660's by a German theologian, of all of the materials that appeared in Europe about Sabbatai Zevi. This archive has only been scratched by Gershom Scholem, myself, David Katz, and a few others. I am hoping to organize a conference in a year or two in Zurich on Sabbatai Zevi in Europe to examine the full effect that the Sabbatai Zevi's Messianic moment had on Christian Europe. Its effect on the Jews is still being assessed, but it was enormous, and greatly shook Jewish confidence in their reading of history for a long long time. Scholem has argued that it gave strength to ahistorical hasidism and spawned what is now reformed Judaism.[52]

Just after the Sabbatai Zevi's conversion to Islam, and the condemnation of the Sabbatai Zevi movement by the Amsterdam Jewish authorities,[53] a figure who will discussed in Allison Coudert's paper, Knorr Von Rosenroth came to Amsterdam to study Hebrew, and obtained a huge collection of unpublished Cabbalistic tracts, some from a disgruntled and apparently disillusioned rabbi, many of which were to appear in print for the first time in the *Kabbala Denudata* of 1677–78. One of the editors, Peter Spaeth, is the last case that I shall discuss. Spaeth was originally a Catholic, a student of the Jesuits, who became a pietist Protestant, and radical Protestant and finally a Jew, who changed his name to Moses Germanus, and became a rabbi in Amsterdam.[54] He certainly qualifies as a Jewish Christian, and he seems to have ended up as a Christian Jew. He became a leader of another Messianic movement centered around the person of a Dane, Oliger Pauli, who claimed to be a descendent of Abraham. (We are told that Oliger Pauli had a court of rabbis around him, which if true, would indicate that they had adopted some form of Christian Judaism, in that Oliger Pauli always remained a Christian, though he claimed to have some Jewish ancestors. Moses Germanus wrote some works arguing that Christianity was a mistake. Jesus was a fine moral rabbi, teaching people how to live. Around the 3rd century he was erroneously converted into a Divinity. Moses Germanus, a Christian who had become a Jew in the full sense of the term, now offered a Jewish way of accepting part of Christianity, namely Jesus as an important ethical teacher.[55] This rendition was taken over in the Bible criticism of Edelman and Reimarus. A companion view that true Judaism is nothing but good ethics appears in the *Memoirs of a Turkish Spy* written in the 1690's.[56]

The various kinds of Jewish Christianity and Christian Judaism surveyed indicate ways attempts at fusing the two traditions played a dynamic and vital role in the 17th century. These fusions were not just oddities, or curiosities. Some of their effects no doubt increased the drive towards a more tolerant world; some led to blind alleys and religious lunacies; and some to transforming Judaism and/or Christianity into just ethical views, thereby creating modern liberal outlooks. The further exploration of ways in which Judaism and Christianity came together in the 17th century may help us understand how aspects of our intellectual world came to be.

NOTES

1. See on this John Leddy Phelan, *The Millenial Kingdom of the Franciscans in the New World,* Berkeley, Univ. of California Press, 1956; and R.H. Popkin, "Jewish Christians and Christian Jews in Spain, 1492 and after," *Judaism*, 41: July 1992, pp. 247–267..

2. Popkin, "Christian Jews and Jewish Christians in Spain," pp. 257–61.

3. See R.H. Popkin, introduction, to Popkin, ed., *Christian Millenarianism and Jewish Messianism in English Literature and Thought*, Leiden, Brill, 1987, and Christopher Hill, "'Till the Conversion of the Jews" in the same volume, pp. 12–36.

4. Cf. Hugh Trevor-Roper,"Three Foreigners:the Philosophers of the Puritan Revolution," in *Religion, the Reformation and Social Change*, London, Macmillan, 1967, pp. 237–293; and Popkin, "The Third Force in 17th Century Thought", in Popkin, *The Third Force in 17th Century Thought*, Leiden, Brill, 1992, pp. 107–111.

5. Juan de Prado hailed the recently abdicated Queen Christina as the long awaited Messiah – who would have expected it would be a woman, he exclaimed! Cited in Yosef Kaplan, *From Christianity to Judaism. The Story of Isaac Orobio de Castro*, Oxford: Oxford Univ. Press, p. 128.

6. It apparently still existed in the late 18th century and was being displayed in Germany. There are rumors that it became the property of the Free Masons. Rabbi Judah Leon, who changed his name to Judah Leon Templo, first tried to give the model to the Queen of England, Henrietta Marie, when she visited England in 1642. Cf. A.K. Offenberg, "Jacob Jehuda Leon (1602–1675) and His Model of the Temple, in J. Van den Berg and E.G.E. Van der Wall, eds. *Jewish-Christian Relations in the Seventeenth Century*, Dordrecht, Kluwer,1988, pp. 95–115.

7. On the joint project to edit and publish the *Mishna* see R.H. Popkin, "Some Aspects of Jewish-Christian Theological Interchanges in Holland and England 1640–1700", in Van den Berg and van der Wall, *Jewish-Christian Relations*, pp. 3–32; and David S. Katz, "The Abendana Brothers and the Christian Hebraists of Seventeenth-Century England, *Journal of Ecclesiastical History*, 40:1989.

8. On Menasseh see Y. Kaplan, H. Mechoulan and R.H. Popkin, *Menasseh ben Israel and His World*, Leiden, Brill, 1989; See also introduction in Menaseh ben Israel, *The Hope of Israel*, ed. H. Mechoulan and G. Nahon, Oxford,Oxford Univ. Press, 1987, pp. 1–95.

9. It was only published long after his death, in Hebrew by rabbi Aboab in 1655 and in Latin in 1677 by Knorr von Rosenroth. Part of the Spanish original was just published a few years ago. On Herrera, see R.H. Popkin, "A Jewish Merchant of Venice," *Shakespeare Quarterly*, 40:1989, pp. 329–331 and Kenneth Krabbenhoft, introduction, Abraham Cohen Herrera, *Puerta del Cielo*, Madrid, Fundacion Univeritaria Espanola, 1987, pp. 11–87.

10. See Cecil Roth, *A Life of Menasseh ben Israel*, Philadelphia, Jewish Publications Society, 1934.

11. See R.H. Popkin, "The First College of Jewish Studies," *Revue des Etudes juives* 143:1984, pp. 351–364.

12. Because, as Dury lamented, the thousand pounds needed, were spent on the troubles in Ireland. Cf. Popkin, "First College of Jewish Studies."

13. See Popkin, "Some Aspects of Jewish-Christian Interchanges,", pp. 8–9.

14. Thomas Thorowgood, *Jewes in America, or Probabilities that the Americans are of that Race,* London, 1650.

15. Cf. the prefatory materials in Thorowgood, *op. cit.*
    On this, see David S. Katz, *Philo-Semitism in England, 1603–1655,* Oxford, Oxford Univ. Press, 1982, chap. 4; and R.H. Popkin, "The Rise and Fall of the Jewish Indian Theory", in Kaplan, Mechoulan and Popkin, *Menasseh ben Israel,* pp. 63–82.

16. It appeared in three editions in English in 1650, 1651 and 1652. The last two editions include an explanation by the translator, Moses Wall, on why he printed the book, namely to bring about the conversion of the Jews. On what is known about Moses Wall, see Popkin, "A Note on Moses Wall", in Mechouldan and Nahon edition of Menasseh's *Hope of Israel,* pp. 165–170.

17. An article on this will appear soon in *Jewish History* by Jacob Barzai.

18. Menasseh ben Israel, *To His Highnesse The Lord Protector ... The Humble Adresses of Menasseh ben Israel,* 1655.

19. See D.S. Katz, *Philo-Semitism in England,* Chaps.5 and 6.

20. As to be expected, one of the charges against Vieria by the Inquistion was that he consorted with a Jewish rabbi, Menasseh Ben Israel. See A.J. Saraiva, "Antonio Vieira, Menasseh ben Israel,et le Cinquième Empire," *Studia Rosenthaliana* 6:1972, pp. 25–56.

21. He had been buying Hebrew books for Christina, and had proposed a Biblioteca Hebrica to her in which he would edit and publish the classical Jewish texts. On his relations with Queen Christina, see Susanna Akerman, *Queen Christina of Sweden and Her Circle,* Leiden, Brill, 1991.

22. On La Peyrère's life and works, see R.H. Popkin, *Isaac La Peyrère, (1596–1676). His Life, Work and Influence,* Leiden: Brill, 1987.

23. Paul Felgenhauer, *Bonum Nunciam Israel quod offertur Populo Israel &c Judae in hisce temporibus novissimus de Messia....,* Amsterdam, 1655.

24. See Popkin, *La Peyrère,* pp. 99–100.

25. See the report of the Swedish diplomat, Bonde, for August 23, 1655, in Michael Roberts, *Swedish Diplomats at Cromwell's Court, 1655–1656, The Missions of Peter Julius Coyet and Christian Bonde,* Camden Fourth Series, Office of the Royal Historical Society, London, 1988, p. 142.

26. A truncated text from Paul's *Romans.*

27. She wrote a pamphlet, *For Menasseth ben Israel. The Call of the Jews out of Babylon,* London, 1656.

28. Cf. Popkin, "The Fictional Jewish Council of 1650: A Great English Pipedream", *Jewish History* 5:1991, esp. pp. 17–20.

29. Katz, *Philo-Semitism in England,* chap. 6; and Popkin, review article on Katz volume, *History of European Ideas* 5:1984, pp. 79–87.

30. Menasseh ben Israel, *Vindicae Judaeorum,* 1656, p. 18.

31. On Nayler, see Mabel R. Brailsford, *A Quaker from Cromwell's Army, James Nayler,* London, 1927; Emilia Fogelkou, *James Nayler, The Rebel Saint,* London, 1931; and Christopher Hill, *The World Turned Upside Down,* London, 1972, chap. 10.

32. On this see R.H. Popkin, "Rabbi Nathan Shapira's Visit to Amsterdam in 1657," in Michman & Levie, *Dutch Jewish History,* Jerusalem: Magnes, 1984, pp. 185–205.

33. Published in London in 1658 by R.W. for Thomas Brewster.

34. It is the leading Kabbalah scholar, Prof. Moshe Idel of Hebrew University, who keeps telling me this.

35. Popkin, "Rabbi Shapira's Visit,", p. 194.

36. *Ibid.* p. 195.

37. *Ibid*, pp. 196–197.

38. David Katz has written up the case. See his "English Charity and Jewish Qualms: The Rescue of the Ashkenazi Community of Seventeenth-Century Jerusalem," in *Jewish History: Essays in Honour of Chimen Abramsky*, ed A. Rapoport-Albert and S.J. Zipperstein, London, 1988, pp. 245–266.

39. See Popkin, note on Serrarius, in Meinsma, *Spinoza et son cercle*, Paris, Vrin, 1983, pp. 277–279.

40. Spinoza, *Tractatus*, Elwes p. 172; Gebhardt, p. 165.

41. Spinoza, *op.cit.*

42. In the Hartlib papers at the University of Sheffield, Ms.25/4/1–7.

43. See Katz, *Sabbath and Sectarianism in Seventeenth-Century England*, Leiden, Brill, 1988.

44. William C. Braithwaite, *The Beginnings of Quakerism*, 2nd edition ed. and revised by Henry J. Cadbury, Cambridge; Cambridge Univ. Press, 1955, esp. chap. xvi.

45. William Penn, *Visitation to the Jews,* in *The Works of William Penn*, London, 1726, Vol.II, p. 853.

46. Margaret Fell, *A Loving Salution to the Seed of Abraham Among the 3 Jews, Where Ever They are Scattered Up and Down Upon the Face of the Earth...Wandering Up and Down from Mountain to Hill. Seeking Rest and Finding None*, 1657.

47. See Popkin, "Spinoza's Relations with the Quakers in Amsterdam," *Quaker History*, 73:1984, pp. 14–28, and " Samuel Fisher and Spinoza," *Philosophia* 15:1985, pp. 219–236.

48. London Friends House Library Ms.Portfolio 17, fols.72–78.

49. Who wrote the memorial to Fisher in the collection of his works, *Testimony of Truth*, London, 1679.

50. This appears on the cover of Popkin, ed., *Christian Millenarianism and Jewish Messianism*.

51. Hanna Swiderska, "Three Polish Pamphlets on Pseudo-Messiah Sabbatai Zevi," *British Library Journal*, 15:1989, pp. 212–216.

52. Gershom Scholem, *Sabbatai Sebi. The Mystical Messiah*, Princeton; Princeton Univ. Press, 1973.

53. Who originally almost to a man were followers. Some leaders like Abraham Peyrera gave up their European business and went to Palestine to set up institutions for the Messianic age. On what happened in Amsterdam, see Kaplan, *From Christianity to Judaism*, chap. 8.

54. On his career, see Hans Joachim Schoeps, *Philosemitismus im Barok* Tubingen,1952, pp. 67–81; and the articles on Spaeth, Johann Peter in the *Jewish Encyclopedia*, 11:484 and in the *Encyclopedia Judaiaca*, 15:219–220.

55. Popkin, "Spinoza, Neoplatonic Kabbalist?" in Lenn E. Goodman, ed., *Neopatonism and Jewish Thought*, New York, SUNY Press, 1992, pp. 387–409, and "Fideism, Quietism, and Unbelief: Skepticism for and Against Religion in the Seventeenth and Eighteenth Centuries," in Marcus Hester, ed., *Faith, Reason, and Skepticism*, Philadelphia, Temple Univ. Press, 1992, pp. 121–154,

56. See Popkin, "A Gentile Attempt to Convert the Jews to Reformed Judaism,"in Shmuel Almog et al eds. *Israel and the Nations. Essays Presented in Honor of Shmuel Ettinger*, Jerusalem, Historical Society of Israel, 1987, pp.XXV–XLV.

ALLISON P. COUDERT

5. THE KABBALA DENUDATA:
CONVERTING JEWS OR SEDUCING CHRISTIANS[1]

The traditional view of the Renaissance and Reformation as periods of philo-Semitism[2] has been qualified in recent years as scholars have increasingly revealed the very real limits to this phenomenon, together with the increasing hostility to Jews and Judaism. The attempt to distinguish between anti-Judaism and anti-Semitism made by Markish, for example, has been undermined by the work of Heiko Oberman, Jerome Friedman, Jonathan Israel and Po-Chia Hsia, among others.[3] In the view of these scholars the enthusiasm of Renaissance Christians for Hebraica, characteristic of Pico della Mirandola and Johannes Reuchlin, was a fragile, ephemeral thing, which was first dampened by the Reuchlin-Pffeferkorn controversy and then fundamentally distorted by the conflicts of the Reformation period. By the mid-sixteenth century the charge of "judaizing" became an all-too-convenient, pejorative epithet for Catholics in their fight against Protestants and for Protestants in their fight against each other. With the reaffirmation of the Vulgate as divinely inspired at the Council of Trent, the Catholic interest in Hebraica, which had always been less than the Protestant, diminished even further. The popular Catholic revival of the late sixteenth and seventeenth centuries further encouraged anti-Semitic sentiments by resuscitating charges of blood libel, which had largely been discredited.[4] In such a situation the embattled Christian Hebraists who were left jumped on the bandwagon of anti-Semitism to prove that they were good Christians because they hated Jews like everyone else.[5]

In his book on sixteenth-century Christian Hebraica, Friedman argues that the Christian Hebraists whose work was most affected by the increasingly anti-Semitic atmosphere were the Lutherans. By 1540s Luther abandoned his earlier conciliatory attitude towards the Jews and wrote the virulently anti-Semitic tracts in which he made it abundantly clear that when it came to interpreting Scripture, Lutherans had nothing whatsoever to learn from Jews. "We do not give a fig for their crazy glosses which have spun out of their own heads," he exclaimed in *On the Jews and Their Lies*. "We have a clear text."[6] The clear text came from faith. As Luther said, "If I know what I believe in, then I know what is written in Scripture, for Scripture contains nothing but Christ and Christian faith."[7]

R.H. Popkin and G.M. Weiner (eds): Jewish Christians and Christian Jews, 73–96.
© 1994 *Kluwer Academic Publishers. Printed in the Netherlands.*

Rabbis were bad and their Talmudic glosses useless; but Kabbalists were even worse[8] because in Luther's view they practicing magic.[9] Luther's vehement attack on magic was part of his larger attack on works as a means to salvation. His hatred of both Kabbalists and Talmudists was in direct proportion to their emphasis on works as pleasing to God and essential to salvation.

Given the vehemence of Luther's anti-Semitism and anti-Kabbalistic sentiment, it is perhaps surprising to find that the largest and most important collection of Kabbalistic texts in Latin in the seventeenth century was edited and translated by a staunch Lutheran, Christian Knorr von Rosenroth (1636–1689).[10] To compound the surprises, von Rosenroth's co-editor was Francis Mercury van Helmont (1614–1698), a Catholic imprisoned and tried by the Roman Inquisition on the charge of "judaizing." He survived that ordeal only to "judaize" even more blatantly before leaving the Catholic Church altogether, first to become a Quaker and finally a non-affiliated "Seeker." Nor is it any less surprising, given the Catholic Church's increasing hostility to Jews during the Counter-Reformation, that von Rosenroth and van Helmont compiled, edited, and published their collection of Kabbalistic texts (the *Kabbala Denudata*) at the court of Christian August of Sulzbach (1622–1708), who had been born a Lutheran but converted to Catholicism as an adult.

How do we explain this enthusiasm for the Kabbalah on the part of a Lutheran Hebraist, a judaizing Catholic-Quaker-Seeker, and a princely Catholic convert? The hundred odd years separating Luther's death from the publication of the *Kabbala Denudata* had clearly effected great changes in the religious outlook of some of those who still considered themselves members of particular Christian denominations. Christian Knorr von Rosenroth, for example, was a staunch enough Lutheran to write a scathing letter to his daughter when she announced that she was going to marry a Catholic.[11] Yet he spent his adult life working for a Catholic Prince and had close relationships with Jews, first as teachers and then as collaborators on the *Kabbala Denudata*. His experience as a student at Leipzig, Wittenberg, and Leiden and his later travels through the Netherlands, France, and possibly England encouraged the ecumenical outlook that was to characterize his mature thought. In addition to theology, law, philosophy, philology, history, and natural philosophy, von Rosenroth began to study oriental languages and Jewish mysticism in Amsterdam under the tutelage of Thomas de Pinedo (1614–79), Isaaac de Rocamora (1601–84), and Rabbi Meir Stern, who was apparently a Rabbi from Frankfurt. He became a proficient linguist in Hebrew, Aramaic, Syriac, Greek, Latin, Arabic, French, Dutch, English, Spanish, and Italian. During the same period he became acquainted with the millenarian Peter Serrarius and various groups of Mennonites and Quakers. It was apparently among these sectarians that von Rosenroth met Francis Mercury van Helmont. In 1659 von Rosenroth became a member of the Deutschgesinnte Genossenschaft on the recommendation of Phillip von Zesen. He later joined another society devoted to the promotion of the German language.[12] As R.J.W. Evans has persuasively argued, these societies were founded to revive and foster the kind of ecumenical humanism characteristic of the Renaissance.[13]

Given this background, it is not surprising that von Rosenroth spent his entire adult life in the service of Christian August of Sulzbach; for Christian August had equally wide interests and ecumenical sympathies. Not only was he intrigued by the Christian Hebraica to the point of subsidizing a Hebrew press, but his policy towards the Jews, whom he invited to settle in Sulzbach in 1666, was both liberal and protective. The charge of ritual murder was brought against the Sulzbach Jews twice during Christian August's regime, in 1682 and again in 1692. On both occasions he actively combatted the charges and ordered corporeal punishment for anyone bringing false accusations against Jews in the future.[14]

On the basis of the recent work on Jewish and Christian millenarians, stimulated (when not actually written) by Richard Popkin, and from the work of certain German historians, all of which deepen Kolakowski's earlier insights,[15] it is apparent that seventeenth-century Europe was criss-crossed by networks of millenarian Christians and Jews who were convinced that the Messiah either had arrived or shortly would. The exhilarating optimism and ecumenicalism characteristic of Pico della Mirandola's *Oration on the Dignity of Man* and *Nine Hundred Theses* resurfaces in the innumerable, though largely forgotten texts of these millenarians. Von Rosenroth's monumental *Kabbala Denudata* exemplifies this genre. Within what appears to be a narrowly esoteric work, one can find the basis for the kind of tolerant ecumenicalism, faith in science, and belief in progress that are generally associated with the Enlightenment, but which had their beginnings far earlier among Italian Humanists. What I am suggesting is that in the court of Christian August of Sulzbach we have evidence for a continuation of the "Rosicrucian Enlightenment" described by Frances Yates in connection with the earlier court of Frederick, the Elector of the Palatine, at Heidelberg.[16] Yates' thesis that Renaissance Hermeticism, with its commitment to the ideal of a *prisca theologia* embracing all religions and its exhilarating faith in man's ability to restore the world to its prelapsarian state, continued to exist even in the pessimistic, dogmatic atmosphere of the Reformation and Counter-Reformation has come under considerable attack. She has been accused, with some justification, of over-generalizing and of making wild extrapolations on the basis of little or no concrete evidence.[17] However, her insights are proving to have more substance that her critics imagined. As I will argue in this paper, the

Court at Sulzbach can be described as "Rosicrucian," in terms of both the broad policy of toleration established by Christian August and the activities and attitudes of people he hired to advise and assist him.[18]

When Christian August took over as ruler of Sulzbach in 1649, he found himself in a delicate political and religious situation as a Lutheran ruler of a territory which was legally subject to the higher authority of his fiercely intolerant Catholic cousin, Philipp Wilhelm of Neuburg. Because of the difficulties of his own situation and on the advice of van Helmont, who was a close personal friend and advisor, Christian August developed a kind of private, ecumenical policy that not only included Catholics, Lutherans, and Calvinists, but also extended to separatist groups, radical pietists, and Jews. In 1652, again on the advice of van Helmont, Christian August came to an agreement with his cousin that Catholics as well as Lutherans would be officially allowed to worship in the Sulzbach territories and that all church assets would be available to both confessions.[19] In 1655 Christian August took the further decisive step of converting from Lutheranism to Catholicism. His conversion was greeted with horror by his immediate Lutheran family, and some Lutheran historians have argued that it was politically motivated, which it was not.[20]

Christian August's conversion was one of a number of similar conversions, for example, that of Ernst von Hessen-Rheinfels, Herzog Johann Friedrich von Braunschweig-Luneburg, and Herzog Christian Louis van Mecklenburg-Schwerin. All these Protestant rulers had been greatly influenced by Archbishop Johann Philipp von Schönborn. Known as the "German Solomon" and the "Prince of Peace," Johann Philipp, was committed to a level of tolerance that was astonishing for the time.[21] For example, he did not refuse to be godfather for Lutheran children; he therefore routinely took part in Protestant religious services. His plans for the reunion of Catholics and Protestants, of which the Pope disapproved, were supported by a number of other ecumenically-minded Lutherans and Catholics, not least of whom was Leibniz, himself a good friend of van Helmont's and von Rosenroth.[22]

Because of the influence of men like Johann Phillipp of Schonborn and Landgraf Ernst von Hessen-Rheinfels,[23] Christian August must have thought that Catholicism offered a greater chance than Protestantism for the kind of universal toleration to which he was committed. (Susanna Akermann suggests that Queen Christina came to the same conclusion.[24]) The men he chose as advisors certainly suggests that he believed this. They were a diverse group, actually recruited by van Helmont. Aside from von Rosenroth, they included Justus Brawe, Clamerus Florin, and Johann Jacob Fabricius, all Kabbalists and theosophists.[25] Another one of Christian August's privy counsellors was the Catholic mystic Johann Abraham Pöhmer.[26]

Christian August's view of Catholicism was radically different from his cousin's and, indeed, from a great many of the Catholics living in the Sulzbach territories. Philipp Wilhelm was appalled by the people attached to the Sulzbach court and took draconian steps to rid Christian August's court of influences he deemed pernicious. He had Brawe, Fabricius, and Florin denounced from the Cathedral at Regensburg with a call for their expulsion;[27] and he worked behind the scenes for the arrest and imprisonment of van Helmont by the Roman Inquisition in 1662, later publishing a pamphlet to justify his actions.[28] Inquisition documents dealing with van Helmont's case give a clear picture of how seriously Catholics viewed the situation at Sulzbach.[29]

Even this brief description justifies, I hope, my description of the Sulzbach court as "Rosicrucian." I would argue further that this "Rosicrucian" orientation explains the emphatic and unusual philo-Semitism characteristic of von Rosenroth, van Helmont, and their patron Christian August. The limitations that historians have increasingly found to be characteristic of sixteenth and seventeenth century Christian philo-Semites do not apply to these three men. Their immersion in the Kabbalah, particularly the Lurianic Kabbalah, led them to advocate a return to what they considered to be the original Jewish Christianity embodied in the Kabbalah. Because they were convinced that this Jewish Christianity predated both the Talmud and the Church Fathers, the doctrinal issues that had divided Christian and Jew for centuries ostensibly became moot. Christians and Jews could at last agree that Jesus was the Messiah and that God was both one and many. The major stumbling blocks in the way of the conversion of the Jews, the belief in Jesus as the son of God and the concept of the Trinity, were therefore eliminated; but they were eliminated in a way that fundamentally undermined these distinctive Christian doctrines, leaving the Sulzbach Kabbalists open to the general charge of heresy and the particular charge of "judaizing."

In his illuminating article "La Kabbala chrétienne en Allemagne du xvi au xviii siècle," Erst Benz describes the kind of religious no man's land that certain Jews and Christians found themselves in as a result of their esoteric, mystical studies:

> ... la Kabbala permet certes d'accepter l'idée que les propheties kabbalistiques au sujet du Messie ont trouvé leur realisation en Jesus-Christ; mais elle n'est pas compatible avec les formules dogmatiques de l'Église au sujet de la Trinité, car elle comporte, avec la doctrine des *Sefirot*, une interprétation differente de la vie intradivine. Ainsi, les kabbalistes juifs en arrivent fréquemment, en partant au judaisme, à faire un pas vers le christianisme; mais ils ne vont jamais jusqu'à l'approbation complète des dogmes chrétiens. Inversement, les kabbalistes chrétiens, partant du christianisme,

évoluent bien souvent de manière à entrer en conflict avec la doctrine tradi-
tionnelle de leur Église, et parfois aussi avec les autorités ecclesiastiques.
C'est ainsi que les groupes esoteriques juifs et chrétiens se retrouvent dans
une sorte de zone frontalière à la limite des deux religions.[30]

When analyzed from a Jewish perspective, the kind of inquiring yet critical
and ultimately skeptical outlook described here by Benz has been characterized elsewhere as typical of the "Marrano mentality" which arose from the
unique experience of Sephardic Jews constrained to live with and encouraged
or forced to convert to an alien religion. Popkin, Petuchowski, Kaplan, and
others who have written about the "Marrano mentality" contend that the kind
of dual allegiance and perspective produced in many Conversos contributed
to the development of the critical, skeptical mentality that led, first, to a non-
dogmatic, essentially non-denominational spirituality and, ultimately, to the
secular thinking characteristic of modern western thought.[31] From a Christian
perspective, the Reformation produced similar conflicting allegiances in the
minds of many Christians, and these conflicts contributed to a similar skeptical and ecumenical outlook. These two mentalities, the "Marrano" and the
post-Reformation Christian meet in the thought of the Sulzbach Kabbalists,
particularly in that of Francis Mercury van Helmont. Van Helmont's and von
Rosenroth's experiences in Amsterdam brought them in contact with Christians and Jews of various religious beliefs. But it was their experience with
Conversos that put a special stamp on their thought, convincing them that the
real difference between Christians and Jews was minimal and easily overcome
by the acceptance of their Christianized version of the Kabbalah. Van Helmont and his fellow Kabbalists provide a further example of how dangerous
Luther's claim to rely on Scripture alone proved to be for dogmatic religious
assertions of any kind. For in trying to understand exactly what the Gospels
meant, they immersed themselves in Jewish sources and Jewish ideas. While
the Sulzbach Kabbalists were all deeply religious, their friendship and col-
laboration transcended conventional Christian denominational boundaries.
For how else could a Lutheran, a Lutheran turned Catholic, and Catholic
turned Quaker/Seeker have otherwise worked together and remained devoted
friends? They were, to use Kolakowski's memorable phrase, *Chrétiens sans
eglise*, although van Helmont was the only one who clearly recognized this
fact.

Notwithstanding van Helmont's more radical position, the philo-Semitism
of each one of the Sulzbach Kabbalists was truly unique. They did not
subscribe to the view of contemporary Christians that the only good Jew was
a potential convert. As Ernestine van der Wall has pointed out, Christian
philo-Semitism did not extend to Jews as Jews, but only to Jews as potential
Christian converts:

...philo-Judaism has to be seen in a conversionist light, which at once indicates the limits of their pro-Jewishness: their philo-Judaism was a conditional sympathy.[32]

Van der Wall makes the excellent point that because many philo-Semites were also mystics and spiritualists who did not care about dogmas and ceremonies, they easily built bridges to other faiths and minimized doctrinal differences. But their ecumenism stopped when it came to the necessity of accepting Jesus as the true Messiah.

Clearly van der Wall is correct in the case of most philo-Semites, and her analysis would at first appear to apply to the Sulzbach Kabbalists as well. Von Rosenroth makes his conversionist aims clear throughout the *Kabbala Denudata*, as well as in his other writings and correspondence. The second part of the *Kabbala Denudata* emphasizes von Rosenroth's missionary intent. It begins with a systematic outline of the doctrines in the *Zohar*, to which von Rosenroth appends parallel passages from the New Testament. Precisely the same technique is used in the *Adumbratio Christiane Kabbalae*, the last treatise in the *Kabbala Denudata*, which was written by van Helmont and published separately because of its imagined importance in the task of converting Jews to Christianity. But a careful reading of the texts reveals that the Christianity proffered to the potential Jewish convert seems very strange and far more Jewish than Christian. For example, their treatment of the central Christian doctrine of Jesus as the Messiah is distinctly unorthodox.

In both von Rosenroth's and van Helmont's discussions the historical, flesh and blood Jesus of the Gospels, who was born of Mary and ordained to die and be resurrected as an expiation for man's original sin, disappears beneath the abstruse doctrines of Kabbalists and Christian mystics. Von Rosenroth and van Helmont identify Christ with one of two figures in the Kabbalah, either with *Adam Kadmon* or with *Seir Anpin*. As van Helmont has his Christian Philosopher say to the Kabbalist in his *Adumbratio Kabbalisticae Christianae*, "Precisely what you call Adam Kadmon, we call Christ."[33] *Adam Kadmon* is the primordial man, who was the first being emanated from the divine light and who contained the souls of all subsequent men within himself.[34] *Seir Anpin* was a composite figure comprised of the six lower *sephiroth*, who played the chief role in the universal process of redemption, or *tikkun*. That von Rosenroth could identify *Seir Anpin* (I use von Rosenroth's spelling)[35] with Christ is not so surprising when one considers that no less an authority than Gershom Scholem describes *Seir Anpin* as the product of God giving birth to himself. I quote the entire passage because Scholem says things about *Seir Anpin* that could easily have persuaded a Christian to identify this figure with Christ:

...The origin of *Zeir Anpin* in the womb of the 'celestial mother,' his birth and development, as well as the laws in accordance with which all the 'upper' potencies are organized in him, form the subject of detailed exposition in the system developed by Luria's followers. There is something bewildering in the eccentricity of these over-detailed expositions – the architecture of this mystical structure might be styled baroque.

Luria is driven to something very much like a mythos of God giving birth to Himself; indeed, this seems to me to be the focal point of this whole involved and frequently rather obscure and inconsistent description....[36]

The identification of Christ with either *Adam Kadmon* or *Seir Anpin*[37] had important unorthodox implications for mainstream Christians, whether Catholic or Protestant. If all souls were originally contained in Adam Kadmon, or Christ, then Christ was essentially in all souls, a shocking notion, when taken literally, because it combined two heresies, pantheism and Pelagianism. This idea hardly squared with the Catholic or Lutheran doctrine of original sin and man's fallen nature. It suggested, on the contrary, that each individual had the potential to save himself by his own efforts and that, indeed, men were potentially, if not actually, divine.[38] I have discussed the Hermetic, Kabbalistic, and Pelagian origins of this view of man elsewhere.[39] I need only stress here how unorthodox such views were because they obviated any need for Christ's sacrifice and death in anything but a metaphorical or allegorical sense and suggested instead that man controlled his own destiny as well as that of the universe. Orthodox Christians routinely dubbed any diminution of Christ's role as "Jewish." The Christian Hebraist Constantine L'Empreur referred with obvious distaste to the Socinian view of Christ as a "Jewish" error: "many people, even some who profess Christianity, do not shrink from frank approval of the Jewish error. They completely reject Christ's expiation for our sins."[40] L'Empreur was right. Socinians, along with other Christian sectarians and mystics, did allegorize Christ's sacrifice as an event repeated in each individual's soul, rejecting the idea that it represented a unique historical episode. One of the main reasons why van Helmont became a Quaker was because he mistakenly believed that the Quaker doctrine of "Christ within" proved that Quakers were essentially Kabbalists at heart. Quakers were, of course, accused of not believing in the historical Christ.[41] One of the charges brought against van Helmont by the Inquisition was precisely this, that he did not believe in Christ as a historical figure:

...Had he lived, the noble Lord Philip Otto from Herzelles...would have spoken about many of Helmont's heinous teachings, which he attempted to instill in this man more than once; namely: that those things must not be believed which the sacred Catholic Church teaches about the conception, nativity, passion, and resurrection of Christ, our Savior. All these things should be understood allegorically, not literally – that Christ is daily conceived, born, suffers, dies, and rises again in true Christians, that is in Helmontians.... The perversity of Helmont is not limited to Catholics, but he tempts Lutherans also with the already mentioned allegorical interpretation of the incarnation and resurrection of Christ along with other impious abominations. If it will be necessary, a renowned man worthy of belief, but not Catholic, will testify concerning this matter.[42]

Because *Adam Kadmon* and *Seir Anpin* were both described by Kabbalists as emanations from God, many Christians rejected them on the grounds of pantheism. The charge of pantheism was the one most often brought against the Kabbalah and its Sulzbach proponents. Henry More wrote at length on the subject. He was followed by Wachter and Basnage, who charged Spinoza with acquiring his pernicious pantheism from the Kabbalah.[43] Henry More took the first fundamental axiom of the Kabbalah to be "ex nihilo nihil posse creari" and wrote a passionate treatise on how sacrilegious it was to "suppose that the divine essence is a corporeal spirit and that the material world is in some way spirit."[44] For More the Kabbalistic doctrine of creation through the *sefirot* supported the dangerous doctrines of pantheism, materialism, and, ultimately, atheism. In regard to its pantheistic implications, More's analysis was correct.[45] The theory that spirit and matter were convertible was a basic Kabbalistic doctrine, just as it was a central tenet of alchemy, Renaissance Hermeticism, and occultism in general.[46] Van Helmont, whose thought derived from all these sources, describes creation in pantheistic terms:

...these are our Position, 1) That the Creator first brings into being a spiritual Nature. 2) And that either arbitrarily (when he pleases) or continually, as he continually understands, generates, etc. 3) That some of these spirits, for some certain cause or reason, are slipt down from the state of knowing, or Penetration. 4) That these Monades or single Beings being now become spiritless or dull, did cling or come together after various manners. 5) That this coalition or clinging together, so long as it remains such, is called matter. 6) That, out of this matter, all things material do consist, which yet shall in time return again to a more loosened and free state. No contradiction is involved in all these. Hence the Creator may also be said to be the efficient cause of all things materiated or made material, although not immediately.[47]

A further doctrine accepted by the Sulzbach Kabbalists, that of *ibbur*, also undermined orthodox Christian views of Christ's essential role in salvation. According to the doctrine of *ibbur*, literally "impregnation," the souls of pious men will be reincarnated into those of sinful mortals in order to help effect their salvation. Here Christ's unique role in salvation is attributed to pious, *mortal* men.

Given these various doctrines taken from the Kabbalah and various strands of Christian mysticism, the stumbling block to the conversion of the Jews identified by van der Wall as the belief in Jesus as the Messiah all but disappeared. The Christ of von Rosenroth and van Helmont is far more Kabbalistic than Christian. This helps to explain why van Helmont apparently accepted Peter Spaeth's conversion to Judaism with equanimity, even encouraging it.[48]

Another unique aspect of the beliefs of the Sulzbach Kabbalists involved salvation and the afterlife. Once again it is apparent that their ideas owe much more to the Kabbalah and unorthodox Christian thought than to either Catholicism, Lutheranism, or Calvinism. In every one of his major works, van Helmont categorically denied the eternity of Hell. In his opinion this was a pernicious doctrine that defiled the character of God and drove men to atheism. He went even further than this, elaborating on the problem of the so-called "virtuous pagans," a problem that had bothered many Christians. How could virtuous pagans be damned eternally for not believing in Christ when they had not been given the chance to believe? Dante had solved the problem by putting his beloved Virgil in Limbo; but his solution seemed mean-spirited to many later Christians. As D.P. Walker has pointed out, orthodox Christian views of hell as a place of eternal torment became increasingly repugnant to many Christians in the seventeenth century. Origen's concept of *apocatastasis*, or universal salvation, anathematized by the Council of Constantinople in 553 A.D., was revived, although the majority of Christians still believed that the orthodox view of hell was the only effective deterrent to vice.[49] Because of their immersion in the Kabbalah, particularly the Lurianic Kabbala, van Helmont and von Rosenroth were far more explicit and adamant in their denial of the eternality of hell than other Christians who leaned towards this view. They accepted the Lurianic doctrine of *tikkun*, or restoration, which posited that every soul would eventually be redeemed and that creation would only come to an end with the perfection and salvation of everything in it, and that meant *everything*, from the lowliest pebble, through plants and animals, and up to men. According to the Lurianic doctrine of metempsychosis, or *gilgul*, every level of creation from the lowest to the highest was filled with souls. Through the process of repeated reincarnations these souls would eventually move up the ladder of creation until they reached perfection. Those souls who needed extra help would be given it through *ibbur*, by being impregnated with stronger, more pious souls placed there especially to help them. This radically optimistic doctrine was wholeheartedly accepted by the Sulzbach Kabbalists. Luria's treatise on the Revolution of Souls was printed in full in the *Kabbala Denudata*. Van Helmont refers to Luria's belief in metempsychosis and the eventual restitution or perfection of all things in many of his writings. His clearest exposition of these ideas occurs in the *Two Hundred Queries Concerning the Revolution of Souls*, which he wrote together with Anne Conway and the Quaker George Keith.[50]

What is so interesting about von Rosenroth's and van Helmont's acceptance of the Lurianic idea of *tikkun*, or the restitution and perfection of all things, in place of the orthodox concept of an eternal hell, is that this belief seems to have been one especially embraced by Amsterdam Jews. It seems likely that van Helmont must have been aware of the divisive and acrimonious debate that had taken place among the Jews of Amsterdam in the 1630s over the nature of hell and divine punishment. This debate among Jews reflected the wider debate in the Christian community between Socinians, Arminians, and Collegiants, on the one hand, who tended to reject the doctrine of predestination and eternal damnation, and Calvinists proper.[51] But the Jewish debate had a special relevance, even poignancy, which the Christian debate lacked, for it became intimately involved with the peculiar problems experienced by Conversos.

The Jewish debate pitted Rabbi Isaac Aboab de Fonseca against Saul Levi Morteira, a senior Haham in the Amsterdam Rabbinate. Aboab, a former Marrano, had been tutored in Kabbalah by Abraham Herrera, himself a former New Christian, who had been a disciple of the Lurianic Kabbalist, Israel Sarug. Aboab embraced the Lurianic doctrine of *tikkun*. Quoting the Mishnaic phrase, "All Israelites have a portion in *olam ha-ba* [the world to come]," as well as all the laws of return and restoration in the Torah, Aboab assured every Jew that he would be saved, no matter what his sins. In his treatise *Nishmat Hayyim*, Aboab flatly states that "whosoever is called by the name Israelite will not suffer eternal punishment even though he may have committed the gravest possible sins."[52] Aboab's doctrine clearly appealed to the many Conversos in Amsterdam because it asserted the inalienable Jewishness of all Conversos, regardless of their past or present associations with Christianity: "This is what our rabbis of blessed memory meant when coining the phrase, "though he sinned, he is still an Israelite" [B.T. Sanh. 44a]. They intended to convey the idea that though he sinned, he was not cut off thereby from the tree but remained a Jew; and even if he apostatized from the Lord and chose new gods, he will again be called a Jew as a result of transmigration and punishments."[53]

Morteira rejected Aboab's teaching on the grounds that it contradicted the "Fathers, the Prophets, the Tanna'im and the Amora'im," all of whom had taught that punishment was eternal.[54] He further objected that such teachings would encourage Conversos to remain as they were or even return to Christianity and that it would discourage those in Spain and Portugal from emigrating and converting back to Judaism.[55] But when Morteira attempted to affirm the eternality of punishment before a congregation, he met with such great indignation that he decided to appeal the matter to the *Beth Din* in Venice. There the matter was dropped as being too sensitive.

The entire episode has been fully described by Alexander Altmann. What especially interested me was his remark that although the debate took place in the 1630s, the documents were copied out in 1648. Van Helmont was in Holland in 1648, attending to the publication of his father's works.   Van Helmont was a close friend of the Collegiant leader Galenus Abrahamsz as well as Adam Boreel, who had published a Hebrew edition of the Mishna with vowels and notes in 1646 with the help of Rabbi Judah Leon Templo, who actually lived with Boreel.[56] Van Helmont was therefore in contact with the circle of philo-Semitic millenarians and their Jewish colleagues and may have actually seen the documents concerning the Aboab-Morteira debate, either at that time or later during the 1650s when Aboab was back in Amsterdam. What convinces me that van Helmont was aware of the debate between Aboab and Morteira is the similarity of Aboab's and van Helmont's arguments against the eternality of punishment. Aboab insisted that God could not punish men eternally for sins which derived from their material, corruptible, and non-eternal part [see #5, 24–34]. Quoting Psalm 62:13: "Also unto thee, O Lord, belongeth mercy; for thou renderest to every man according to his work," Aboab comments, "i.e. according to his work performed by him who is non-eternal, and dost not measure him, a mere creature, against thee who art eternal, for thou art not adversely affected by the evil deeds of men." This was one of the major arguments van Helmont used to deny the existence of an eternal hell. The major difference between Aboab's and van Helmont's views is that van Helmont did not restrict universal salvation to Jews but extended it to everyone.

Altmann claims that it was common knowledge among Amsterdam Jews that Uriel da Costa had rejected Christianity because the dread of eternal damnation had tormented his youth and that he rejected the same doctrine when avowed by Jews.[57] Van Helmont had the same reaction; he believed that the doctrine of an eternal hell was what turned men away from God. The fact that there were both Jews and Christians who categorically denied that hell was eternal was one important reason why van Helmont and von Rosenroth came to believe that the Lurianic Kabbalah, with its doctrine of *tikkun*, offered a meeting ground for Christians and Jews. As van Helmont says:

> is it [the doctrine of *tikkun*] not like to prove of great service to the con-
> version both of Jews and Gentiles, to whom the denial of this one thing
> with some others, is of no small offense and stumbling block to many, both

Heathens and Jews, who conclude the Divinity of the modern Christians cannot be good while their philosophy is so bad. Besides, many Doctrines maintained by some Christians, concerning Reprobation, Original Sin, Infinite Damnation and the like, do give great occasion to many, both Jews and Gentiles, to suspect the whole Doctrine is false, and many of them do bless themselves from the God of the Christians, as being not the true God, but an Idol of their own making, whom they have so shaped and framed after their own dark and foolish Imaginations.[58]

The attempt to make Christianity less offensive to Jews had been the ostensible goal of many Christians concerned with converting the Jews long before the publication of the *Kabbala Denudata*. Pico della Mirandola, Reuchlin, Postel, La Peyrère, and other Christian Hermeticists and Kabbalists had from the Renaissance onwards emphasized the compatibility of Judaism and Christianity largely by minimizing or ignoring the very real doctrinal differences. They did this by returning to what they considered to be the *prisca theologia* common to all religions. In the sixteenth and seventeenth century radical Protestant philo-Semites tried a new tactic to convert Jews. Rejecting Catholic tradition, they offered Jews the promise of a return to the apostolic past of early Jewish-Christianity stripped of the more offensive doctrines of the incarnation, resurrection, and the Trinity. The problem was, how could one find out exactly what apostolic Jewish-Christianity was? This required delving into Jewish sources to discover what the customs and beliefs of early Jewish-Christians were. These investigations provided the rationale for those Christians, such as the Sabbatarians, who embraced Jewish customs.[59] To their Christian critics, the Sabbatarians provided a cautionary example of how delving into Jewish sources could undermine Christian beliefs and result in "judaizing."

At the same time that Protestants were trying to reconstruct Jewish-Christianity, they tried to convince the Jews that their own later tradition of Rabbinic Judaism based on the Talmud was, like Catholic tradition, a spurious addition. According to George Williams certain New Christians were attracted by this vision of a common meeting ground. The attraction of New Christians to a simplified, rationalized Christianity was paralleled by the effort made to simplify Judaism by New Christian and Marrano converts back to Judaism. What is interesting about the Sulzbach Kabbalists is that their appeal to the Jews to convert and to Christians to unite combines the Renaissance *prisca theologia* tradition with the radical Protestant appeal for a return to simplified apostolic Jewish-Christianity. Emphasizing the importance of publishing the principle Kabbalistic text, the *Zohar*, von Rosenroth says:

Because I suspect that so great a separation of Christian religions arose from no other cause than from such great diversity among Christians of philosophical principles and metaphysical definitions, which constitute, as it were, the left hand of theology (because many confess that philosophy is the servant of theology), it immediately occurred to me that I should hunt out that same ancient philosophy which flourished at the time of Christ and the Apostles and which appears to have flowed from the stream of the sacred oracles.... As I was about to examine those ancient opinions about God and other spiritual and theological questions, I fell upon this most ancient book of the Jews, which is called the *Sohar*, or *Book of Splendor*. Although I might seem to assail the antiquity of this work on account of its modern division into chapters, nevertheless, I discovered that the chapters themselves and teachings, which ought rather to be called fragments, are ancient enough and amply set forth the most ancient opinions and hypotheses. Not having, therefore, been frightened away by the incredible difficulty of the style or by the very abstruse covering of enigmas with which it teemed, I entered the path, worn by few, traversed by no one I knew, and, furthermore, filled with so many hard stones, uneven places, chasms, precipices, and such mud that it is not surprising so many, put in dread, abandoned it with disgust. Nevertheless, I pressed on. Nor to this day have I succumbed to the tediousness of the journey. I shall sketch for you in a few words what gold and whatever gems I have thus far dug out of this dirt and what hope leads me further.

First, indeed, the field of the most ancient Jewish theology reveals itself very clearly [in this source], the boundaries of which it was scarcely permitted to know to this very day, since that [theology] flowed in another way than that revealed by the modern teachers of this people.[60]

For von Rosenroth the Kabbalah represents the *prisca theologia* and it is entirely distinct from what modern Rabbis teach the Jews because it predates the Talmud and represents the actual teaching of the first Jewish Christians. When von Rosenroth complains of the tediousness of his work and describes the difficulties he has experienced in separating the few Kabbalistic gems and nuggets of gold from all the remaining rubbish, one suspects that his protestations do not really represent his own views but were designed to forestall the criticisms of Christian anti-Semites, just as in other places he attempts to forestall the criticisms of Jews. The Sulzbach Kabbalists did find themselves caught at times between the two.[61]

The belief that Christianity was implicit in the Jewish Kabbalah was the assumption of a long line of Jews who had converted for precisely that reason.[62] In 1280 Abulafia says that some of his students converted because they had applied the Kabbalistic practice of transposing letters to the phrase

"I sit in the shade to which I aspire" (Song of Songs) in such a way that they came up with the phrases "I love his cross" or "in the shadow of the crucified one." Alfonse de Valladolid (Abner of Burgos) explicitly refers to the Kabbalah in discussing his own conversion in 1320. He maintained the doctrine of the Incarnation was implicit in the concept of the *shehkina*, and he identified *metatron* of the Kabbalah with Jesus on the grounds that some thirteenth-century Kabbalists had interpreted *metatron* to mean "envoy." Although orthodox Jews began to argue strongly against this kind of Christian interpretation, even going as far as to argue that Christians were simply bad Kabbalists, who had derived such doctrines as the Trinity from a misunderstanding of the Kabbalah,[63] the practice continued. As Benz points out, Pico learned about the Kabbalah from the New Christian Flavius Mithridates. In 1512 Abraham Farisol, author of the anti-Christian polemic, *The Shield of Abraham*, described how Jewish converts to Christianity employed the idiom of the *Zohar* and other Kabbalistic texts to justify the Incarnation of God, his nativity, and resurrection. He pointed out that on the basis of the doctrine of the emanation of the *sefirot* Christians could argue that Jews already accepted the idea of multiplicity in God and that therefore the doctrine of the Trinity should not prove a stumbling block to conversion.

As Ernestine van der Wall has shown, the philo-Semitic millenarians in mid-seventeenth-century Amsterdam were well aware of the usefulness of the Kabbalah in converting Jews. In October, 1647, for example, Moriaen wrote to Hartlib, lamenting the fact that there are so few Christians expert in the Kabbalah. Moriaen thinks that Christians should pay someone to study the Kabbalah and publish his findings with the conversion of the Jews specifically in mind. He proposes that Boreel take on this important task.[64] The arrival of Rabbi Nathan Shapira, a renowned Kabbalist, in Amsterdam in 1657 reinforced the belief among Christian millenarians that the Kabbalah was indeed a *potentissima tela contra lapidem cor Hebraeorum*, as Pico had described it centuries before.[65] Popkin has described how Shapira was willing to recognize Jesus as the Messiah because he subscribed to the Lurianic view that the spirit of the Messiah reappeared at different times in history.[66] Shapira further encouraged the millenarians to think that the gulf between Christians and Jews was not so great by asserting, first, that Kabbalists believed Isaiah 53 actually did refer to the Messiah[67] and, second, that Jews could accept the Sermon on the Mount as the authentic teachings of the Rabbis. As Popkin points out, Shapira's remarks left Serrarius convinced that Shapira was "almost" a Christian and Dury that the conversion of the Jews was imminent. As Boreel's and Serrarius's close friend van Helmont undoubtedly shared the view that the Kabbalah offered a powerful means to convert the Jews. Caspar Kohlhans, one of van Helmont's oldest friends and a Quaker, claimed that van Helmont was a committed Kabbalist as early as 1660.[68] After Boreel's death, he may have been designated as the one to take on the task that Moriaen had allotted to Boreel. His meeting with von Rosenroth, who was well grounded in Hebrew, Syriac, and Aramaic, would then have been additionally fortuitous.

From the foregoing examples I hope I have provided enough evidence to suggest that the Philo-Semitism of the Sulzbach Kabbalists was indeed unique. Convinced they had rediscovered the original, authentic Jewish-Christian teachings of Christ and his disciples, they accepted complex Kabbalistic doctrines that simply could not, and did not, meet with the approval of the Christian community at large. Henry More, for one, was revolted by the convoluted philosophy of the Kabbalah. How, he asked, in a treatise von Rosenroth included in the *Kabbala Denudata*, could the Kabbalah hope to explain the difficulties in Scripture when it was itself so abstruse? Allegories and enigmas are not explained by further allegories and enigmas.[69] Eventually rejecting the Kabbalah, More advocated his version of Christianity instead, which he believed was simple, clear and more concerned with ethics than doctrine.

What is so interesting, and perhaps paradoxical, is that for all the abstruseness of their thought, and even because of it, the Sulzbach Kabbalists actually ended up with a far more tolerant and ecumenical outlook than More and many other thinkers who have been singled out for their enlightened religious views. By accepting the Lurianic Kabbalistic doctrine of *tikkun*, which categorically denied the eternality of hell and postulated the salvation and perfection of every created thing, von Rosenroth and van Helmont undercut the need for any institutionalized system of belief. Anyone could and would be saved. This was the basis for one of the Inquisition's charges against van Helmont: "...Helmont maintains without doubt that anyone in his own faith, of whatever kind, may be saved."[70] If everyone could be saved, whatever his faith, then believing in specific doctrines or specific sacraments was clearly unnecessary. Obviously, this way of thinking was not tolerable in the eyes of the Inquisition, as another charge against van Helmont makes clear:

> ...he has professed...that confession and the doctrine of the divine Eucharist is unnecessary and superfluous.... He maintained vehemently that our baptism with material water is not necessary, but it is sufficient for a man if he marks himself with the character of a Christian by engaging rightly in good works with a certain inner fervor.[71]

Although the Lurianic doctrine of *tikkun* could logically lead to the kind of uncommitted, ethical humanism that van Helmont embraced at the end of his life, he was the only one of the three Sulzbach Kabbalists to take this radical step. Von Rosenroth and Christian August remained within the Lutheran and Catholic Church respectively. For whatever reasons (and that is the subject of another paper), they were able and willing to accept the outward constraints of the institutionalized Church to which they belonged. Van Helmont could not. In his case, the search for church unity within a Christian framework had developed into a true spirit of toleration. The short declaration prefacing his *Adumbratio Kabbalisticae Christianae* succinctly sums up his attitude and beliefs:

> Quaero, non pono: nihil determino dictans:
> Conjicio: conor: confero: tento: rogo:
> Judaeos capto: meliori tramite ductor
> Si fueris, cedo: quaeritur una salus.

(I question; I do not assert, saying I determine nothing. I conjecture; I make trial; I compare; I test; I enquire; I court the Jews. If you have a guide to a better way, I yield.)

The last description we have of van Helmont's religious views comes from Leibniz, who describes him in terms consistent with this declaration, as a "seeker," a man without religious affiliation:

> Monsieur Francis Mercurius, Baron of Helmont, son of the famous physician of that name, is an old acquaintance of Madame, the Electress of Hanover. He had been a Roman Catholic, but subsequently a Quaker and while at Hanover called himself a Seeker.[72]

The Sulzbach Kabbalists are unique in another way as well. The primary motivating force behind their ecumenicalism was not millenarianism in the classic Christian sense of anticipating the decisive moment of Christ's second coming. Their exceptional tolerance and commitment to peace and brotherhood sprang from another source, their personal experiences of the suffering and desolation caused by the Thirty Years' war. Because of the war von Rosenroth and his family were forced to flee his birthplace, Alt-Raudten, a town then in the Silesian principality of Wohlau. That childhood experience shaped much of his mature poetry with its recurring theme of longing for peace. Christian August's childhood and adult life were both shaped and scarred by the war, as were van Helmont's. This is not to say that the Sulzbach Kabbalists were not millenarians,[73] simply that their millenarianism was shaped far more by the optimistic and meliorist Lurianic doctrine of *tikkun* than by the violent apocalypticism of the Book of Revelations. It consequently stressed the ultimate redemption of all of God's creatures through their own efforts rather than their judgement and (in most cases) condemnation by God.

Another unique aspect of Sulzbach philo-Semitism was the complete absence of anti-Semitism. Beneath the surface of much ecumenically-minded and ostensibly philo-Semitic prose lurks real intolerance and dislike for the Jews as fellow human beings. (I remind the reader of Ernestine van der Wall's observation that for most philo-Semites the only good Jew was a convertible Jew.) One of the most astonishing example of this appears in Johann Jacob Schudt's detailed account of Jewish customs. Like many other Christians, Schudt refers with great dismay, indeed horror and disgust, to Johan Peter Spaeth's conversion to Judaism and his taking of the name Moses Germanus.[74] (Spaeth's case is especially interesting because he himself attributed his conversion to the period he spent helping von Rosenroth edit the *Kabbala Denudata*.) Schudt was obviously interested in Jews and had sympathy for them. Yet he could not transcend stereotypes. He is, for example, well aware of the many Christian prohibitions limiting the ways in which Jews could make a living, but he refuses to believe that these have anything to do with the fact that Jews engage in usury. Jews practice usury because they are too lazy to do any real work. Furthermore, if they do work with their hands, they are bad at it. To prove this he gives the amazing example of Moses Germanus's circumcision. Schudt explains that because it was done by a Jewish carpenter (!), it was bungled, causing Moses Germanus great and long-term pain.[75] Schudt was a well-respected Hebraist like von Rosenroth, but the two men were worlds apart when it came to seeing Jews as fellow human beings.

When I first described van Helmont's Kabbalistic theories in a lecture at the Warburg Institute many years ago, I was asked if he was insane. To the twentieth-century questioner he may well appear to have been, but for those who have spent time reading about the bitter and bloody religious battles of the early modern period, van Helmont's philosophy comes as a breath of fresh air. A number of his contemporaries obviously felt the same way. Leibniz begins his epitaph for van Helmont with the lines, "If he had lived among the Greeks, he would now be numbered among the stars."[76] But the last word must be left to van Helmont's long-time friend, Benjamin Furly, a highly educated, intelligent man, and a Quaker, who, like van Helmont, eventually left the society. Writing to William Penn about the book in which van Helmont gives the fullest account of the Lurianic theory of *tikkun*, he reveals how highly he thinks of van Helmont as someone whose outlook was far ahead of his times:

...when thou readst, I doubt not but thou wilt see that it goes further than any System yet publikly receivd by any [sect?] of christians to the clearing the Divine providence, Justice, mercy & wisdom of god & rendring the most perplext articles of the Christian faith, easily conceivable to the meanest as well as largest capacity. So it is with me notwithstanding all the hot Zeale with which some pursue it, and him in England, stigmatizing him as a Papist, a Jesuit, yea a kind of Atheist, which rude, unmannerly, and unmanly treating of a man of his quality, age, reputation in the world, harmless deportment, going up & down doing good to all & harm to none, especially if we consider with all that he is a forreigner, every ingenious Englishman should be ashamed of & blush at; I hope if he, or any of his perswasion in some of those things should come thither they shall not be so hunted as Foxes, but received as Christians, & not be held unchristian for an opinion which if Christ did not [teach?] his disciples he at lest did bear[est?] with in them, & therefore must neither be in it self destructive of faith in [god?] nor of a holy conversation. But I shall forbear Apologizing, & leave the booke to Apologize for it self....[77]

NOTES

1. I would like to thank the Herzog August Bibliothek in Wolfenbüttel for their generous support which gave me the opportunity to do the research for this paper.
2. Hans J. Schoeps, *Philosemitismus in Barock: Religions und geistegeschichtliche Unter-suchungern* (Tübingen: J.C.B Mohr, 1952).
3. Shimon Markish, *Erasmus and the Jews*, tr. Anthony Olcott (Chicago: University of Chicago Press, 1986); Heiko Oberman, *The Roots of Anti-Semitism in the Age of Renais-sance and Reformation*, tr. James I. Porter (Philadelphia: Fortress Press, 1984); Jerome Friedman, *The Most Ancient Testimony: Sixteenth-Century Christian-Hebraica in the Age of Renaissance Nostalgia* (Athens, Ohio: Ohio University Press, 1983); Jonathan Israel, *European Jewry in the Age of Mercantilism* (Oxford: Clarendon Press, 1985); R. Po-chia Hsia, *The Myth of Ritual Murder: Jews and Magic in Reformation Germany* (New Haven: Yale University Press, 1988).
4. Po-chia Hsia, *op. cit.*(note 3), pp. 218, 222, note 76.
5. Friedman, *op. cit.* (note 3), p. 181.
6. *Luther's Works*, ed. Jaroslav Pelikan & Helmut T. Lehmann (Philadelphia: Fortress Press, 1971), 47: 196.
7. Quoted in Friedman, *op. cit.*, p. 132.
8. Amos Funkenstein's "Changes in the Patterns of Christian Anti-Jewish Polemics in the 12th Century" (*Zion*, 33:125–44) deals with an analysis of the types of Christian attacks on Biblical and Rabbinic exegesis, philosophical argumentation, and attacks on the Talmud. Scholem does not see any real Christian knowledge of the Kabbalah during the 13th century, and it seems that only with the emergence of Pico della Mirandola do we see this source entering the Christian orbit alongside the Talmud. Simha Assaf's *On the Debate over the Publication of the Books of the Kabbalah* (Jerusalem: Mossad Ha-Rav Kook, 1946) analyzes the fear of Jews at the Ferrara Rabbinic Synod (1554) that publication of the *Zohar* would provide Christians with an arsenal of post-Talmudic arguments against the Jews (see Kenneth R. Stow, "The Church and the Jews: From St. Paul to Paul IV," *Bibliographical Essays in Medieval Jewish Studies*, II, KTAV, 1976).
9. "They invent many lies about the name of God, the tetragrammaton, saying that our Lord was able to define this name (which they call *Schem Hamphoras*), and whoever is able to

do that, they say, is also able to perform all sorts of miracles. However, they cannot cite a single instance of any men who worked a miracle worth a gnat by means of this *Schem Hamphoras*" (Luther's Works, *op. cit.*, v. 47, 256).

10. Martin Friedrich discusses the attitude of seventeenth-century Lutherans towards Jews in *Zwischen Abwehr und Bekehrung: Die Stellung der deutschen evangelischen Theologie zum Judentum in siebzehnten Jahrhundert* (Beitrage zur historischen Theologie, no. 72, Tubingen: J.C.B. Mohr, 1988). His conclusion that seventeenth-century Lutherans had some toleration but no real respect or appreciation for Jews and little concern with missionizing emphasizes the uniqueness of von Rosenroth's position.

11. *Herrn Christian Knorrs von Rosenroth, Hochfürstl. Pfaltz-Sultzbachischen Hof-Raths und Cantzley-Direktoris Schreiben an seine älteste Fräulein Tochter, womit er sie für dem Abfall, als sie mit einem Catholischen Herrn von Schütz vermählet worden, wiewol vergeblich gewarnet. In: Sammlung von Alten und Neuen Theologischen Sachen ... aufdas Jahr 1738*: 413–432.

12. For a bibliography of von Rosenroth see K. Salecker, *Christian Knorr von Rosenroth (1636–1689)*, Leipzig: Mayer & Muller, 1931, and my entry on von Rosenroth in *Grundriss der Philosophie*, forthcoming.

13. R.J.W. Evans, "Learned Societies in Germany in the Seventeenth Century," *European Studies Review* 7 (1977): 129–51.

14. J.C. Wagenseil, *Benachrichtigungen wegen einiger die Judenschafft angehende wichtigen Sachen ...* (Leipzig, 1705), pp. 32–3.

15. Leszek Kolakowski, *Chrétiens sans Église: La conscience religieuse et le lien confessionel au xviie siècle*. Traduit de Polonais par Anna Posner (Paris: Gallimard, 1969).

16. Frances A. Yates, *The Rosicrucian Enlightenment* (London: Routledge & Kegan Paul, 1972).

17. Brian Vickers, "Frances Yates and the Writing of History," *Journal of Modern History* 51 (1979): 287–316.

18. For a description of the ecumenical policy promoted by Christian August, see Klaus Jaitner, "Der Pfalz-Sulzbacher Hof in der europäischen Ideengeschichte des 17 Jahrhunderts," *Wolfenbütteler Beitrage: aus den Schatzen der Herzog August Bibliothek*, hrsg. Paul Raabe (1988): 273–404; Manfred Fincke, "Toleranz und 'Discrete' Frömmigkeit nach 1650: Pfalzgraf Christian August von Sulzbach und Ernst van Hessen-Rheinfels," *Frommigkeit in der frühen Neuzeit: Studien zur religiosen Literatur des 17. Jahrhunderts in Deutschland*, ed. Dieter Breuer (Amsterdam: Rodopi, 1984).

19. G. Neckermann, *Geschichte des Simultaneum Religionis Exercitium im vormaligen Herzogthum Sulzbach* (Regensburg, 1897).

    Van Helmont, "Memoirs," British Library, Sloane 530: "Being at the Emperor's Court in 1650 a prince of the Empire sent to me a Gentleman with a letter desiring me (since he heard I was lodg'd apart from the Court) that as I passed through the Empire I would be pleased to call upon him which accordingly I did. Now this prince being a Lutheran, the warrs having driven him out of his Country, and almost an half part of his subjects made Catholicks, and after the peace was made in Germany he had power given to him to reforme the religion by turning out the Catholick Clergy, and supplyed their rooms with Lutherans, when I therefore was arrived at his court among many matters concerning which he was pleased to ask my advice I counseled him that he should divide the Rooms of the clergy between the religions mentioned, for which peaceable endeavour I gaind afterwards the hatred of both."

20. The horrified reactions of Christian August's mother are printed in full in G. Ch. Gack, *Geschichte des Herzogtums Sulzbach* (Leipzig, 1847), who, as a Lutheran, accuses Chris-

tian August of caring more for earthly political power than spiritual good (p. 308).

21. A further indication of Johann Phillipp's unusual tolerance is revealed by the effect on him of his meeting with Friedrich Spee. When he became Bishop of Würzburg in 1642, Johann Philipp was one of the first imperial princes to stop all witch trials in his jurisdiction. Friedhelm Jürgensmeier, "Johann Philipp von Schönborn, " *Frankische Lebensbilder*, Bd. 6 (1975), pp. 161–184. Also see Heribert Raab, "Das 'discrete Catholische' des Landgraften Ernst von Hessen-Rheinfels (1623 bis 1693). Ein Beitrag zur Geschichte der Reunionsbemühungen und der Toleranzbestrebungen im 17. Jahrhundert," *Archiv für Mittelrheinische Kirchen-Geschichte* 12 (1960): 175–198; Manfred Fincke, "Toleranz und 'Discrete' Frömmigkeit nach 1650: Pfalzgraf Christian August von Sulzbach und Ernst van Hessen–Rheinfels," *op. cit.* (note 18).

22. While on a trip in 1670 Leibniz remained for a full month (longer than anywhere else) at Sulzbach with von Rosenroth in order to study the Kabbalah: "De Cabala Hebraeorum multum olim locutus sum cum Domino Knorrio, auctore Cabalae Denudatae, viro magnae et multiplicis doctrinae, egregiique in publicum animi." Letter to Bourgnet, G. G. Leibniti, *Opera Omnia*, hsg. von L. Dutens, 1768, Bd 6, p. 204.

23. The depth of Landgraf Ernst's philo-Semitism was also unusual. He published a treatise, *Der discrete Catholisher*, in 1666 in which he included the Jews among those who would be saved. See Heribert Raab, "Das 'Discrete Catholische'.. ," *op. cit.; Idem,* "'Sincere et ingenue etsi cum Discretione.' Landgraf Ernst van Hessen-Rheinfels (1623–93) über eine Reform von Papstum, Römischer Kurie und Reichskirche," in *Beiträge zu kirchlichen Reformbemühungen von der Alten Kirche bis zu Neuzeit. Festgabe für Erwin Iserloh*, hrsg. Remigius Baumer (Paderborn/Munchen: Ferdinand Schöningh, 1980), pp. 814–30; Manfred Finke, "Toleranz und 'Discrete' Frömmigkeit nach 1650: Pfalzgraf Christian August von Sulzbach und Ernst von Hessen-Rheinfels," *op. cit.* (note 18).

24. Susanna Akerman, *Queen Christina of Sweden and her Circle: The Transformation of a Seventeenth-Century Philosophical Libertine* (Leiden: E.J. Brill, 1991).

25. Gack (note 20) describes these men as follows: "ihre Lehren stimmten mit den Irrlehren jener Sekten überein, die unter dem Namen Quäker, Weigelianer und Wiedertäufer bekannt seien (p. 321). Arnold says that Fabricius was influenced by the theosophy and pansophy of Arndt and Weigel (*Kirchen- und Ketzerhistorie*, vol. 3/4, 151).

26. At Christian August's express wish, Pöhmer translated a mystical treatise entitled *Reiches Gottes in der Seele oder wie eine Gottsuchende Seele das Reich Gottes, nach einem geistlichen Tode, in ihr selbst finden, behalten und geniessen solle....* This was printed at Sulzbach.

27. A fascinating series of pamphlets and petitions exists in the Herzog August Bibliothek, Wolfenbüttel, denouncing Philipp Wilhelm's charges and testifying to the orthodoxy of the men he wished to have expelled.

28. *Motiven und Ursachen/ umb welcher Willen der Durchleuchtigste Fürst und Herr/ Herr Philipp Wilhelm/ Pfaltzgraf bey Rheyn/ u. Herrn Franciscum Mercurium, Freyherrn von Hellmont/ zu Kützingen gefänglich annehmen/ und von dar nach Rohm führen/ lassen/ allermassen dieselbe/ dem auch Durchleuchtigsten Fürsten und Herrn/ Herrn Christiano Augusto, Pfaltzgrafen bey Rheyn/ u. Auf dero Fürstliche Durchleucht. bewegliches anhalten/ endlich Schrifftlich communicirt worden.* (Bibliothek der evangelischen Kirchengemeide, Sulzbach, no date). I would like to thank Dr. Manfred Finke for sending me a photocopy of this document.

29. Archivio Segreto Vaticano, Archivio della Nuziatura di Colonia 81.

30. Ernst Benz, "La Kabbale chrétienne en Allemagne du xvi au xviii siecle," in *Kabbalistes Chrétiens: Cahiers de l'Hermetisme.* Directeurs: Antoine Faivre & Frederick Tristan

(Paris: Editions Albin Michel, 1979), pp. 111–2.

31. See, for example, R. H. Popkin, *The History of Scepticism from Erasmus to Descartes* (Berkeley: University of California Press, revised and expanded edition, 1979); *idem, The Third Force in Seventeenth-Century Thought.* Brill's Studies in Intellectual History (Leiden: E.J. Brill, 1992); Y. Kaplan, *From Christianity to Judaism: The Story of Isaac Orobio de Castro* (Oxford: Oxford University Press, 1989); and J. Petuchowski, *The Theolgy of Hakam David Nieto: An Eighteenth-century Defense of the Jewish Tradition* (New York: KTAV Publishing House, Inc., 1970).

32. Ernestine van der Wall, "The Amsterdam Millenarian Petrus Serrarius (1600–1669) and the Anglo-Dutch Circle of Philo-Judaists," in J. van den Berg & E. van der Wall, *Jewish-Christian Relations in the Seventeenth Century. Studies and Documents* (Dordrecht: Kluwer Academic Publishers, 1988), p. 73.

33. p. 5, paragraph 13.

34. Scholem, *Major Trends in Jewish Mysticism* (New York: Schocken Books, 1961), pp. 265, 279. In van Helmont's view *Adam Kadmon* was also Adam. In a letter to Thomas Burnet, Leibniz refers to van Helmont's belief that Jesus and Adam were one and the same: "...Mr. Mercurius van Helmont croyoit que l'ame de Jesus-Christ étoit celle d'Adam, et que l'Adam nouveau reparant ce que le premier avoit gasté, c'estoit le même personnage qui satisfaisoit à son ancienne dette" (Leibniz to Thomas Burnet, 26 May 1706 in O. Klopp ed., *Correspondance de Leibniz ave l'Electrice Sophie de Brunswick-Lunebourg.* London: Williams & Norgate, 1874, v. 3, 217).

35. *KD*, 2, p. 80–81: "Quaeritur: annon Adam Kadmon sit *logos* seu secunda Persona Divinitatis? Respondeo. Ex ista Hypothesi, nisi fiat insignis notionum Confusio, id non posse deduci. Cum nempe juxta Scripturae verba in divinis omnium retinenda sit appellatio Filii; haec sanè, si Judaeorum vulgo reddi debet tolerabilis, nulli personarum Judaicarum applicari poterit, quam Seir Anpin, qui secundum generalem Numerationum conceptum reperitur in Tiphereth, à Cabbalistis propriè atque constanter Filius appellatur; etaim primogenitus sex comprehendens Numerationes à Gedulah usque ad Jesod. Pater vero secundum istam hypothesin est Chochmah, cui Binah ad intergritatem personae Androgynae constituendam annexa est. Clauditque decadem non minus quam triadem Spiritus Sanctus, seu Malchuth. Appositè omnia ad Sensusm Cabbalisticum.... Atque sic Christus in compendium redigisse videtur totam Cabbalam, discipulis suis in pietatis potissimum praxi exercendis, sufficientissium.

36. Scholem, *op. cit.* (note 34), pp. 270–1.

37. One might well ask why von Helmont and von Rosenroth did not agree on which Kabbalistic figure represented Christ. The following statement from Scholem provides a possible answer: "The five principal *parzufim* of *Arikh Anpin, Abba, Imma, Ze'eir Anpin*, and *Nukba de-Ze'eir* constitute the final figure of *Adam Kadmon* as it evolves in the first stages of *tikkun*, which is quite different from the figure of *Adam Kadmon* that existed before the breaking of the vessels." Hence *Ze'eir Anpin* is ultimately part of *Adam Kadmon*. (G. Scholem, *Kabbalah*. New York: New American Library, 1978, p. 142).

38. Moshe Idel, *Kabbalah: New Perspectives* (New Haven: Yale University Press, 1988); *idem*, "The Magical and Neoplatonic Interpretations of the Kabbalah in the Renaissance," *Jewish Thought in the Sixteenth Century*, ed. B.D. Cooperman (Cambridge, Mass.: Harvard University Press, 1983): 186–242.

39. Allison P. Coudert, "Henry More, the Kabbalah, and the Quakers," in *Philosophy, Science, and Religion in England (1640–1700)*, ed. R. Kroll, R. Ashcraft, & P. Zagorin (New York: Cambridge University Press, 1992), pp. 31–67.

40. Peter T. van Rooden, "Constantijn L'Empreur's Contacts with the Amsterdam Jews and

his Confutation of Judaism," in *Jewish-Christian Relations in the Seventeenth Century,* *op. cit.* (note 32), p. 62.

41. This became the subject of a prolonged debate, which eventually had the effect of pushing the Quakers in a more conservative and orthodox direction.

42. Indictment of the Inquisition, Rome, July 5, 1662. Achivio Segreto Vaticano, Archivio della Nunziatura de Colonia 81.

43. Richard H. Popkin, "Spinoza, Neoplatonic Kabbalist?," in *Neoplatonism and Jewish Thought,* ed. L. Goodman (vol 7 in *Studies in Neoplatonism: Ancient and Modern,* R. Baine Harris, General Editor). New York: State University of New York Press, 1992, pp. 387–409.

44. Henry More, "Fundamenta Philsophiae sive Cabbalae Aeto-Paedo-Melissaeae, quae omnem Creationem proprie dictam negat, Essentiamque supponit Divinam quasi Corporeo-Spiritualem, Mundemq; Materialim aliquo modo Spiritum...," *Kabbala Denudata, Apparatus in Librum Sohar, pars secunda...,* pp. 293ff.

45. "For Luria and his followers, there is no break in this continuous process of evolution. This fact makes the problem of Luria's theism doubly acute, for the pantheistic implications of this doctrine are too manifest to require emphasis" (Scholem, *Major Trends in Jewish Mysticism, op. cit.,* p. 272).

46. Brian Vickers, "Analogy and Identity," *Occult & Scientific Mentalities in the Renaissance,* ed. Brian Vickers (Cambridge: Cambridge University Press, 1984), 117.

47. *A Cabbalistical Dialogue in Answer to the Opinion of a Learned Doctor in Philosophy and Theology, that the World was made of Nothing* ... (this was first published in Latin in the *Kabbala Denudata, Apparatus in Librum Sohar,*1677, pp. 308ff.), p. 4.

48. Popkin, "Spinoza, Neoplatonic Kabbalist?," *op. cit.* (note 43), p. 399; Johann Jacob Schudt, *Jüdische Merckwurdigkeiten...* (Frankfurt & Leipzig, 1714), i, p. 273, iv, p. 194.

49. D.P. Walker, *The Decline of Hell* (Chicago: University of Chicago Press, 1964).

50. *Two Hundred Queries moderately propounded concerning the Doctrine of the Revolution of Humane Souls, and its Conformity with the Truth of the Christian Religion...* (London, 1684).

51. Alexander Altmann, "Eternality of Punishment: A Theological Controversy within the Amsterdam Rabbinate in the Thirties of the Seventeenth Century," *Proceeding of the American Academy for Jewish Research* 40 (1972): 1–88.; Ernst Benz, "Der Mensch und die Sympathie aller Dinge am Ende der Zeiten," *Eranos Jahrbuch,* xxiv (1955), pp. 157ff.

52. *Ibid.,* p. 11 [text A, lines 1 & 2].

53. *Ibid.,* 22.

54. *Ibid.,* pp. 11–12.

55. *Ibid.,* 18.

56. The edition has Manasseh ben Israel's name on the title page rather than Boreel's for reasons explained by Richard Popkin ("Some Aspects of Jewish-Christian Theological Interchanges in Holland and England 1640–1700," in *Jewish-Christian Relations in the Seventeenth Century,* ed. J. van den Berg & E.G.E. van der Wall. Dordrecht & Boston 1988).

57. *Ibid.,* p. 19.

58. *Two Hundred Queries moderately propounded concerning the Doctrine of the Revolution of Human Souls, and its Conformity with the Truth of the Christian Religion...* (London, 1684), pp. 163ff.

59. Friedman, *op. cit.* (note 3); David Katz, *Sabbath and Sectarianism in Seventeenth-Century England* (Leiden: E.J. Brill, 1988).

60. *Kabbala Denudata, Apparatus in Librum Sohar, Pars Secunda* (after p. 740).

61. See for example the less than enthusiastic reaction to the *Kabbala Denudata* on the part of Christians like Johann Jacob Schudt (*Jüdische Merkwürdigkeiten....* Frankfurt & Leipzig, 1714), Johann Christoph Wagenseil (*Benachrichtingungen wegen einiger die Judenschafft angehende wichtigen Sachen....* Leipzig, 1705), Johann Andrea Eisenmenger(*Entdecktes Judenthums... .,* Königsberg, 1711), the Jewish convert Peter Spaeth, who became known as Moses Germanus (letter to F.M. van Helmont, Hamburg, Staats- und Universitätsbibliothek, Suppellex. ep., v. 26, pp. 67ff.), and van Rosenroth's description of the reaction of the Jewish community in general (*Kabbala Denudata*, 11 (1), pp. 18–19).

62. Ernst Benz discusses these converts in "Kabbalists Chrétiens," *op. cit.* (note 30).

63. Benz gives the example of Profiat Duran, who argued in (1397) that Christians had obtained their doctrine of the Trinity from a misunderstanding of the Kabbala.

64. Ernestine van der Wall, "Johann Stephen Rittangel's Stay in the Dutch Republic (1641–1642) in *Jewish-Christian Relations in the Seventeenth Century, op. cit*(note 32).

65. Pico della Mirandola, *Heptaplus*, ed. E. Garin (Florence, 1942), p. 348.

66. Richard H. Popkin, "Rabbi Nathan Shapira's Visit to Amsterdam in 1657," in *Dutch Jewish History*, ed. J. Michman & T. Levie (Jerusalem: The Institute for Research on Dutch Jewry, 1984), p. 194.

67. Ernestine van der Wall, "The Amsterdam Millenarian Petrus Serrarius (1600–1669) and the Anglo-Dutch Circle of Philo-Judaists," *Jewish-Christian Relations, op. cit.*

68. C. Kohlhans, *Dilucidationes quaedam valde necessariae in Gerardi Croesi Historiam Quakerianam...* (Amsterdam, 1695), pp. 120–1.

69. H. More, "Ad Clarissium ac Eruditissimum Virum N N... de rebus in Amica sua Responsione contentis in ulterior Disquisitio," *Kabbala Denudata*, I, 2, p. 179.

70. Informatio de Helmontio, May/June 1662. Archivio Segreto Vaticano, Achivio della Nunziatura di colonia 81.

71. *Ibid.*, document no. 3, "Indictment."

72. O. Klopp, *Correspondenz von Leibniz mit der Princzessin Sopie* (Hanover, 1873) ii, p. 8.

73. See for or example, the letters between von Rosenroth and George Keith in the Herzog August Bibliothek, Wolfenbüttel.

74. See the reference to this conversion in Richard Popkin's paper in this volume.

75. Johann Jacob Schudt, *Jüdische Merkwurdigkeiten....* (Frankfurt & Leipzig, 1714), pt. 2, Bk vi, ch. 12, pp. 169–170.

    Nil patre inferior jacet hic Helmontius alter,

    Qui Junxit varias mentis et artis opes;

76. Per quem Pythagoras et Cabbala sacra revixit,

    Elausque potest qui dare cuncta sibi.

    Quod si Graja virum tellus et prisca tulissent

    Secula, nunc inter lumina prima foret.

    (Leibniz added the following note to explain his reference to Elaus: "Hippias, patria Elaus, professione Philsophus, qui omnia quibus opus, ipse sibi manu sua elaborare poterat.") The epitaph is in Hanover, Niedersächsische Landesbibliotek, LBr. 389, MS Helmont, fol 130.

77. Furly to Penn, 23 July, 1684 [13 July in the English calendar], *The Papers of William Penn*, ed. Richard S. Dunn & Mary Maples Dunn (Philadelphia, University of Pennsylvania Press, 1981–6), ii, letter no. 185.

ARTHUR H. WILLIAMSON

6. BRITISH ISRAEL AND ROMAN BRITAIN:

THE JEWS AND SCOTTISH MODELS OF POLITY

FROM GEORGE BUCHANAN TO SAMUEL RUTHERFORD

Traditionally, George Buchanan and John Knox have personified two poles of the Scottish Reformation. Both were Protestants. Both were revolutionaries and leading apologists for the upheavals of the 1560s. But their views of these events and of the place of religion in society differed drastically.

The humanist Buchanan – poet, philologist, professor – first entered Scottish political and cultural life in the 1530s as a critic (and enemy) of the Franciscans, endorsed the Henrician Reformation and especially dissolution of the monasteries, and later approached society in his enormously influential political writings from a position which might well be described as anti-scriptural. Surely the only anti-clerical layman ever to serve as the Moderator of the Church of Scotland, Buchanan's Calvinism promoted a highly politicized, neo-Stoic ethics.[1]

The preacher and reformer John Knox became increasingly persuaded that the godly society could only be derived from the experience of the ancient Hebrews. Like so many sixteenth-century Scots, both lay and clerical, Knox saw himself as a latter-day "prophet". As such, he could interpret the meaning of scripture both past and present (even if he could not add to the text). A reformed Scotland would thus prove to be a highly biblicist society, indeed a society modeled remarkably closely on the Old Testament. It was also a society created in the "latter days" of the world, articulating and realizing events which would, seemingly, precipitate the eschaton.

So runs tradition. And of course it is broadly correct. Yet European thought between the late fifteenth century and the late sixteenth century possessed a truly extraordinary plasticity, and easy verities often enough require qualification and rethinking. Richard Popkin has recently shown us the complex tissue of apocalyptic expectations in the world of Cardinal Ximenes, a world at once brutally intolerant of Iberian Jewry and yet reformist and even Judaized. Still other scholars have observed that, in early modern Europe, anti-Semitism and philo-Semitism, intolerance and toleration, derive from common cultural materials and have a remarkably intertwined history.[2]

The essay which follows seeks to suggest that the widely accepted picture of revolutionary Scotland is too pat and that closer examination will reveal a

R.H. Popkin and G.M. Weiner (eds): Jewish Christians and Christian Jews, 97–117.
© 1994 *Kluwer Academic Publishers. Printed in the Netherlands.*

world quite different from what we would anticipate. If Knox embraced the experience of the ancient Jews and a political order derived almost exclusively from the Old Testament, and if Buchanan denied at length the significance of that experience, their attitudes towards Judaism nevertheless simply confound our expectations. An Old Testament society could be an important step toward Judaizing and philo-Semitism, but it was not in itself sufficient. A classical aristocratic vision might well find the Jews irrelevant (or, worse, aculturate pagan Ciceronian anti-Semitism), but that too need not happen. The dynamics which we could begin to recognize as the source of modernity only appear, in the anglophone world, during the decades which straddle the turn of the century and, effectively, the union of the British crowns.

GEORGE BUCHANAN AND THE JEWS

> "Of Judaism I have never thought."
> "...there are no Jews in Scotland." –
> George Buchanan, before the Lisbon Inquisition, 1550[3]

It has long become a commonplace to note that Buchanan's political thought is secular in the sense that it radically restricts the relevance of scripture, revelation, and, for that matter, even natural law to politics. His major work of political theory, the *De Juri Regni apud Scotos: Dialogus*, emphatically insists that the "holy experience" of the Hebrew commonwealth offered no guidance to other societies precisely because of its unique sacred character. The Jewish kings and judges had been appointed by God through a divinely instituted formula. All other societies created legitimate authority by an act of popular will which was sustained through a mutual or reciprocal contract between rulers and ruled. Because God ruled in Israel by establishing their rulers, when the ancient Jews eventually rejected these procedures, the Lord declared that they had thereby rejected Him. As all other governments derived their legitimacy from the governed and could legitimately be overthrown, the two forms of political authority were not only completely different, "but precisely the opposite."[4]

In a broadly similar way Buchanan severely contextualized and thereby detached the New Testament – and especially *Romans* – from the contemporary political world. At one point Buchanan simply dismissed Paul with heavy irony: "I feel you are quite right in giving so much weight to Paul that one sentence of his has predominated over all the writings of all philosophers and jurists."[5] At another moment when Paul turned out to be right, it was because he agreed with Aristotle rather than the other way around. In the end, the precedence of scripture simply dissolved before the vast diversity of human institutions and experience.

I can instance from the records of many nations many beneficial laws of which there is no example in the Scriptures. ...if nothing is to be done without prior example, how few of our civil institutions and laws will be left to us! The greater part of these are not based on ancient precedent, but are evolved to deal with new and unprecedented crimes as they arise.[6]

If scripture signally failed to provide a political model, it also failed to offer Buchanan a time scheme of human development. One searches his great Scottish history, the *De Rerum Scoticarum Historia*, in vain for sacred prophecy and the historical redemption. Only Galfridian prophecy appears, and its propagators – Merlin and Gildas and their like – are blasted as frauds in what must be one of the most blistering critiques of these traditions to appear in the sixteenth century.[7]

Buchanan's great project was to imagine Scotland as a classical *politeia* and convert its aristocracy into classical citizens. His preoccupation was therefore "vertew and manheid" – to use the words of one of his contemporaneous popularizers[8] – to be realized in a world populated by austere, civic-minded patriots whose selfless moral autonomy allowed for an effective articulation of society's good. He perceived these values as operating centrally within Scotland's enormously long history, a story in which the ancient Scottish virtue underwrote the nation's independence by resisting corruption, vice, luxury, dependence, effeminacy, irrationality, and, in so saying, tyranny.

With Jewish antiquity so rigorously excluded and with such intensely classicized values so completely his concern, the Jews surely become so marginalized within Buchanan's project as virtually to disappear altogether. It is therefore surprising indeed to learn that Buchanan faced, among others, the charge of Judaizing before the Lisbon Inquisition in 1550 – which, because of the trial, is the most fully documented period of the scholar's life. Buchanan was accused of "fleeing Scotland because he was a heretic and a Jew, who said that he might partake of the Passover Lamb; and five others, who were with him in this heresy, were all burned alive." The charge originated with Portuguese academics in 1548 and found support from Simon Simson, a Scottish professor of theology at the Sorbonne, and apparently from another Scot, John Stewart, a regent of the Parisian College of Sainte Barbe – an institution with which Buchanan had earlier been associated. The tradition thereafter had a long history indeed. It would be picked up and embroidered upon by James Laing, another doctor of the Sorbonne and Catholic controversialist, who claimed that Buchanan's "Ebionite" madness went so far as to urge the Scottish king, James V, in Lent, to "eat the paschal lamb if you wish to achieve salvation."[9] According to Laing, no less a figure than the theologian John Mair was summoned and commented, "Whoever says, Most Christian King, that you should eat the paschal lamb, he would wish you to become

a Jew and live as the Jews do." Somewhat later a Scottish priest, David
Chambers, also promoted the tradition in a work eventually published by the
Parisian Oratorians, and Buchanan's Jewish scandal would become standard
stuff for subsequent Catholic annals and even the history of the University of
Paris, eventually finding its way into Pierre Bayle's dictionary.[10]

Buchanan himself dismissed the "fable" of the paschal lamb which,
he claimed, was the first he had heard of such a thing (*fabula illa agni
paschalis...de qua hodie primum audivi*).[11] His inquisitors knew that he was
an Old Christian and that there were no Jews in Scotland, and they did not
long pursue the matter. Secular commentators since Bayle have also agreed
with Buchanan. And with reason. There is no doubt that five heretics were
burned in Scotland in 1539 and that Buchanan was probably associated with
them and saved only by his intimate connection with the Scottish court.
There is no doubt that he fled to England, sought the patronage of Thomas
Cromwell, and then left for France with Cromwell's fall and Henry's new
conservatism.[12] But it is hard to imagine how Judaizing might be understood
in Scotland, a country which had never had a medieval Jewish community
and where Judaism could only have had the most limited meanings.

Yet, whatever the origin of Buchanan's Judaizing reputation, the assertion
does acquire a kind of cogency when seen within its peculiar French context.
Within that context a rather different Buchanan emerges. Shortly after he
returned to Paris from England in 1539, he went on to join André de Gouvea
and his colleagues who were reorganizing the college of Guyenne at Bordeaux. Buchanan had come to know de Gouvea and many of his associates
during his previous stay in Paris (c. 1525–1534) when they were all at the
College of Sainte Barbe. More important, the de Gouveas were a leading
Portuguese New Christian family – oddly enough, a matter largely ignored
by historians of both Scotland and Portugal.

Originating from Béjà, a significant center for Marranism, the de Gouvea clan established itself in France in about 1500 when Diogo de Gouvea
and his brother-in-law arrived in response, it is said, to rising Portuguese
intolerance.[13] Like many within the New Christian community, the de Gouveas continued to have close relations with Portugal and even with its government. There appears to have been considerable travel back and forth
between the two countries. At the same time the main community at Bordeaux also developed close relations with elements of the local parlementaire
elite – as is well-known, the seigneur de Montaigne, father of the celebrat-
ed philosopher, married the daughter of a Portuguese New Christian – but
the community nevertheless always led a precarious existence. Most of the
leading New Christians were merchants, although some were physicians, but
Diogo and his four nephews – André, Antonio, Marcial, and another Diogo

– initially established themselves as humanist scholars at Sainte Barbe in Paris. André de Gouvea would subsequently have an extraordinary career not only as a scholar but also as an administrator. Indeed, he had that rarest of administrative privileges, the opportunity to organize a world-class faculty as the principal of the College of Guyenne at Bordeaux and again as the principal of the College of Arts at the University of Coimbra in Portugal. The faculty which de Gouvea attracted to Guyenne embraced a wide range of opinion. Many were also Portuguese New Christians – among whom, much more than with their Spanish counterparts, crypto-Judaism exerted a powerful influence. Some like João de Costa and Diogo de Teive probably were (or became) sincere converts. Others were variously radical. Antonio de Gouvea was strongly anti-clerical, was initially favorable to reform, but may have ended his days with his thinking "tinged with scepticism."

Another professor, Jean Gelida, found himself in difficulty because his wife did not sufficiently conceal her Judaism. Although André de Gouvea himself was widely suspected of heterodoxy (and many saw Guyenne as subversive to the faith), his own views are unclear and there is no direct evidence that he actually was a marrano. Perhaps the archetypal university administrator, he contrived to have good relations with the fiercely reactionary local bishop, while at the same time he proved instrumental in securing the charter from Henri II which formally recognized the Portuguese New Christian community – and effectively founds modern French Sephardic Jewry.[14] Buchanan was personally close to all of these individuals, especially André. He much later recalled that he had joined the group of them who set out to reestablish the University at Coimbra in part because, with them, he would be "among family and friends" (*inter propinquos et familiares*).[15]

In France then Buchanan inhabited an environment which was not at all philo-Semitic, but was significantly crypto-Jewish. Publicly it normally appeared faultlessly Catholic – though many knew and still more suspected otherwise – while internally it was informed by elements of Jewish religious culture and identity. In this environment Buchanan wrote his two great tragedies which served as the annual play to be performed by the students of the college. The more complex play, *Baptistes, sive calumnia tragoedia*, which dramatizes the story of John the Baptist, has typically been seen as basically a discussion of political tyranny. That is how Buchanan sought its exculpation before the inquisitors – the tyrannical Herod like Henry VIII, the martyred John like Thomas More. Buchanan again stressed its anti-tyrannical message, though also noting its religious significance, in his dedication of the play to the young James VI in 1577 (after all, James' religion was thought to be secure). But the drama, although profoundly political, concerns a great deal more than a "speculum" for classically conceived tyranny. It is also about prophecy, reform, and ultimately – as some recent critics have observed[16] – it concerns judging language and appearances.

That the play should reflect favorably upon the experience of a prophet, something altogether missing from his formal political writings, is itself significant.[17] But the truly striking feature is the way it treats the nation of the Jews. The Jewish priesthood is by no means composed of cardboard villains – and still less of proto-Christians. The young rabbi Gamaliel insists against the older, repressive rabbi Malchus that the Baptist must be given a chance to prove his insight, which, if wrong, needs be confronted at least initially with reason rather than authority and repression. Pride, violence, and arrogance, Gamaliel comments in a voice not unlike Buchanan's poem to Cromwell, "was not this regimen which raised high our fore-fathers."[18] The Jewish community, represented by the chorus, seems still more favorable to the Baptist. Yet even Malchus is not altogether unambivalent. To be sure, he defends clerical authority by the absolutist (for Buchanan, tyrannical) argument: "the man in authority...must be his own law; if he sins, God is there to witness and punish him for his crime."[19] He is obsessed with tradition, seeks the "concordia" provided by social hierarchy and deference, is utterly distrustful of the "plebs", and is fully prepared to calumniate the prophet to King Herod by insisting that religious reform will mean political revolution. But Malchus *does* know that things are deeply wrong in Israel and that some of the things the prophet says have merit. The flashpoint of course is the authority of the clergy and their immunity from judgement, which causes Malchus to "burst with anger." "Am I to listen to this in silence?"[20] Now all of this is in context quite remarkable. The profoundly anti-Judaic attitudes virtually everywhere in late medieval and early modern Europe made it almost inevitable that reformers would compare the persecuting Catholic hierarchy to the pharisaical priesthood and that they should see themselves as the successors to the early Christians. As the Jews persecuted the original Christians, so too did the medieval church now persecute the reformers of the sixteenth century – latter-day Jews persecuting latter-day Christians. This trope would reach Scotland in a powerful way at least by the 1550s. But not a trace of this sort of thing is to be found in Buchanan. The Jews are simply ourselves.

Much ink has been spilled trying to determine at what point Buchanan became a Protestant and to analyze his writings within this framework. Nineteenth-century historians have discovered Protestantism early on in Buchanan's career, while twentieth-century historians have denied this claim. But surely these matrices are une questione mal posée, for the plasticity of the times often does not easily allow for highly-wrought theological categories. From an early date Buchanan visibly sought reform and was vocal in this pursuit as security and circumstance allowed. In *Baptistes* the prophet speaks of "silent watch-dogs" and of the hierarchy as devouring rather than feeding its flock (both subsequently standard Protestant and then puritan shibboleths).[21] Moreover, Buchanan was prepared to admit to the inquisitors that he had accepted a most radical reading of the *Revelation*.

> The Babylon which is described in the Apocalypse I at one time imagined to be Rome, and thought the same city was indicated by the woman; but when I took counsel with myself that all interpretation of the prophets in respect to future events is perilous, inasmuch as the greatest part of such prophecies is only understood when the event is manifest, I at once suspended my judgement in this matter and readily admitted that herein I am as ignorant as the multitude.[22]

An amazing admission! Whether Buchanan had read John of Patmos as meaning the city of Rome or the Roman church, it was the stuff of revolution. It was the framework from which the Reformation acquired historical intelligibility. It inherently implied radical change.[23]

Still, for Buchanan in the end, the test of the prophet became less a matter of illumination than of common sense. Malchus asks John if he is the prophesied Christ "promised to our fathers," and he is not. Malchus asks if he is "the expected prophet", and he is not. Malchus asks if he is Elias, and again he is not. Then on what possible basis, demands the by now exasperated Malchus, can John presume to instigate a new baptism? The prophet's answer is poetic, claiming to be the voice of a new era, and Malchus comments, "what traps this fellow lays, how he deceives with ambiguities!" Does John have any miracles to prove his authority? No, yet again. But then does Malchus have any miracles at hand for his own authority? John's claim ultimately turns on the assertion:

> If I speak the truth and do what is right, why must anyone impose silence upon me? But if I speak falsehoods, you who are learned must demonstrate this to me in my ignorance.[24]

The crux of the issue had already been posed by Malchus earlier on in the scene when he asked John, "Did God, then, bid you utter these sentiments?" John replies, "Truth bids all proclaim what is true."[25] Neither revelation nor tradition – neither revolutionary Protestant saint nor hysterical clericalist reactionary – therefore could inherently provide the test of truth. Only open discourse could hope to do so, and consequently the prophets of the sixteenth century simply had to be heard.[26] Although they reached quite different conclusions in both politics and religion, Buchanan was indeed a professor fully worthy the young Michel de Montaigne. It is perhaps only appropriate that the boy performed – almost certainly in drag – principal roles in Buchanan's tragedies while at the college of Guyenne.[27]

Even King Herod turns out to be a more complicated figure than we might expect. His decision to destroy the prophet results from a tricky political judgement. He will protect the monarchy at the risk of alienating the populace. But Buchanan's call for fair play for prophets, for openness, for public discourse, is such that no claim for "reason of state", as it would soon be called, can countermand it. Prudential calculation, inherently a private act, cannot legitimately supplant public decision-taking. Only the latter environment permitted (and was underwritten by) civic virtue and the ethical judgement derived from Stoic autonomy. Herod did not simply make a bad call, he played the tyrant. To be sure, he was a sophisticated tyrant – whose arguments were immediately recognizable in contemporary France – but a tyrant nevertheless.

At the heart of *Baptistes*, however, lies neither tyranny, nor reform, nor prophecy, but authenticity. Nearly every scene features some comment on people misrepresenting themselves through language or other forms of disguise. Malchus, Gamaliel, and the chorus repeatedly make this point.[28] The most striking instance in the drama is Herod himself who ostensibly is constrained to kill the prophet by the calumny of Malchus, the "royal lust" stimulated by Queen Herodias, and the dancing of Salome. Herod protests and proclaims in the most fulsome language the obligations of a just king against the tyrannous urgings of Salome, but in fact she is coercing him to a political decision which he has actually already taken.[29] What he proclaims and what he truly is, are radically different, and this is at least potentially true for all of the characters, including John.

The tension between language and truth, appearance and reality, was of course an ancient topos, but surely no group in the sixteenth century experienced that tension as severely as did the marranos. Those associated with them, like Buchanan, had to be acutely aware of it, and it is tempting to think that the drama's obsession with false appearances derives at least in part from this association. His plea for openness to latter-day prophets may well have extended to the descendants of the original types.

The trial in Lisbon came in the wake of a wave of anti-Jewish-New Christian sentiment and of unfettered Inquisition activity after 1547.[30] Specifically, it is today seen as having been prompted from several sources.[31] The Jesuits, it is thought, sought control of the University at Coimbra, and certainly the debacle enabled them to achieve this end. At the same time, the trial would probably not have taken place but for a split within the de Gouveas: a long-term power struggle between the elder and strenuously orthodox Diogo and his nephew André whose religious views were much more dubious. The initial trigger was a disgruntled Guyenne alumnus, João Pinheiro. In addition to the tale of Buchanan's Judaizing in Scotland, Pinheiro spoke of a meal at Advent in Bordeaux in which meat was eaten, at which the monastic orders and the Church generally were criticized, and at which the human origins of fasting, Advent, and Lent were discussed.[32] Is it possible that Pinheiro happened upon a seder or at least a celebration of half remembered family traditions? If so, Buchanan may well be one of the first post-medieval Scottish intellectuals to participate in such an event. The paschal lamb story in Scotland, perhaps originating from a misapprehension of similar kinds of conversation, may now have become reality in the world of the Portuguese emigre community.

George Buchanan's thought, so immersed in Graeco-Roman classicism, so ostensibly separated from Hebraic traditions, in fact took its earliest form in a deeply, if ambiguously, Judaized environment. There exists some reason for thinking that some of his writings may even have been a response to it.

JOHN KNOX AND THE JEWS

"Two thinges perchance may move you to esteme these histories [from the Old Testament]...to apperaine nothing to you. Fyrst, because you are no Jewes but Gentiles: & secondarely, because you are no kinges, but nobiles in your realm. ...it is a thing more then certein, that whatsoever God required of the Civile Magistrate in Israel or Juda concernyng the observation of true religion during the tyme of the Law, the same doth he require of lawfull Magistrates professing Christ Jesus in the tyme of the Gospell." – John Knox, *The Appellation...Addressed to the Nobility and Estate of Scotland*, 1558[33]

John Knox was a prominent example of the sixteenth century prophet whose hearing Buchanan had promoted in the 1540s. Like the prophets of old, he understood the meaning of scripture – the standard it set and the reform it therefore required. Although the illumination of the latter-day prophets could not enable them to add to the text (all that was needed was already in hand) or demonstrate its power through miracles (those demonstrations had already occurred), it certainly did mean that they had responsibilities of awesome proportions. They were called upon to guide the reconstruction of Christian society – and the establishment of righteousness and justice. They also interpreted God's activities in the world: not only the plagues and triumphs which all communities encountered, but as well the great programmatic design inherent within the human experience, whose imminent conclusion was expected by them virtually without exception. As John had announced the coming of Christ, so they now announced his long-awaited return.

God's Word, the sole instrument of salvation, necessarily loomed large within this context. How large, however, was a matter of considerable argument. For several reasons, scripture played a particularly important role in Knox's perceptions. He stressed its role in imagining and legitimating society.

> ...yf anie think, I say, that they [the Gentiles] were not bounde to the same obedience which God required of his people of Israel, [at] what tyme he confirmed his leage and covenant with them, the same man appeathe to make Christ inferior to Moses, and contrarious to the law of his heavenlie Father. And thererfore I fear not to affirm that the Gentiles (I mean everie citie, realm, province, or nation amongst the Gentiles, embracing Christ Jesus and his true religion) be bound to the same leage and covenant that God made with his people of Israel, [at] what tyme he promised to roote out the nations before them...the Gentiles [are] no lesse bounde then somtyme were the Jewes.[34]

Knox's insistence upon the covenant and in some ways upon the ancient judicial law (including such matters as excluding women from public office) was strikingly emphatic. To be sure, he would rely upon other sources of political authority – councils, custom, Roman Law, Natural Law, the examples godly emperors, etc. – but none could possess the "firmitie" and stability of scripture. In an increasingly fragmented world which was so manifest to the sixteenth century, in a world where tradition and human authority appeared increasingly suspect and even corrupt, scripture alone spoke with a clear and uniquely compelling voice. Scripture alone overcame particularist custom: it spoke with equal cogency to all communities, and thus equally to both England and Scotland – thereby providing the common vocabulary vital to Knox's British perspective and British aspirations.[35] And of course scripture alone could save.

From the later 1550s onward Knox became ever more deeply immersed in an Old Testament vision of reformed society and of the politics which would create it. The covenant, the defeat of idolatry, the attendant reform of manners and morals, the political fortunes of Christian society were all imagined as a direct extension of the experience of the ancient Jews. The Hebrew Commonwealth provided the model of polility and, more than that, it provided the spirit and mentality for government, society, and piety. Knox became increasingly impatient with those who found scripture insufficient and looked to other sources of cognition.

I am not ignorant that as the Israelites lothed manna, because that every daye they sawe and eat but one thinge, so some there bee now-a-dayes (who will not be holden of the worste sorte) that after once reading some parcelles of the Scriptures, do commit themselves altogether to prophane authors and humain lectures, because that the varietie of matters therin conteined doeth bringe with it daily delectation, wher contrariwyse within the simple Scriptures of God the perpetuall repetition of one thinge is fashious and werysome. This temptation, I confesse, may enter in God's elect for a time, but impossible it is that therin they continew to the end.[36]

To be sure, Knox was here discussing personal piety in a "most wholesome cousell..tuiching the daily exercise of God's most holy and sacred Word." But just this attitude towards the Jewish past constantly informed his understanding of the political world. Just this view – as presented in the *First Blast of the Trumpet against the Monstrous Regiment of Women* – of course led him to serious difficulty with the newly-formed Elizabethan establishment. But much more was at issue than the obvious embarrassment to the succession of the new queen. His narrow appeal to the ancient Jewish commonwealth, as London's new bishop John Aylmer angrily stressed, also ignored the English common law, and his response to Knox was to a significant extent a patriotic one. But, additionally, it more broadly concerned political epistemology. In a voice not altogether unlike Buchanan's, the Bishop of London insisted that the special experience of ancient Israel could not supplant the particular history of specific countries. He did grant – as Buchanan might not have – that the Bible was "a paradise wherein are to be found all the best hearbes and frutes that be." Yet only a man "unskilled in the diversities of times and histories" would mistake the Jewish law of succession for "the constant and unchangeable will of God."

> all antiquitie of time, all histories and monumentes, cannot be conteined in so lyttle rometh. Wherefore if men will decide weightie matters, hanging uppon antiquitie, they will not only counsell with the Bible, but exercise them selfe in aunciente stories.[37]

Knox's biblicism – and probably his Britain as well – held little appeal for Aylmer.

Knox thus emerges as one of the more uncompromising defenders of the relevance of ancient Judaism and one who sought unhesitatingly for himself and his society the persona of the ancient Jews. There is surely more than one sense in which Knox might legitimately be accused of being a Judaizer. Further, if anyone wanted to be like the ancient Hebrews, then a whole range of technical tools would become vital. Surely Jewish language and learning therefore ought to be integral to Knox's project. And in theory that would soon extend to a concern with a huge range of pre and post-pharisaical traditions.

Ultimately it should lead to the European Ghetto and to contemporaneous Jewish culture – and to a philo-Semitic fascination with Judaism.

Yet that did not happen. Instead, Knox adopted the analogy which identified early Christians with the reformers and their persecutors with the Jews. Spain's militant persecution of heresy in the later 1550s was necessarily arresting to any observer and certainly to Knox. By their blood-thirsty behavior, "the odious nation of Spaniards" indicated that they "were ignorant of God, ennemeis of his truth, deniers of Christ Jesus, persecutors of his true members, and haters of all vertue." And perhaps that was only natural. Were they not in fact Jews – "as histories do witnesse and they themselves confesse." They were thus simply manifesting the deep-seated "despit" which they bore "against Christe Jesus." As their "forefathers" had crucified him, so they now "make plaine warre against all true professors of his holie Gospell." Bloody Mary Tudor was of course of Spanish descent – her promoters, it seems, had apparently even linked her to "the roote of Jesse" – and, for Knox, the fires of Smithfield seemed to be its consequence.[38] Knox was of course unaware of a remark which Philip II had made only two years earlier: "All the heresies in Germany, France, and Spain have been sown by the descendants of Jews."[39] It is hard to imagine what his response might be.

Both Buchanan and Knox were in some sense and perhaps several senses anti-Semitic. But Buchanan's classicist and anti-scripturalist attitudes did not prevent him from participating in and perhaps speaking to a crypto-Judaic world. Knox's profound absorption in the world of the Old Testament did not lead to a preoccupation with Jewish learning and culture – and still less with a concern for Jewish involvement in the latter days. The transformations which made the Jews relevant to Christian aspirations lay over the horizon with the next generation. Knox died in 1572 at about the age of 60. Buchanan died in 1582 at the age of 76. The changes which refigured the matrices for perceiving both Jews and society occurred largely in the years following 1590. From them arose the foundations of early modern British political culture.

JEWISH PROMISE AND BRITISH HOPE:
THE WORLD OF THE ANGLOPHONE BAROQUE

George Buchanan began his intellectual life, it seems, seriously concerned with the meaning of the Judaeo-Christian apocalypse. John Knox was always immersed in these ideas and saw himself directly involved in precipitating the prophesied end of days. But this perception of the world acquired everywhere in Europe new depth, specificity, and potential during the decades straddling the year 1600. During those years apocalyptic expectations about the future became much more specified, articulate, and hopeful. A vast flowering of speculation about a Protestant imperium took place in Germany, in Scandinavia, and, with the regnal union of 1603, in Scotland. Much of this speculation was founded upon an integration of apocalypticism and magic. These decades marked the historical high point of Protestant academic astrology and – altogether ignoring Calvin's objections and Luther's unease – and witnessed as well enormous interest in Parcelsianism, number mysticisms, Neo-Platonism, and even cabala. Such expectations issued in Rosicrucianism and the magico-scientific utopias of Andreae, Campanella, and Bacon. It is no accident that the first Faust book appeared at the end of the sixteenth century (1587) – to be translated into English, Dutch, and French during the next decade. During the 1590s the Swede Johannes Buraeus (Bure) launched his enormously learned fusion of "Gothic" historiography, Neo-pythagoreanism, Runic Studies, and apocalypticism – a project which eventually envisioned a final "dominium maris Baltici." In fact, these years saw increasingly confident prophetic projections in many parts of Europe and the beginnings of modern millenarian speculation. At this time, it seems, the former New Christian, now re-born Jew, Abraham Cohen de Herrera began his immersion in the Lurianic cabala which would eventually find fruition in the extraordinary *Puerto de Cielo*. It is hardly surprising that these years saw an altogether new fascination with Jewish traditions (often but not always mystical) and, most important, the beginnings of apocalyptic philo-Semitism.[40]

In the anglophone world these developments culminated with the great English philo-Semites, Hugh Broughton and Thomas Brightman. In the short term both had only limited impact on England – although their later influence, especially Brightman's, would prove enormous, far greater in fact than most historians of the southern kingdom have explored or even recognized. Brightman's impact in Scotland, however, was immediate and important. Both James Melville on the Presbyterian left and Patrick Forbes of Corse on the Episcopalian right would find his *Revelation of the Revelation* to be of immediate and signal importance.[41]

Forbes would write the first commentary on the *Revelation* derived from Brightman, would draw on such Jewish works as the mystical, anti-scholastic commentaries of Rabbi "Menachem" (almost certainly Rabbi Moses ben Nahman), and reportedly ended his days corresponding with a learned Jew about the Jewish expectation that the Messiah would come in about the year 1650. His son and successors, known today as the Aberdeen doctors, would continue and deepen this interest. The younger Forbes for example lined his spiritual diary with references to the Hebrew text from scripture and on occasion determined their meaning through the targums and the commentaries of Rabbi "Abenezra" [Eben Ezra] and "Sal. Iarchi" [Rashi].[42]

Robert Pont, a founding father of the Scottish Reformation and junior contemporary of John Knox, survived into the early years of the seventeenth century and contributed significantly in the 1590s to the deepening apocalyptic interest. He drew occasionally on Jewish prophetic traditions (specifically that of the Rabbi Elias), but this interest was distinctly limited and largely conversionist, and his attitude toward "that miserable nation" of the Jews is characteristic of an earlier generation. It contrasts with the thinking of Pont's parishioner, John Napier of Merchiston, who had a much more deeper and less contentious interest in Jewish learning. Like many late sixteenth century Scottish intellectuals, Napier was well aware of Jewish magical traditions, and publicly he declared his neutrality about them.

> ...there are books of the Jews, containing (as they alledge) doctrines proceding from the mouthes of the Patriarchs, affirming every great Angel of 7 to rule the world 490 yeares: which wee (wanting the warrant of scripture) can either affirm nor condemn.[43]

This kind of concern goes well beyond Knox and even Pont. It is very much in the spirit of the 1590s and early 1600s throughout much of Protestant Europe.

During the early decades of the seventeenth century the Presbyterian tradition drew even more strongly on Jewish traditions than did its Episcopalian competitor and found itself even more philo-Semitic. The Old Testament biblicism, inherited from the days of John Knox, now converged with a far more articulate and future-oriented apocalypticism. The covenanted Scots (or, in more expansive moments, the covenanted Britons) acquired a status not unlike the ancient Jews. They participated in and thus would redeem Jewish hope and promise in the latter days. That central Presbyterian revolutionary, the key drafter of the National Covenant, the lawyer Archibald Johnston of Warriston firmly believed that passages of the Old Testament spoke to Scotland – and uniquely to post–1560 Scotland – every bit as much as they did to the Davidic Age. But if Britons became the latter-day Jews in the vision of the covenanters, the "real" Jews did not become irrelevant as a result. Quite the contrary, the Scottish revolutionaries saw them as vital partners in the historical redemption. The advent of Christianity had not abrogated their covenant with God, and their special role complemented and was even integral to Scottish dreams. Revolutionary leaders like Samuel Rutherford and Andrew Cant saw the "calling of the Jews" as the direct analogue to Jewish hope for the gentiles in *Canticles*, and that event would be of monumental importance. Cant's earliest sermons launching the covenanting movement took time to assure his audience, among other things, that the Jews would join them "shortly". Rutherford who had been exercised about the role of the Jews in the culminating events at least since the early 1630s, wanted a formal conference with them. It is almost touching to hear Rutherford as he tried to reassure the nervous covenanting troops in 1640 – when for the first time in nearly a century a Scottish army crossed the English frontier – by noting that the Jews were about to join their old "husband". Scots and Jews had indeed become brethren in the world created within the revolutionary northern realm.[44]

Not all Scottish Presbyterians, however, embraced either the new apocalypticism or the Jewish model. David Hume of Godscroft (c. 1560–1630) was a leading intellect within the Presbyterian party, who both self-consciously and in the view of his contemporaries was the successor to George Buchanan. He fully accepted the notion of a Scottish covenant with God derived from the so-called Negative Confession of 1581 – the standard Presbyterian view. He fully accepted the Presbyterian church polity as advanced by his colleagues. However, he had remarkably little to say about the apocalyptic future. His references to Antichrist and the sacred drama were consistently metaphorical. Like Buchanan he looked to the great families to uphold Scottish integrity and its fundamentally civic character.[45] He had virtually nothing to say about Jews or Judaism. There exists not the slightest indication of anti-Semitism, so far as I have been able to determine, anywhere in the corpus of Godscroft's writing. Such topics were simply not a part of his political vision. That extraordinary politician, the Marquis of Argyll, may well have accepted Godscroft view. Certainly there was talk about triumvirs and dictators in the years about the 1641 settlement.[46] But the classical model and the country Calvinism associated with it – so much in the shadow of its Hebrew competitor – could hardly prove as persuasive in the excited years after 1637. Its triumph – in a politically sanitized form – would occur only later, as apocalyptic hopes and eschatological dreams faded before political disaster.[47] The importance of the Jews to British political culture would decline accordingly.

Knox and Buchanan had laid the foundations for British Israel and Roman Britain. But these competing, and yet interpenetrating, political visions only assumed many of their characteristic implications – among them philo-Semitism and anti-Semitism – in the wake of the Union of Crowns.

NOTES

* I wish to thank the Committee for Research and Creative Activity at California State University, Sacremento for funding a research trip essential to the completion of this essay.

1. The best introduction to Buchanan's classical sources has been provided by Roger Mason, "Rex Stoicus: George Buchanan, James VI and the Scottish Polity," in *New Perspectives on the Politics and Culture of Early Modern Scotland*, ed. by John Dwyer et al. (Edinburgh, 1982), pp. 9–33. See also A.H. Wiliamson, *Scottish National Consciousness in*

the Age of James VI: The Apocalypse, the Union, and the Shaping of Scotland's Public Culture* (Edinburgh, 1979), ch. 5.

2. R.H. Popkin, "Jewish Christians and Christian Jews, 1492 and After," in *Judaism* 41 (1992), pp. 248–67; see for example A.H. Williamson, "The Cultural Foundations of Racial Religion and Anti-Semitism," in *Lingering Shadows: Freudians, Jungians, and Anti-Semitism,* ed. Aryeh Maidenbaum (Boston, 1991), pp. 135–55.

3. "De Iudaismo nunquam cogitavi." *The Trial of George Buchanan before the Lisbon Inquisition...,* ed. by James M. Aitken (Edinburgh and London, 1939), pp. 36, 37, 56n.1.

4. *The Art and Science of Government among the Scots* [= *De Jure Regni apud Scotos: Dialogus*], trans. by D.H. MacNeill ([Glasgow], 1964), pp. 72–3, 96, 65–6, 82; original edition (Edinburgh, 1579), pp. 70, 96, 62, 80.
   Quod si Iudaeorum reges a ciuibus puniti non sunt, hi non magnopere ad nostrum institutum faciunt. Non enim ab initio a ciuibus creati, sed a deo illis fuerunt. (p.80)
   [What does it matter that the kings of the Jews were not punished by their subjects? The point has little bearing on our monarchies, for these kings were not originally appointed by citizens; they were given to them by God. (MacNeill, p. 82)]

5. MacNeill, p. 73; 1579 edition, p. 71: *"Quod autoritatis tantum in Paulo esse statuas, ut apud te monium Philosophorum & jure consultorum scriptis una eius sententia praeponderet, recte mihi facere videris."*

6. MacNeill, p. 82; 1579 edition p. 79–80: *"Possum apud multas nationes plurimas ac saluberrimas recensere leges, quarum in sacris libris nullum est exemplum. ...Quod si nihil sine exemplo geri placet, quota ciuilium institutorum pars nobis restabit? quota item legum? Maxima enim earum pars non ex veteri exemplo est desumpta, sed adversus nouas, & sine exemplo fraudes sancita."*

7. George Buchanan, *History of Scotland [De Rerum Scoticarum Historia],* trans. James Aikman (Edinburgh, 1827), 1:233, 236–44. For Buchanan, Merlin was "an egregious impostor and cunning pretender."

8. The anonymous author of "ane Declaratioun of the Lordis iust quarrell," in *Satirical Poems of the Time of the Reformation,* ed. by James Cranstoun, Scottish Text Society (Edinburgh, 1891), 1:57.

9. Aitken, *Trial of George Buchanan,* pp. 118–27. James Laing (1502–94), *De vita et moribus atque rebus gestis haereticorum nostri temporis* (Paris, 1581).

10. David Chambers (Camerarius), *De Scotorum Fortitudine, Doctrina, & Pietatae, ac de ortu & progressu haeresis in Regbis Scotiae & Angliae, libri quartor* (Paris, 1631), p. 269; Egrasse Du Boullay, *Historia Universitatis Parisiensis* (Paris, 1673), 6:935 (repeating Laing); Henri de Sponde (Spondanus, 1568–1643), *Annalium eccesiasticum... Cardinalis Caesaris Baronii Continuatio* in Bayle, *The Dictionary Historical and Philosophical of Mr. Peter Bayle* (London, 1734), 2.184; Antoine Varillas (1624–1696), *Histoire des Révolutions arrivée dans l'Europe en matière de Religion* (Paris, 1688), 6.165; John Durkan, "Buchanan's Judaising Practices," in *Innes Review* 15 (1964) pp. 186–7. Chambers' manuscript history was "recovered" by one "R.P. Jean Morin, prestre de la congregation de l'oratoire de Jesus-Christe."

11. Aitken, *Trial of George Buchanan,* pp. 6, 7. Buchanan told the inquisitors that in Scotland during the 1530s he was influenced by a Dominican – "an exceptionally famous preacher" – who defended eating meat during Lent by saying even Christ ate it at that time with his apostles. This, he suspected, was the source of the paschal lamb story.

12. Despite his assertions to the contrary before the Inquisition. His claim to have been a spy for James V is simply preposterous. Buchanan's poems to Henry and to Cromwell ("under whose protection the revived religion of our ancestors flourishes" – "floret pietas rediviva

parentum") provide the real indication. (Philip J. Ford, *George Buchanan, Prince of Poets* [Aberdeen, 1982], pp. 154, 155)

13. In 1526 the mission to João III of that extraordinary prophet-adventurer, David Reubeni, apparently spoke to the messianic hopes of "many Marranos" there – as well as elsewhere in Portugal. (Y.H. Yerushalmi, "Prolegomena," to Alexandre Herculano, *A History of the Origin and Establishment of the Inquisition in Portugal*, trans. by John C. Branner (New York, 1972), p. 48) It is likely that de Gouvea and his brother-in-law came to France in the wake of the Lisbon pogroms of 1506 and the legalization of New Christian emigration from Portugal in the following year. (Yerushalmi, pp. 43–4)

14. Théophile Malvezin, *Histoire des Juifs à Bordeaux* (Bordeaux, 1875/1976), pp. 88–145; Henry Léon, *Histoire des Juifs de Bayonne* (Paris, 1893), pp. 16–26; I.D. Mcfarlane, *Buchanan* (London, 1981), pp. 29–30, 34, 80–1, 95–8; Ford, *Buchanan*, p. 123 n.12; Donald M. Frame, *Montaigne: A Biography* (New York, 1965), ch. 2.

For the persistence of Jewish identity and practice among Portuguese New Christians in relative contrast to Spanish New Christians (and the reasons for it), see Perez Zagorin, *Ways of Lying: Dissimulation, Persecution, and Conformity in Early Modern Europe* (Cambridge, MA, 1990), p. 47, and more esp. and compellingly Yerushalmi, pp. 34–55. Even the assessment of de Costa and de Teive remains potentially problematic in light of the case of their successor faculty member, Antonio Homem, more than two generations later. Homem held nothing less than the prime chair of canon law at the University of Coimbra and was a noted preacher and confessor. Yet he was discovered to have been the leader of a group of *conversos*, including canons and students at Coimbra, which met in secret to observe Jewish holy days, fasts, and other commandments of the Mosaic Law, and he was executed in 1618. (Zagorin, pp. 60–1)

15. *Georgii Buchanani Vita. Ab ipso scripta biennio ante mortem*, in Aitken, *Trial of George Buchanan*, pp. xx, xxi.

16. Rebecca Buchnell, *Tragedies of Tyrants: Political Thought and Theatre in the English Renaissance* (Ithaca and London, 1990), pp. 108–15; at a more abstruse and de-politicized level, Timothy J. Reiss, *Tragedy and Truth: Studies in the Development of Renaissance and Neo-Classical Discourse* (New Haven, 1980), ch. 2.

17. The College de Guyenne would not have constrained him to adopt biblical themes. His colleague, Marc Antoine Muret, wrote *Iulius Caesar* (1544) which was produced and which apparently gives Brutus' republicanism a respectful hearing. Buchanan is said to have taken the play as "a celebration of Brutus' pia facta." (Gordon Braden, *Renaissance Tragedy and the Senecan Tradition: Anger's Privilege* (New Haven, 1985), p. 126; cf. Hans Baron, *The Crisis of the Early Italian Renaissance* (Princeton, 1966).

18. "Non haec parentes ratio nostros extulit"; cf. the "pietas rediviva parentum" promoted by Thomas Cromwell. (George Buchanan, *Tragedies*, ed. by P. Sharratt and P.G. Walsh [Edinburgh, 1983], pp. 103, 137; Ford, *Buchanan*, p. 154, see note 11 above)

The 1642 translation captures more of the voice of the period: "Truly, *Malchus*, you shoot far from the marke that you suppose we can defend our dignity with pride and arrogancy, or with strength of arms; our parents were not by such means advanced." (*Tyrannical-Government Anatomized: A Discourse concerning Evil-Counsellors*, printed by order of the House of Commons [London, 1642], p. 6)

Interestingly, Gamaliel's plea for open debate anticipates in some ways one of Buchanan's few statements before the inquisitors which we can confidently take at near to face value: "For when I had grasped the fact that from my earliest years I had been badly educated in grammar, rhetoric, and dialectic, I resolved that I must listen to the opinions of all, but swear allegiance to no master. This consideration took me further so that I thought I should listen to any argument on any subject. Accordingly when the Lutherans, relying on their opponents' ignorance, advertised themselves, and Christian men [i.e. the Catholic hierarchy], brooking ill the public questioning of what they considered stable and sound beliefs, answered by abuse rather than by argument, it generally happened that the minds of the weaker brethren would waver because they believed that it was from lack of proofs that the orthodox resorted to abuse and for the same reason they did not venture to disclose their feelings to everybody; so, not daring to seek help, they were bogged in the mire."

[*Nam cum ab ineunte aetate in grammatica rhetorica et dialiectica male institutum me intellexissem, statui mihi omnium opiniones audiendas, in nulius magistri verba iurandum. Ea ratio me provexit longius ut nihil non audiendum in quavis re putarem. Itaque cum Lutherani, freti adversariorum ignorantia, sese ostentarent, Christiani homines quae ipsi firma et soilda putarent in disquisitionem vocari moleste ferrent, et conviciarentur magis quam responderent, factum est plerumque ut infirmiorum animi nutarent quod inopia probationum eos ad convicia descendere crederent et ob eandum causam suos sensus non auderent omnibus nudare; dum auxilium petere non audebant in luto haerebant.*] (Aitken, pp. 32, 33)

A critique of scholasticism (and presumably also of John Mair) became a critique of authority generally. Undoubtedly, the restoration of the learning of antiquity (i.e. of our parents) and the restoration of the original faith "of our parents" were closely connected for Buchanan.

19. "Qui praest...lex ipse sibi sit; si quid autem erraverit, est qui scelestum cernat et plectat deus." (Buchanan, *Tragedies*, pp. 136–7; 102, lines 141–3)

20. "Disrumpor ira; tacitus haec ut audiam?" (Buchanan, *Tragedies*, pp. 150; 117, line 734)

21. Buchanan, *Tragedies*, pp. 150–1; 118, lines 745, 773. Before the Inquisition Buchanan insisted that he followed the orthodox Barthélemy Masson (Latomus) against Martin Bucer on the subject of vows (Aitken, pp. 12, 13). Yet his other tragedy, *Jephthes*, which centrally concerns this topic, presents a highly problematic picture (despite his asserion about it to the inquisitors). The carefully-wrought arguments against Jephthal's ill-considered vow which will sacrifice his daughter may well seem persuasive, and the tragedy may then result from the king's stubborn insistence on being trapped by his words. Buchanan's later remark to the Inquisition, in which he condemns those fathers who sentence their children to monastic lives, may come closer to his real sentiments (Aitken, pp. 14, 15). Monastic vows manifestly never impressed him.

22. Aitken, *Trial of George Buchanan*, pp. 36, 37: "*Babylonem quae describitur in Apocalypsi aliquando Romam putavi, ac eam etaim designari per mulierem; verum mecum reputarem in prophetis de re futura omnem interpretationem esse periculosam, quippe cum maxima pars tum demum intellegatur ubi eventus est manifestus, statim in ea re suspendi sententiam ac facile passus sum cum multis id ignorare.*"

23. Today people (of any faith) will with good reason think of the Inquisition as a truly evil organization with a truly evil agenda. But moderns rarely think of it as inept and plain stupid. Buchanan's trial is striking for its incompetence and for its palpable lack of enthusiasm. The inquisitors neglected the dynamite in Buchanan's gratuitous admission (which surely resulted from his view being widely known in France) and instead took up his apparent rejection of prophecy.

"Asked, with reference to that which he had said in his Confession, that all interpretation of future things in the Prophets was dangerous, if he held that all the doctors who interpreted the prophecies as to the future were dangerous or had erred; he said that many of them interpreted truly, although many erred, and that he had erred in making the proposition universal." (Aitken, *Trial of George Buchanan*, p. 108)

24. *Ibid.*, pp. 152, 119, lines 822–24: "Si vera dico, recta facio, cur mihi quisquam imperare debeat silentium? Sin falsa, doctus imperitio id indica." The conversation earlier in this paragraph occurs on pp. 150–1.

25. *Ibid.*, pp. 150; 118, lines 765–6: *"Te iussit igitur ista proloqui deus?"* *"Iubet profari vera cunctos veritas.*

26. There is an echo of this idea in the *Dialogus* when Buchanan insists that many judges are better than one.

    For not only do they see and understand more in the mass than any one man by himself, but even more than any one individual who excels them in cleverness and skill. Indeed a large number is generally a better judge of all matters than one man. For each individual has some particular good points, and if these points be grouped together we get an excellent result...many men are slow and undecided while others are impulsive and rash; but if they are brought together in a crowd they will produce a kind of balance and that moderation we look for in every type of creativeness. (MacNeill, p. 42)

    Non enim solum plus vident ac sapiunt multi, quam unus quilibet eorum seorsum, sed etiam quam unus, qui quemuis eorum ingenio & prudentia praecedat. Nam multitudo fero melius quam singuli de rebus omnibus iudicat. Singuli enim quasdam habent virtutum particulas, quae simul collatae unam excellentem virtuem conficiunt. ... Similiter in hominibus alijs tarditas & cunctatio, alijs praeceps termeritas obest, hae in multitudine commixtae tempermentum quoddam & quam in omni genere virtutis quaerimus mediocritatem pariunt. (1579 edition, p. 33)

    In a similar vein Buchanan seemed to regard lawyers (*jurisconsultus*) as a species orator whose trade was basically rhetorical – conducted according to the rhetoricians' rules that have been carefully handed down" (*rhetoroum praecepta dilligentissime tradita*). (MacNeill, p. 43; 1579 edition, p. 34)

27. Montaigne, *Essais*, I.xxvi (Paris, 1946), p. 187: *"J'ay soustenu les premiers personages ez tragedies latins de Buchanan, de Guerente, et de Muret qui se representerent en nostre college de Guyenne auecques dignite."* [I have played the principal parts in the Latin tragedies of Buchanan, Guerente, and Muret which were performed in our College de Guyenne with a certain pomp.] (quoted in Mcfarlane, *Buchanan*, p. 94; cf. Bushnell, *Tragedies*, p. 82). The exceptionally young Montaigne would surely have been called upon to perform the role of the puella (Salomé) in *Baptistes*. Buchanan apparently also served as a tutor for Michel at the Montaigne château – as later did his Scottish student, the Coimbra alumnus John Rutherford, subsequently a professor at St. Andrews and supporter of the Reformation (John Durkan, "John Rutherford and Maintaigne: An Early Influence?," in *Bibliothèque d'Humanisme et Renaissance* 41 (1979), pp. 115–22.

28. Malchus: John "has beguiled the simple folk with the appearance of stern sanctity" (p. 135); "I have seen men parading an austere sanctity in dress, so that they readily fostered the belief that they were moderate and simple in mind" (pp. 151–2).

    Gamaliel: "However much we may flatter ourselves, be proclaimed as blessed, or be considered godlike, holy, chaste, and dutiful by the common folk, none of us is free from the greatest vices" (p. 136); "We have long ago transformed the sense of virtue because we shine with no virtue; but in our arrogance we deceive the ignorant crowd with shining claims to it" (p. 139).

    Chorus: "An assumed modesty cloaks the shameless; the cover of piety conceals the impious" (p. 140); "Feigned devotion cloaks the cruelty of tyrants, the fringed robe wicked manners. Naked virtue hides herself in thin rages in the shade of a rustic hut" (p. 141).

29. Bushnell, *Tragedies*, p. 111; Buchanan's thought is so irreducibly political that both Queen Herodias and Salome speak mainly about politics – even if rather more coarsely than does Herod. Sexual desire enters quite late on and quite marginally. It ultimately does not motivate the king's action.

30. Alexandre Herculano, *History of the Origins and Establishment of the Inquisition in Portugal*, ch. 10. A number of prominent New Christian families left Portugal at that time – as did several members of the Coimbra faculty, including Buchanan's brother Patrick. In this context occurred what appears to be Buchanan's only anti-Jewish outburst, a poetic attack on his colleague Belchior Beleago who, he apparently believed, had denounced him to the Inquisition. Beleago had called him a Jew, and he called Beleago a Jew back. Buchanan was wrong on both counts. See *Omnia Opera*, ed. by Thomas Ruddiman (Edinburgh, 1715), II.63 ("In Beleagonem").

31. Aitken, *Trial of George Buchanan*, pp. liii–lviii; Buchanan indicates in his *Vita* that his move was motivated by French political and religious instability and by his intimate association with the Portuguese faculty. This is undoubtedly true, but the key must surely be the enthusiastic patronage of King João III. James V's patronage at the Edinburgh court really launched his career, preserved him against his arch-enemy, Cardinal Beaton, and saved him in the time of persecution. The failure to obtain such patronage from Cromwell and Henry VIII in 1539 prompted him to move on to France. The patronage of Mary Stewart brought him back to Scotland. The subsequent patronage of the revolutionary Scottish government in the name of the infant James VI (whom of course he was to tutor) must have been simply ideal from his perspective.

    The Portuguese themselves had always maintained close connections with kin and allies still living within the kingdom, and movement back and forth occurred in times of intensified persecution or of relaxation. Moreover, they also continued to have significant links with the Portuguese government and its representatives in France. André de Gouvea undoubtedly also felt secure in the move because he had obtained French naturalization – a major achievement which was granted in 1536 and formally conferred with great solemnity the following spring by no less than the seigneur de Montaigne, then sub-mayor of Bordeaux. (Malvezin, *Histoire*, p. 102)

    Buchanan's religious beliefs at this time are particularly obscure. He assured the inquisitors that de Gouvea had resolved his earlier doubts about the real presence in the mass (derived from a reading of Augustine) through the works of Fisher and Clichthove. This is very hard to assess. Buchanan was extremely concerned to establish a clear terminus to his heterodoxy, when he realized his errors and reconciled himself to the traditional faith. Although he showed a more cautious attitude at Bordeaux than in Edinburgh or London – understandable enough in context – he still continued to write critically of the church (Ford, *Buchanan*, p. 47)

32. Mcfarlane, *Buchanan*, p. 105.

33. John Knox, *Works*, ed. by D. Laing, Wodrow Society (Edinburgh, 1846–52), 4:490–1.

34. *Ibid.*, 4:505–6.

35. See Williamson, *Scottish National Consciousness*, pp. 11, ff.

36. *Works*, 4:135. He subsequently commented

    I wyll more gladly spende xv houes in communicating my judgemente with yow, in explanyng as God pleases to open me any place of Scripture, then halfe ane houre in any matter besyd. (138)

    Readers of his complete works will likely find this plausible.

37. John Aylmer, *An Harborowe for Faithful and Trewe Subiectes...* ([Strasbourg], 1559), pp. [31–2].

38. Knox, *Works*, 4:411–12.
39. Cited in Williamson, "Cultural Foundations," p. 136.
40. Robin Bruce Barnes, *Prophecy and Gnosis: Apocalypticism in the Wake of the Lutheran Reformation* (Stanford, 1988), p. 184, also pp. 119, 135, 139, 177, 181, 187, 201, 216 and esp. chs. 4 and 5; Martin Brecht, "Chiliasmus in Würtemberg im 17. Jahrhundert," in *Chiliasmus in Deutschland und England im 17. Jahrhundert*, ed. by Klaus Deppermann et al. (Göttingen, 1988), pp. 25–49; E.M. Butler, *The Fortunes of Faust* (Cambridge, 1952/1979), p. xiii; Frances Yates, *The Rosicrucian Enlightenment* (London, 1972); Yates, *Giordano Bruno and the Hermetic Tradition* (London, 1964); Susanna Åkerman, *Queen Christina of Sweden and Her Circle* (Leiden, 1991); Åkerman, "Queen Christina of Sweden and Messianic Thought," in *Sceptics, Millenarians and Jews*, ed. by David Katz and Jonathan Israel (Leiden, 1990), pp. 142–60; Kenneth Krabbenhoft, "The Structure and Meaning of Herrara's *Puerto del Cielo*," in *Studia Rosenthalia* 16(1): 1; David Stevenson, *The Origins of Freemasonry: Scotland's Century, 1590–1710* (New York, 1988); A.H. Williamson, "Scotland, Antichrist, and the Invention of Great Britain," in *New Perspectives on the Politics and Culture of Early Modern Scotland*, ed. by John Dwyer et al., pp. 34–58.
41. A.H. Williamson, "The Jewish Dimension of the Scottish Apocalypse: Climate, Covenant, and World Renewal," in *Menasseh Ben Israel and His World*, ed. by Yosef Kaplan et al. (Leiden, 1989), pp. 7–30.
42. Scottish Record Office: CH12/18/6 (Forbes' diary), fols. 175–6; I am most grateful to Dr. David Katz for the suggested identification of Rabbi "Menachem"; Williamson, "Jewish Dimension."
43. John Napier, *A Plaine Discovery of the Whole Revelation* (Edinburgh, 1593), pp. 8–9. He later commented that:

    ...the Jews also have books of antiquity, deviding the government of the earth among 4 great Angels and under the, to be many inferior angels. But these assertions being more curious than certain or pertinent to us to know, we leave this... (p. 118; cf. p. 336 of the 1611 edition)

    Cf. Robert Pont, *A Newe Treatise of the Right Reckoning of Yaers and Ages of the World* (Edinburgh, 1599), p. 22.
44. Williamson, "Jewish Dimension"; Williamson, "Latter-day Judah, Latter-day Israel: The Millennium, the Jews, and the British Future," in *Chiliasmus in Deutschland und England im 17. Jahrhundert*, pp. 119–49; "A Patriot Nobility? Calvinism, Kin-ties, and Civic Humanism," in *Scottish Historical Review* (forthcoming).
45. Williamson, *Scottish National Consciousness*, chs. 4 and 5.
46. E.J. Cowan, *Montrose for Covenant and King* (London, 1977), pp. 47, 54, 93–4, 148.
47. A quite analogous phenomenon occurred in England. See, for example, Steven Zwicker, "England, Israel, and the Triumph of Roman Virtue," in *Millenarianism and Messianism in English Literature and Thought, 1650–1800*, ed. by Richard H. Popkin, (Leiden, 1988), pp. 37–64.

DAVID S. KATZ

7. JEWISH SABBATH AND CHRISTIAN SUNDAY
IN EARLY MODERN ENGLAND

A Frenchman, writing home in 1659, confessed that he had failed to understand why the English Calvinists believed themselves to be following a form
of that religious doctrine laid down in Geneva. "The religion of England,"
he remarked, "is preaching and sitting still on Sundays."[1] This observation
points to one of the most distinguishing features of English religious life,
the English Sunday, devoted to religious edification and complete abstinence
from ordinary weekday activity. The strict English attitude towards the Sabbath was and always has been radically different from that which prevailed
even in Protestant areas on the Continent. Indeed, it has been argued that
Sabbatarianism is perhaps the only important English contribution to the
development of Protestant theology in the first century of its history.[2] Strict
Sabbatarianism was also one of the permanent effects of the Puritan rule in
seventeenth-century England. Even after the Restoration of the king in 1660,
when the two decades of the Cromwellian period were regarded as a time
of temporary national insanity, the almost Judaic observance of the Sunday
rest continued to be a deeply rooted part of English life and culture. Most
importantly, the general question of Sabbath observance itself reflects the way
in which the biblical text and Jewish religious observance were understood
in post-Reformation England.

   The explanation for the phenomenon of English Sabbatarianism must in
the first instance be sought in the light of the Puritan emphasis on a direct
understanding of the word of God as it appears in the Bible, without priest-
ly intermediaries. Although it was during the sixteenth and seventeenth
centuries that the Old Testament regained a place of honour beside the newer partner that was thought to have superceded it, the extent to which the
Mosaic law might be binding on Christians was still a thorny question. The
Elizabethan religious settlement included among its thirty-nine articles the
affirmation that "the Law given from God by Moses, as touching Ceremonies
and Rites do not bind Christian men, nor the Civil precepts thereof ought of
necessity to be received in ay Commonwealth."[3] Yet it was extremely difficult to find convincing theological justification for the partial exclusion of
Old Testament injunctions, especially for Puritans who located the ultimate
authority for their actions in both biblical books. Even for moderate Puritans, the Old Testament was still seen as a useful model, perhaps somewhat

R.H. Popkin and G.M. Weiner (eds): Jewish Christians and Christian Jews, 119–130.
© 1994 *Kluwer Academic Publishers. Printed in the Netherlands.*

inexact, for the ordering of temporal affairs. This turn of mind was given fullest rein at the high-water mark of the English revolution, in 1653, when Cromwell forcibly dissolved Parliament and prepared to put to the test godly notions about the best way to reorder government and society. But the ideas expressed then were hardly new: when the radicals sought guidance from the past, they turned to Jewish sacred history and the books of Moses.

Among the most interesting ideas which emerged in the early 1650s was a plan to model the new parliament on the Jewish Sanhedrin of seventy members. The main obstacle seems to have been that seventy members alone would comprise an assembly which would be much too small to represent adequately all of the English counties, Scotland, Ireland and Wales. Cromwell later claimed that he had therefore fixed 140 members on this Judaical basis, and indeed until the last stage it had been intended to summon only 130 men to the nominated parliament.[4] A very strong biblical element appears at the very outset of the short life of Barebone's Parliament, then, and illustrates, like Sabbatarianism itself, the penetration of the Old Testament ideas and values into the realm of political action.

This Jewish orientation is also apparent in the debates over legal reform which threatened to divide Barebone's Parliament. The ultimate hope was that "the great volumes of law would come to be reduced into the bigness of a pocket book, as it is proportionable in New-England and elsewhere".[5] The reference was to the radical code of laws which had been enacted in Massachusetts in 1643 and revised the following year as "The Laws and Liberties".[6] One of the comprehensive plans which was not finally accepted in Massachusetts was John Cotton's "Moses his Judicials", so called because it aimed at being a synthesis between the biblical commandments and common law practice. Although other plans were thought to be more workable, Cotton's code was printed in England and appealed to radical instincts everywhere.[7] The 1655 edition included a preface by William Aspinwall the Fifth Monarchist. Others who advocated adopting the Mosaic law included John Brayne, *The New Earth* (London, 1653), and John Spittlehouse, *The first Addresses* (London, 1653). As it was, the final code had numerous biblical overtones: the list of capital offences included idolatry, blasphemy, witchcraft, adultery, rape, sodomy, kidnapping, and cursing or smiting a parent. As Professor Woolrych puts it, "the Bible and the Statutes at Large were almost equally consulted in the framing of it", this "first modern code of the Western world".[8]

Certainly, then, the Old Testament was widely regarded as a legal authority with a divine claim on the obedience of Christians. Yet even the faithful of New England argued that not all the injunctions of the Jews applied to them. These were the "ceremonial" laws whose authority had ended with the coming of Christ. Jewish dietary regulations and the prohibitions against mixing linen and wool fell into this superceded category, which included many of the 613 commandments in the Old Testament.

But what was one to do about the Sabbath? Its authority derived from the very most central text of the Old Testament, the Ten Commandments, to which was accorded special respect even by those who argued that Christ had fulfilled and abrogated the Mosaic law. Nine of the commandments could easily be incorporated into existing codes of behaviour: murder, theft, and adultery were sins in any man's law. But the fourth commandment proved more difficult to assimilate by New England-style Puritans and more moderate churchmen alike. The first problem was that God had ruled that on the Sabbath "thou shalt not do any work, thou, nor thy son, nor thy stranger that *is* within thy gates". Before the Civil War, both Church and State positively encouraged recreation and sports after the Sabbath prayer; this sacreligious state of affairs was somewhat ameliorated afterwards. The second and insurmountable difficulty was the divine definition that "the seventh day *is* the sabbath of the LORD".[9] The Commandment stated very clearly that Saturday was the Sabbath, not Sunday, and the intention of this Mosaic rule was hardly disputed at any time. The Sabbath question in early modern England was two-fold, therefore, both in regard to the manner and the day of observance.

Let us look first at the more widespread problem of the proper way in which the Sabbath day should be honoured, whenever in occurred. Strict Sabbatarianism in its earliest English form was a doctrine associated with the unreformed Catholic Church. Even in medieval England the assumption remained that there was a moral core to the fourth commandment apart from its ceremonial husk.[10] The notion that Sunday should be spent in good works was eventually codified in legislation prohibiting Sunday markets. This Roman Catholic Sabbatarianism aroused the hostility of the Lollards because no justification could be found in the New Testament for this practice.[11]

So too did the Continental Reformers reject Sabbatarianism as another evil papistical invention, along with pilgrimages and prayers to saints. The Church's habit of linking the Sabbath with saints' days in ecclesiastical legislation only reinforced this view.[12] "If anywhere the day is made holy for the mere day's sake," Luther advised, "then I order you to work on it, to ride on it, to feast on it, to do anything to remove this reproach from Christian liberty."[13] Calvin made a point of playing at bowls on Sunday to demonstrate his own attitude to the question.[14] Tyndale protested that "we be lords over the Saboth and may yet change it into the Monday, or any other day, as we see need...Neither needed we any holy day at all, if the people might be taught without it."[15]

Until the later sixteenth century, the English Protestant position regarding the Sabbath was similar to that which prevailed in Reformed circles on the Continent. During the reigns of Henry VIII and Edward VI the Church in England took a middle ground: with the Lutherans they denounced the superstitious observance of the Lord's Day, but with the Catholics they promoted Sunday as a day given over in normal circumstances to worship, good works, and religious education.[16] By 1573, however, Richard Fletcher, a future bishop of London, could complain that it "is said crediblelly in the countrie that... it is no greater a sinne to steal a horse on Munday then to sell him in fayre on the Sunday; that it is as ill to play at games as shoutinge, bowlinge on Sundaye as to lye with your neyghbors wiffe on Munday".[17] Learned theological treatises provided the academic justification for this increasingly popular view. Richard Greenham led the way in 1592 with his *Treatise of the Sabbath*, followed three years later by his son-in-law Nicholas Bownde's study of *The Doctrine of the Sabbath*. By the Civil War fifty years later, it could even be claimed that "England was at rest...till they troubled Gods Sabbath".[18]

It is clear that this change in attitude was not officially inspired. Elizabeth vetoed a bill for "the better and more reverent observing of the Sabbath day" in 1585 and ensured that a similar or identical measure would not escape the Lords' committee when the issue came up again in 1601. J.E. Neale points out that these were not Puritan measures: the first attempt at passing the bill was probably the legislative result of the collapse of the old scaffolding about the bear pit in the Paris Garden during a crowded Sunday performance, killing eight people and injuring many more. This tragedy seemed to confirm a growing popular feeling that Sabbath abuse might have unforeseen and unpleasant consequences. "Her action may have been determined mainly by a resolve not to let Parliament interfere with any religious questions," Neale suggests, "but there can also be little doubt that she preferred a Merry to a Puritan England. What she had done was to veto a measure on which both Houses had set their hearts; and her chief statesman, Burghley, had been on the committee that steered in through the Lords."[19]

When James I passed through Lancashire in 1617 on his way back from Scotland, he had occasion to "rebuke some Puritans and precise people" for the "prohibiting and unlawful punishing of our good people for using their lawful recreations and honest exercises upon Sundays, and other Holy-days, after the afternoon sermon or service". James took advice with the local bishop and decided that every man was free to amuse himself on Sunday afternoon unless the Puritans could convince him otherwise.[20] The following year, in 1618, James extended this proclamation for Lancashire to the entire kingdom as the Declaration of Sports, where he positively encouraged traditional recreations on Sunday, excepting "bear and bull-baiting, interludes and at all times in the meaner sort of people by law prohibited, bowling." The hope was that all able-bodied men would engage in sports that had some military value, especially archery. His son Charles I reissued the Declaration in 1633, noting that if Sunday sports were banned, "the meaner sort who labour hard all the week should have no recreation at all to refresh their spirits". Charles ordered that the Declaration be read from the pulpits of all parish churches, a step which his father had abandoned in the face of stiff opposition, even from the archbishop of Canterbury.[21] The popular sort of Sabbatarianism, on the other hand, is best illustrated by the possibly apocryphal story of the London clergyman who first read the Declaration of Sports and then the Ten Commandments: "Dearly beloved," he told his congregation, "ye have heard the commandments of God and man, obey which you please." Measures for enforcing Sabbath observance appeared in the parliaments of 1621, 1624, and 1625 as well, and some of them became law.[22]

The explanation for this popular support of Judaical Sabbath observance on Sunday has long puzzled historians. "The good and evil effects of this self-imposed discipline of a whole nation, in abstaining from organized amusement as well as from work on every seventh day," wrote Trevelyan, "still awaits the dispassionate study of the social historian."[23] The Victorian historian S.R. Gardiner thought that one of the features of the Jewish Sabbath which was attractive to religious radicals was that it was incumbent upon them as individuals, not as members of any congregation. They could therefore observe the strict Sabbath quietly at home, and avoid any legal or social reprisals.[24] M.M. Knappen, the religious historian, saw the rise of Sabbatarianism was the natural result of a social need for orderly religion. In his view, the notion of a strict Sabbath worked its way up from the bottom and was in origin the medieval Catholic doctrine which had survived in Anglican teaching and religious legislation. Only in the seventeenth century, especially after the tragedy at the Paris Garden, did Sabbatarianism become a characteristically Puritan issue.[25] A more dramatic explanation of popular support for the Jewish Sabbath concentrates on the economic utility of a regular day of rest. Margaret James was the pioneer of this approach more than half a century ago, and no doubt drew some measure of inspiration from Weber's remarks on the Protestant ethic. Margaret James noted that although Puritans were anxious to observe the day of rest with great severity, and though "religious exercises might be reserved for Sundays, the week was fully occupied in the work of economic salvation." The Puritan obsession with work was one of the reasons that they campaigned for the suppression of saints' days, which were economically unproductive. Parliament could therefore be assured of support from business interests when it passed an ordinance in 1647 abolishing festivals and declaring the second Tuesday in every month as an arbitrary secular holiday. The religious enthusiasm which had been distributed over a large number of festivals was now concentrated on the strict observance of the Sabbath.[26]

This economic approach to the Sabbath question was utilized by Dr Christopher Hill in his study of pre-revolutionary English society. Dr Hill argues that the Puritans promoted the Jewish Sabbath as a *regular* day of rest, in contrast to the haphazard hundred or so saints' days which were compatible with the agricultural society of medieval England. The newly emerging industrial society, on the other hand, required a more regular framework in order to develop further. The Puritan objection to saints' days, then, was part of their general assault on the existing social and economic order. Following Margaret James, Dr Hill notes that the fourth commandment also enjoins us to *work* on the remaining six days; the Sabbath day was meant to be a day of recovery from a hard working week. Sunday sports would continue to be popular in the countryside, where the medieval agricultural life was still dominant. In the modern industrializing cities, however, the emphasis would be on Sunday rest. Soon, the Puritans came to see this Sabbath day of rest as a time for religious edification, and began to argue that *rest* days should be deducted from ordinary work days, as would be done in the legislation of 1647 which created the Tuesday secular holidays. Generally, then, Hill claims, we should see the Puritan attack on Sunday sports as an attempt to impose the ethos of an urban civilization, particularly the new concern for labour discipline, on the whole realm, especially its dark corners. The Crown here again supported the economically backward areas of the country, which would be Royalist in the civil war, against the values of the "industrious sort of people".[27]

On this basis, Hill is able to explain why nothing like the English Sunday developed in other Calvinist countries. Hill argues that the answer is to be sought in the peculiar features of economic and social development in England, where an industrial and urban way of life was established on a national scale earlier than elsewhere. The "industrious sort of people", the early capitalists, required a new ethos and protection from overwork, which they could obtain by championing the Sabbath as a day of rest. The monarchy and the medieval landed class, however, encouraged traditional sports as a harmless occupation for idle agricultural workers. In Dr Hill's view, the Bible had little influence on the creation of strict Sabbatarianism, which derived from the pressures and demands of society, only afterwards justified by an apposite biblical text. "There were plenty of Bibliolators among the Puritan Sabbatarians;" Dr Hill explains, "but there was also a rational case for the Sunday rest. It was the habit of the age to find Biblical texts to justify men in doing what they would have done even if no texts could be found."[28] Yet certainly not all biblical interpretation was utilitarian. As is often the case, one finds the most sensible approach in the writings of unfashionable classic authors. J.R. Tanner, writing in 1930 about James I's Book of Sports, insisted that the Sabbatarian controversy is "vastly more important than it appears at first sight. The fundamental conflict was after all between those who contended for the exclusive authority of the Bible and those who contended for the co-ordinate authority of the Church." This debate, Tanner continues, was part of the controversy which included the question of whether the Church might institute ceremonies not mentioned in the Bible, provided they were not contrary to the spirit of the law. It was only another application of their principle when the Puritans claimed for Sunday the characteristics of the Jewish Sabbath.[29] So too in the nineteenth century, Gardiner emphasized the biblical origins of the Puritan's strict Sabbath observance: "The precepts of the Fourth Commandment were, according to his interpretation, of perpetual obligation. The Christian Lord's Day was but the Jewish Sabbath, and it was the duty of Christian magistrates to enforce its strict observance." The opponents of the strict Sabbath, on the other hand, argued that the Christian Sunday was a human rather than a divine institution, handed down by oldest Church tradition, and that therefore the Church was free to determine the exact form of its observance.[30]

Tanner and Gardiner bring us back again to the Old Testament and the second part of the fourth commandment. If, as they argue, the Sabbath question was primarily religious in nature, why have historians consistently revealed a blind spot towards the most radical of Sabbatarians, those who followed the commandment to the letter of the law and observed God's holy Sabbath on the seventh day, on Saturday? James I noted with distaste that "all such kind of people...encline to a kind of Judaism".[31] Dr Hill claims that it is especially in "the fierce discussions as to whether God intended Saturday or Sunday to be observed as the day of rest" that an element of "mere irrational Bibliolatry" enters into the Sabbath question. Indeed, the determination of the time of Sabbath observance was not a dilemma that began with the Puritans in seventeenth-century England. Only about one hundred years after Jesus made his dramatic declaration that the "sabbath was made for man, and not man for the sabbath", Christians began using the expression "Lord's Day" as their exclusive designation for Sunday.[32] Certainly by the fourth century the Sabbath was no longer observed on Saturday in accordance with Jewish law, but had been transferred to Sunday, perhaps in commemoration of the Resurrection, but more likely as a means of distinguishing Christians from Jews.[33]

We need to pay careful attention to the important distinction between the acceptance of the Church's insistence of Sunday as the Sabbath day and the belief in the continuing existence of a morally binding Sabbath. As we shall see, many churchmen and indeed less educated practitioners of the Christian faith were quite willing to accept the second principle, while finding no conclusive scriptural authority for the first.

The promulgation of the Book of Sports in 1618 only intensified the general Sabbatarian debate and with it the problem of justifying Sunday as the day to observe the word of God in all its Mosaic rigour, for one could hardly obey one part of the commandment with uncompromising strictness while altering the other part completely. The first attempt to eliminate this ambiguity in a dramatic and highly public way was that of John Traske (1585–1636), the famous Jacobean Judaizer, who kept a whole range of Jewish laws, from the Sabbath to Passover. By the beginning of 1618, Traske and his sect of Judaizing Saturday-observers could no longer be ignored, even though the king seemed to be rather more amused than incensed at Traske's well-known practices. He was sentenced in Star Chamber on 19 June 1618 to be kept close prisoner in the Fleet for the rest of his life, given a monetary fine of unpayable proportions, and was finally whipped across London, branded in the forehead with the letter J, and nailed to the pillory by his ears. Traske recovered, renounced the open observance of the Saturday-Sabbath, and eventually joined the Baptist Church led by Henry Jessey. One of Traske's followers seems to have converted the Judaism in Amsterdam.[34]

But the silencing of Traske and his little band by no means put an end to those who were willing to cut the Gordian knot of biblical fidelity, or who were brave enough to air their doubts in public. It was Theophilus Brabourne (1590–1661) who, after Traske, did the most for propagating the belief in the Saturday-Sabbath in England before the outbreak of the civil war. Brabourne, a native of Norwich, the son of a Puritan hosier, began to write on the Saturday-Sabbath in 1628, but was not committed to prison until six years later. Brabourne appeared before Laud and High Commission, and was pronounced "a Jew, a heretic and schismatic, and adjudged him worthy to be severely punished." During the Interregnum he was free to promote these doctrines once again, although he seems to have steered clear of the organized churches which observed the Saturday-Sabbath. After the Restoration he wrote several pamphlets concerning liberty of conscience, while upholding the royal supremacy in religious affairs. Some of Traske's followers may have migrated to Brabourne's circle of acquaintances after 1636, but in any case in contemporary minds the two men were inextricably linked. As Peter Heylyn the royalist historian of the Sabbath wrote, "their Opinions, so farre as it concerned the *Sabbath*, were the very same; they onely making the conclusions, which of necessitie must follow from the former premisses".[35]

By the time Peter Heylyn wrote his comprehensive five hundred page history of the Sabbath in 1636, the validity of the seventh-day Sabbath was already an idea that had taken root in the fertile soil of the English religious landscape during this period. For in that year Henry Jessey, the pioneer of the Baptist movement in England, was appointed pastor of the Jacob Church, the mother church of the English Baptists and of the English semi-separatist tradition. And Henry Jessey observed the Sabbath on Saturday. His adoption of that straight-forward understanding of the fourth commandment would be crucial for the later development of Saturday-Sabbatarianism into an organized religious sect during the period of the civil war. His advocacy of the readmission of the Jews to England and his friendship with Menasseh ben Israel was the practical application of his respect and admiration for the Jewish tradition. Jessey's own interests in Hebrew, biblical studies, contemporary Jewry, millenarianism, and in the Baptist movement itself ensured that these would be the controlling themes of Saturday-Sabbatarianism as a whole even after the Restoration.

Indeed, in a sense this is the story of the remarkable persistence of a revolutionary religious belief in seventeenth-century England, powerful and convincing enough to survive the watershed of the king's return in 1660 and to continue into modern times. The Saturday-Sabbath gradually became institutionalized in a non-conformist sect in which the ideological foundation was sufficient to unite men who on political grounds should have been the most bitter of enemies, including millenarians, Fifth Monarchists, neutrals and Royalists alike. That these men and their followers could amicably join forces after the Restoration is testimony to the power of religious ideas which might overshadow the political affiliations of the Civil War. Most importantly in the long term, in the latter part of the seventeenth century Saturday-Sabbatarianism was transplanted into English America, to Rhode Island, where thanks to a motley coalition of Quakers, Freemasons, and Jews the sect would flourish as the Seventh-Day Baptists. This group would be instrumental in the foundation of the Seventh-Day Adventists after the "Great Disappointment" of 22 October 1844 when Jesus declined to arrive manifestly as scheduled, and in the theological development of Fundamentalism at the beginning of the twentieth century. But far more crucial than the institutional survival of the Seventh-Day men are the ideas which had been highlighted by their struggle against disintegration, and which continue to run through English and American Protestantism in the following centuries. It is well known that one of the most important theological results of the Protestant Reformation was that the Old Testament regained a place of honour next to the New, but the precise application of this distinction was never satisfactorily resolved, and at different points in religious history the problem of the Old Testament and of the Jewish antecedents of Christianity erupts with disturbing clarity. In the seventeenth century, in a culture which prized linguistic precision and confessional allegiance, this issue became centered around the observance of the Seventh-Day Sabbath, that day of rest that had been ordained in the Ten Commandments, the central text of the Old Testament which was revered by Christians of all persuasions. Those worried by the need to observe all of the Ten Commandments literally found the problem of the Old Testament brought home with terrifying power, for they were forced to make a public demonstration of their faith by putting aside Saturday, a working day, as the day of rest.

A good deal has already been written on the persistence of certain social and political creeds from the beginning of the English Civil War, thorough the American and French Revolutions, down to 1917, concepts revolving around a wider franchise, land reform, and other views especially associated with the Levellers, the Diggers, and other radicals. But the Jewish Sabbath in a Christian context became a potent unifying theme to bring within the fold men whose political views differed so dramatically. What needs to be looked at again is the *religious* bequest of that sparkling period, especially the Jewish heritage of Protestantism, by focussing on such issues as the conviction that the Old Testament, and especially the Ten Commandments, was given to all mankind, in all its severity, including the Seventh-Day Sabbath, and examining its institutional and historical consequences.

For many religious radicals, the Bible, including the Old Testament, provided a model for conduct, religious observance, and even for solving intellectual and scientific problems. This was more than irrational bibliolatry, but rather in their eyes the practical application of the divine knowledge revealed to the Jews in the word of God. So too had Thomas Münzer and his rebellious Germaasants in the 1520s raised the cry of "God's word, God's word". "But my dear fellow", Luther objected, "the question is whether it was said to you".[36] The Saturday-Sabbatarians of seventeenth-century England thought they knew the answer.

NOTES

1. [Anon.], *A Character of England* (London, 1659), repr. *Harleian Miscellany*, ed. T. Park (London, 1808–13), x. p. 192.
2. M.M. Knappen, *Tudor Puritanism* (2nd edn, Chicago, 1970), p. 442.
3. H. Gee and W.J. Hardy, *Documents Illustrative of English Church History* (London, 1896), p. 477; E.C.S. Gibson, *The Thirty-Nine Articles* (London, 1898).
4. John Rogers, *To...Cromwell. A few Proposals relating to Civil Government* (London, 1653), broadsheet; Edmund Ludlow, *Memoirs*, ed. C.H. Firth (Oxford, 1894), i. pp. 358–9; Anthony Morgan to Henry Cromwell, 3 Mar. 1657: *The Writings and Speeches of Oliver Cromwell*, ed. W.C. Abbott (Cambridge, USA, 1937–47), iv. pp. 418–19; *Clarke*

Papers, ed. C.H. Firth (Camden Soc., 2nd ser., 49, 54, 61, 62, 1891–1901), iii. 4, iv. 21; *Thurloe State Papers*, ed. T. Birch (London, 1742), i. 240; *Cal.S.P.Dom., 1652–3*, pp. 339–40; B.S. Capp, *The Firth Monarchy Men* (London, 1972), pp. 63, 117–18; *Staffordshire and the Great Rebellion*, ed. D.A. Johnson and D.G. Vaisey (Staffordshire, 1964), p. 72.

5. L.D. [Samuel Highland], *An Exact Relation* (London, 1654), repr. *Somers Tracts*, ed. W. Scott (2nd edn, London, 1809–15), vi. 266–84, esp. p. 278; A. Woolrych, *Commonwealth to Protectorate* (Oxford, 1982), p. 271.

6. *Ibid.*, p. 272.

7. [John Cotton], *An Abstract or the Lawes of New England* (London, 1641).

8. Woolrych, *Commonwealth*, p. 272.

9. Exod. xx. 8–11.

10. M.M. Knappen, *Tudor Puritanism* (2nd edn, Chicago, 1970), pp. 443–4; S. Bacchiocchi, *From Sabbath to Sunday* (Rome, 1977), pp. 16–55.

11. E.g. 12 Rich. II, c.6; 27 Hen. VI, c.5: see J. Wigley, *The Rise and Fall of the Victorian Sunday* (Manchester, 1980), pp. 204–8 for a list of statutes.

12. Knappen, *Puritanism*, pp. 444–5.

13. Quoted in C. Hill, *Society and Purirtanism* (2nd edition, New York, 1967) p. 210.

14. R. Cox, *The Whole Doctrine of Calvin about the Sabbath* (Edinburgh, 1860), p. 91.

15. William Tyndale, *An Answer to Sir Thomas More's Dialogue*, ed. H. Walter (Parker Socl, xxxviii, 1850), pp. 97–8.

16. Knappen, *Puritanism*, pp. 445–6; Hill, *Society*, pp. 149–50: see e.g. 5 and 6 Edw. VI, c.3 (repealed under Mary but re-enacted in 1604) which authorized harvest labour on Sunday 'or at any times in the year when necessity shall require to labour, ride, fish or work any kind of work, at their free wills and pleasure'.

17. Dr Williams's Lib., MS Morrice B II, f. 9v: quoted in P. Collinson, 'The Beginning of English Sabbatarianism', *Stud.Ch.Hist.*, i (1964), p. 208.

18. Thomas Shepard, *Theses Sabbaticae* (London, 1649), preface, sig. B; W.U. Solberg, *Redeem the Time* (Cambridge, USA, 1977), pp. 1–2. A similar viewpoint can be found in William Gouge, *Gods Three Arrows* (London, 1631), p. 5; and from John Dod, preaching in Coggeshall: *Cal.S.P.Dom., 1636–7*, p. 514. Cf. W. Hunt, *The Puritan Moment* (Cambridge, USA, 1983), pp. 259, 274.

19. J.E. Neale, *Elizabeth I and her Parliaments* (London, 1953–7), ii. pp. 58–60, 394–5.

20. J. Tait, 'The Declaration of Sports for Lancashire (1617)', *Eng.Hist.Rev.*, xxxii (1917), 561–8. Tait located a copy of this hitherto lost document in *Manchester Sessions*, i, ed. E. Axon (Rec. Soc. Lancashire & Cheshire, xlii, 1901), pp. xxiv–xxvii.

21. *The Constitutional Documents of the Puritan Revolution*, ed. S.R. Gardiner (3rd edn, Oxford, 1906), pp. 99–103: Declaration of Sports re-issued 18 Oct. 1633. For the background to this action, see S.R. Gardiner, *History of England... 1603–1642* (2nd edn, London, 1883–4), iii. pp. 248–52; vii. pp. 318–23; *Vict.Cnty.Hist., Somerset*, ii (1911), pp. 43–6; T.G. Barnes, 'County Politics and a Puritan Cause Celebre: Somerset Churchales, 1633', *Trans.Roy.Hist.Soc.*, 5th ser., ix (1959), pp. 103–22; R.C. Richardson, 'Puritanism and the Ecclesiastical Authorities', in *Politics, Religion and the English Civil War*, ed. B. Manning (London, 1973), pp. 15–16.

22. Gardiner, *History*, vii. 322; C. Russell, *Parliaments and English Politics 1621–1629* (Oxford, 1979), pp. 96–7, 157, 183, 234, 276; *idem*, 'The Parliamentary Career of John Pym, 1621–9', in *The Elizabethan Commonwealth*, ed. P. Clark *et al.* (Leicester, 1979), p. 152; *Commons Debates 1621*, ed. W. Notestein, *et al.* (New Haven, 1935), ii. pp. 96; iii. 299; iv. 377–8.

23. G.M. Trevelyan, *History of England* (3rd edn, London, 1945), p. 453. The two most thoughtful pieces of work are Hill, *Society*, chap. 5: 'The Uses of Sabbatarianism'; and Collinson, 'Beginnings'. See also R.L. Greaves, 'The Origins of English Sabbatarian Thought', *Sixteenth Cent.Jnl*, xii (1981), pp. 19–34; K.L. Sprunger, 'English and Dutch Sabbatarianism and the Development of Puritan Social Theology (1600–1660)', *Church Hist.*, li (1982), pp. 24–38; K.L. Parker, 'Thomas Rogers and the English Sabbath: The Case for a Reappraisal', *Church Hist.*, liii (1984), pp. 332–47 and his 1984 Cambridge Univ. Ph.D. thesis, 'The English Sabbath, 1558–1649', now published by Cambridge University Press. See also D.S. Katz, *Sabbath and Sectarianism in Seventeenth-Century England* (Leiden, 1987). An older work, still useful, is M. Levy, *Der Sabbath in England* (Leipzig, 1933). For the Sabbath in later times, see Wigley, *Victorian Sunday*; and D. Eshet, 'The English Sunday: Sabbatarianism and Social Order in England, 1780–1867' (M.A. thesis, Tel-Aviv University, 1992), now being expanded as a Ph.D. thesis for UCLA. The primary sources are meticulously catalogued in R. Cox, *The Literature of the Sabbath Question* (Edinburgh, 1865). See also M. Weber, *The Protestant Ethic and the Spirit of Capitalism*, trans. T. Parsons (New York, 1958), p. 167.

24. Gardiner, *History*, iii. p. 247.

25. Knappen, *Puritanism*, pp. 447–9.

26. M. James, *Social Problems and Policy During the Puritan Revolution* (London, 1930), pp. 9, 14–15, 21.

27. Hill, *Society*, chap. 5, *passim*.

28. *Ibid.*, esp. pp. 146, 159, 167, 172, 209, 213, 216.

29. *Constitutional Documents of the Reign of James I*, ed. J.R. Tanner (Cambridge, 1930), p. 49.

30. Gardiner, *History*, vii. pp. 318–19.

31. Tait, 'Declaration', p. 565.

32. Mark ii. 27.

33. Bacchiocchi, *Sabbath*, p. 17.

34. See D.S. Katz, *Philo-Semitism and the Readmission of the Jews to England, 1603–1655* (Oxford, 1982), chap. 1.

35. P. Heylyn, *The History of the Sabbath* (London, 1636), pp. 259–60. On Brabourne, see Katz, *Philo-Semitism*, pp. 34–8.

36. Martin Luther, 'How Christians Should Regard Moses', in *Works*, ed. J. Pelikan and H.T. Lehman (St Louis and Philadelphia, 1955–67), xxxv. p. 171, from the sermon of 27 Aug. 1525.

JAMES E. FORCE

8. NEWTON, THE LORD GOD OF ISRAEL
AND KNOWLEDGE OF NATURE

INTRODUCTION

In the nineteenth century, the triumvirate of W.E.H. Lecky, John W. Draper, and Andrew D. White eagerly cataloged an all out "warfare" between modern science and religion, a "conflict" in which science "rose" and religion, generally categorized as superstitious and irrational, "fell."[1] Today such Whiggish historiography is out of fashion given our inability to ignore the impact of the design argument and our ever widening understanding of the role religion played in the thinking of such private men as, for example, Isaac Newton. Basil Willey speaks for the majority of twentieth century historians when he writes of the "holy alliance between science and religion" in eighteenth century England.[2]

Even so, such an eminent historian as Norman Hampson has written that "However orthodox men like Descartes, Locke and Leibniz might be, their Christian orthodoxy was tacked on to systems of thought which were logically viable without it."[3] Richard S. Westfall, after skillfully tracing how numerous seventeenth century English thinkers attempt to synthesize science and religion, finally concludes that "the skepticism of the Enlightenment was already present in embryo among them. To be sure, their piety kept it in check, but they were unable fully to banish it."[4]

Too frequently modern historians write as if the tension which some modern scholars are able to observe in the thought of early modern thinkers, if only "in embryo," was problematic for them as well as for us.[5] More sophisticated modern interpreters readily acknowledge an intimate "union" between Newton's theology and his science in his *private* thought but, for these writers, Newton remains a fundamentally typical modern scientist whose public science may be, and therefore is, epistemologically and metaphysically disconnected from any private theological views he may have held. Even if Newton is an extreme metaphysical voluntarist who emphasizes the absolute primacy of God's providential control over his creation from beginning to end and even if he simultaneously adopts an Arian Christology and is keenly interested in understanding historically fulfilled events in prophetic history, the *Principia* is still the *Principia*. Newton's universe becomes thereby theologically neutered:

R.H. Popkin and G.M. Weiner (eds): Jewish Christians and Christian Jews, 131–158.
© 1994 *Kluwer Academic Publishers. Printed in the Netherlands.*

Newton's universe, when stripped of metaphysical considerations, as stripped it would be, is an infinite void of which only an infinitesimal part is occupied by unattached material bodies moving freely through its boundless and bottomless abyss, a colossal machine made up of components whose only attributes are position, extension, and mass.[6]

In contrast, I wish to attempt to analyze Newton's universe in Newton's terms. I wish to argue that his extremely voluntaristic notion of the Lord God of Israel, a God of total power and absolute "dominion," affects every aspect of his metaphysics including his approach to a scientific understanding of nature.

My starting point will be to assess Newton's understanding of the Lord God of Israel. Given Newton's intensive, wide-ranging theological interests, it is no surprise that he is fascinated by the Jewish religious experience. Newton's interest in the Jews includes such topics as Old Testament geography, Jewish religious ritual, how the various Jewish apostasies prefigure later Christian apostasies, the equivalent relationship between prophetic images in the Book of Daniel with "synchronal" images (i.e., those which describe the same event) in the Book of Revelation, and the exact shape of Ezekiel's temple down to the last Biblically correct cubit.[7]

According to Richard S. Westfall, in the late 1670's or early 1680's, Newton becomes keenly interested in Judaism because of his growing conviction that ancient Jewish rites and ceremonies are prophetic "types" and thus an important key to understanding the meaning of scriptural prophecies. Westfall rightly insists that Newton's obsession with understanding the exact size and shape of the Jewish temple (as well as with Jewish ritual observances in general) derives from Newton's view that the temple's very shape, along with the rites conducted there, is a microcosmic symbol of the heavenly Jerusalem and that the Temple is a "type" which prefigures the world to come.[8]

Differing in emphasis, Frank E. Manuel has pointed with equal justification to the similarity between Newton's heretical Arianism and the supreme monotheism of the Jewish faith. Manuel writes of the Jews that:

> In their best monotheistic period after Moses had restored the law, they came as close as any people to Newton's idea of true religion, and there is a temptation to judaize him, especially if one constricts the definition of historical Judaism to its rationalist formulation in the works of Moses Maimonides.[9]

Neither of these points of emphasis is exclusive and both are accurate as far as they go. What I wish to do in this paper is to show why we must synthesize these two perspectives and then extend and clarify them in order to appreciate fully why and how Newton becomes so interested in the God of the Jews.

This synthesized focus will show how Newton's theology may be categorized as that of a "Judaizing" Christian and of how his subsequent theory of the nature of the "Lord God" affects his natural philosophy. In Part I of what follows, I examine the question of Newton's methodology for interpreting revelatory scripture both in the Jewish scriptures and in the New Testament and consider the degree to which Newton's method differs from that of the "Carites," the Kabalists, and the rabbinical Talmudists. Newton effectively constricts what counts as important in the historical strands of Judaic Biblical interpretation to the "rationalist" approach of Moses Maimonides while dismissing other schools within the Jewish tradition. In Part II, I address how Newton's particular method of "systematizing" the Bible produces, in his manuscript entitled the *Irenicum*, the ultimate statement of Newton's own Christian-Maimonidean creed in which he makes a clear distinction between what theological doctrines must be absolutely believed for salvation ("milk for babes") and what doctrines may be speculated about ("strong meat for elders"). Further, I will show that Newton's creed structurally resembles Maimonides' statement of the Jewish creed in the *Perek Helek*, a famous chapter in Maimonides' commentary on the Mishnah. In Part III, I examine how Newton's understanding of and reverence for what he terms (in his *General Scholium*) "the God of *Israel*, the God of Gods, the Lord of Lords" directly affects his view of the method human beings must bring to their probings of nature and nature's laws and of his views regarding the limits of human understanding in seeking such knowledge. Finally, in Part IV, I present new evidence for the plausibility of arguing that Newton's conception of the God of Israel directly influences his epistemological expectations in his natural philosophy.

Thus approached, Newton's thought as a whole presents a systematic unity of startling coherence. Indeed, I will argue that the central unifying priniciple of Newton's thought, the key to understanding its uniquely integrated quality, is his conception of the nature of the Lord God of Dominion.[10] What will become clear from my argument is that Newton's extreme voluntarism, his emphatic focus upon God's attributes of freedom and power, is the logically unifying principle of both his interest in Jewish religion and his science. Newton's interest in the Jews centers around his obssession with the Lord God of the Jews as that God revealed himself to Moses and the Prophets and not with what various rabbinical commentators or Kabalists have said about that revelation. He also is interested in how the Lord God will reveal himself again, both to the Jews and to their covenental successors, the true Christians, as he brings to pass the promised prophetic future. Newton's conception of the Lord God of Moses, i.e., his understanding of the God of the Jews at the highwater mark of Jewish monotheism, becomes the basis for his own heartfelt, but heretical, Judaized Christianity which in turn becomes crucial to his "rules" for approaching the study of natural philosophy.

I. NEWTON'S MIDDLE PATH BETWEEN THE CARAITES AND THE CABBALISTS

The interest on the part of Newton in Jewish temple rituals as allegorical *types* which symbolically prefigure future prophetic visions and, hence, serve as an aid in understanding what those visions signify is an integral part of the larger question of his approach to interpreting scripture as a whole. Newton's interest in interpreting the scripture of the Jews is well known. The Temple rituals of the Jews pointed to by Westfall as *types* which aid us in understanding the meaning of prophecies become a part of the larger question of what Newton conceives to be the best method of interpreting Biblical prophecy in general. Many Christians besides Newton hoped that the customs of the Jews will aid the understanding of apostolic Christianity.[11] Newton believes that the Hebrew Bible is particularly unique and important as a guide in understanding God. While Newton believes that it is simply a historical fact that "The Israelites fell into great troubles several times & every time their worship was interrupted & their Antiquities scattered," he also believes that the historical documents and records of the Egyptians, Assyrians, Babylonians, Persians, Medes, Greeks, and Romans "by means of various warrs & revolutions have been long since lost." Newton asserts that:

> ...the Records of the Jews have above all others escaped the shipwracks of time. They have been frequently in danger but by Providence have escaped tho not without some damage.[12]

Newton maintains that the "Records" of the Jews divide into three parts: the Laws in the books of Moses, the future visions in the books of the later Prophets, and the Hagiographa which Newton calls the "historical books."[13] Of these three sorts of "Records," the "Laws" and the "Prophets" were the least corrupt due to Ezra's institution of their public reading in the Jewish synagogues following their return from their Babylonian exile: "By reading the Law and the Prophets in the Synagogues, those books have been kept freer from corruption than the *Hagiographa*."[14]

For Newton, too, "Christ and his Apostles laid the stress of religion upon the Law and the Prophets."[15] Thus, by Newton's day, there are FOUR sorts of reliable revelatory "Records" and all of them are exclusively Jewish in origin or grow out of the Jewish intellectual and religious context. Newton writes that:

> We have *Moses*, the Prophets, and Apostles, and the words of Christic himself; and if we will not hear them, we shall be more inexcusable than

the *Jews*. For the Prophets have foretold that as *Israel* often revolted and brake the covenant, and upon repentance renewed it; so there should be a falling away among the Christians, soon after the days of the Apostles; and that in the latter days God would destroy the impenitent revolters, and make a new covenant with his people. And the giving ear to the Prophets is a fundamental character of the true Church. For God has so ordered the Prophecies that in the latter days *the wise may understand, but the wicked shall do wickedly, and none of the wicked shall understand*, Dan. xii. 9, 10. The authority of Emperors, Kings, and Princes is human. The authority of Councils, Synods, Bishops, and Presbyters, is human. The authority of the Prophets is divine, and comprehends the sum of religion, reckoning *Moses* and the Apostles among the Prophets: and *if an Angel from Heaven preach any other gospel*, than what they have delivered, *let him be accursed.*[16]

For Newton, misinterpreting these "Records" thus has dire consequences for an individual's personal salvation. Misinterpreting them simultaneously severely injures the church. Newton writes, for example, of the prophetic visions in the Revelation of St. John that:

They are the counsels of God & so ye most wise, & fittest for ye end to wch they are designed: And that end is the benefit of ye Church to guide & preserve her in ye truth. For to this end are all ye sacred prophecies in both ye old & new Testament directed, as they that will consider them may easily perceive.[17]

Getting the scriptures right preserves the Church in truth and the soul from damnation. Newton's avid interest in the rules which guide his interpretative efforts become clearer in this context. We must have instructions for how to read our sources. Too much depends on reading them correctly. And yet the prophetic scriptures, according to Newton,

are wrapt up in obscurity, & so framed by the wisdom of God that ye inconsiderate, ye proud, ye self-conceited ye presumptuous ye sciolist, ye sceptic, they whose judgmets are ruled by their lusts, their interest, ye fashions of ye world, their esteem of men, the outward shew of thing [sic] or other prejudices, & all they who, of how pregnannt [sic] natural parts soever they be, yet cannot discern ye wisdom of God in ye contrivance of ye creation: that these men whose hearts are thus hardned [sic] in seeing should see & not perceive & in hearing should heare & not understand. For God has declared his intention in these prophecies to be as well that none of ye wicked should understand as yt ye wise should understand.[18]

Most of Newton's famous manuscript on "methodizing" the Apocalypse of St. John is a highly technical exposition in which Newton attempts to "synchronize" the prophetic language of the pouring out of the vials with the the sounding of the trumpets, i.e., to illustrate that these prophetic images signify the same event.[19] But interlaced with his rules for interpreting these particular prophecies is evidence of Newton's general approach to detecting God's meaning in the words of other prophets such as Moses, the apostles, and Jesus.

The general problem in interpreting all these basic sources and in getting to God's intended meaning in them reduces for Newton to a problem of textual moderation, i.e., of walking a middle path between those who might be called absolute literalists and those who read each and every passage as an allegory. For Newton, a "Rule" for interpreting "ye words & language in Scripture" is that the interpreter must prefer neither sort of reading exclusively. The interpreter, instead, must choose:

> those interpretations wch are most according to ye litterall meaning of ye scriptures unless where the tenour & circumstances of ye place require an Allegory.[20]

In Newton's view, the most famous and tragic mistake of the school of strict literalists occurred when the Jews rejected Jesus because they could discern no literal kingdom following his preaching such as their literalistic interpretations of the messianic prophecies had led them to expect. Likewise, in Newton's view, Modern Christian interpreters who insist on a literalistic fulfillment of messianic prophecies regarding events which precede the second coming (in order to force these events into the apocalyptic scenario as "a demonstration in Euclide") are mistaken. To the simple-mindedly literalistic Christians of his day who wish to be certainly convinced by a concretely literal "Signe" of the coming of the messiah, Newton poses a question. Are you not, he inquires of such literalists:

> like ye Scribes & Pharisees who would not attend to ye law & ye Prophets but required a Signe of Christ? Wherefor if Christ thought it just to deny a signe to that wicked & adulterate generation notwithstanding that they were God's own people, & the Catholique Church; much more may God think it just that this generation should be permitted to dy in their sins, who do not onely like ye scribes neglect but trample upon the law & ye Prophets, & endeavour by all possible means to destroy ye faith wch men have in them, & make them disregarded.[21]

Interpreting the serpent who deceived Eve as an actual snake is another example of excessive literalism among Jewish interpreters. Following Joseph Mede, Newton writes that this serpent must be understood allegorically or "symbolically" and that a strictly literal interpretation will not do. Newton writes that Eve's serpent:

is no more a real serpent then ye Dragon in the Apocalyps is a real Dragon or then then [sic] the Beasts in John and Daniel are real Beasts. Tis only a symbol of the spirit of delusion & therefore ye curs of this serpent for deceiving Eve must be interpreted accordingly. Whence I conceive it will amount to no more then this, That *because this Spirit had deceived Eve he should be represented by, & symbolically become the most accursed of all Beasts,* even the serpent which eats dust & goes upon its belly.[22]

But if the strictly literalistic approach to understanding crucial scripture prophecy can lead to error if it is always followed, so, too, does an absolute adherence to a purely allegorical method lead to error. In this instance, Newton again compares the problems of allegorically minded contemporary Christian interpreters with the overly literal Jewish interpreters at the time of Christ but this time he points out that at least those ancient Jewish interpreters did not make the mistake of interpreting the descriptions of the second coming as purely allegorical or symbolic as modern Christians often do. Newton inquires:

Or how knowest thou that the christian church if they continue to neglect [the prophecies of the second coming], shall not be punished even in this world as severely as ever were the Jews? Yea will not ye Jews rise up in judgment against us? For they had some regard to these prophesies insomuch as to be in generall expectation of our Saviour about that time when he came, onely they were not aware of the manner of his two comings; they understood ye description of his second coming, & onely were mistaken in applying that to ye time of his first coming. Consider therefore, if ye description of his second coming was so much more plain & perspicuous then that of ye first, yt ye Jews who could not so much as perceive any thing of ye first could yet understand ye second, how shall we escape who understand nothing of ye second but have turned ye whole description of it into Allegories.[23]

Beyond all of Newton's specific positions regarding "methodizing" the "synchronizations" of St. John's prophetic visions, there is revealed in this manuscript his general disgust with reading all passages as exclusively literal or allegorical. Perhaps the most widely known, though least recognized, instance of Newton's adherence to a middle path is in his letter to Thomas Burnet from January 1681 in which he carefully distinguishes between the literal meaning of the words of Moses concerning the work of the seven days of creation and their occasional allegorical or "poetical" meaning. In Genesis 1:16, Moses states that on the fourth day of creation, God made two great lights: "the greater light to rule the day, and the lesser light to rule the night." To accept literally that the sun and moon (and stars) were created completely on the fourth day contradicts reason and so justifies an allegorical interpretation. Allegorically, or "poetically," this text means that the light of the sun, moon, and stars became completely visible to any who would have seen it from earth on the fourth day, i.e., they were created in a sense "but only as they were lights to this earth" and gave the "appearance of lights in ye firmament to enlightenthe earth."[24] But Newton immediately applies the brakes and refuses to depart any further from the literal sense of the text as Burnet had done in Burnet's allegorical interpretation that no real seas were created on the third day. Newton continues:

> Thus far perhaps one might be allowed to go in ye explaining ye creation of ye 4th day, but in ye third day for Moses to describe ye creation of seas when there was no such thing done neither in reality nor in appearance me thinks is something hard.[25]

Through his references in Yahuda 1, Newton reveals his knowledge of the Jewish literalist school of interpretion, a school still extant in his day and which he may have known about if he read the books in his library.[26] Newton, in short, may well have known of the Jewish sect of literalists known as the Caraites. Richard Simon explains that the Caraites differ from the "*Rabbinists*, who make the Fables of the *Talmud* and the Conceits of their Ancestors, go hand-in-hand with the Sacred Books of Scripture."[27] Simon cites the example given by the Caraite Aron ben Joseph of the sort of absurd and irrational fables which have been given authority and status among Talmudic rabbis. According to Simon, the Caraite interpreter, Aron ben Joseph, "relates the pleasant Account which these Doctors [i.e.,the "Rabbinists"] give of the Serpent mention'd in the beginning of *Genesis*: For the *Rabbinists* and *Cabalists, That he was as big as a Camel....*"[28]

Ben Joseph, according to Simon, then goes on to mention:

> the Allegorical and Cabalistic Interpretations of these same Doctors, which he substantially refutes, adding these words, *In these sorts of Expositions, and the like, they lean only upon the Authority of their Fathers.* Afterwards, inveighing against such as abuse the Word of God, after this manner, Wo be to him, (says he) that has the Impudence to use it thus.[29]

The positive method of the Caraites, as described by Simon, is to keep as close to the "Grammaticisms" of the text as possible and to array as many "Various Readings" as necessary to make the choice of the one which is "closest to the Letter of the Text."[30] Prideaux explains that in such comparisons of the "Various Readings" the Caraites are content to utilize in this task the "Opinions of the former Doctors, as human helps for the interpreting and the better understanding of the written word, as far as they shall find them conducive thereto, but not to equal them to the written word it self, which all the other *Jews* do."[31] Newton, if indeed he had read the books in his own library by Simon and Prideaux and was aware of the Caraites, may have felt sympathetic to their emphasis upon the words of scripture and he may have regarded them as allies in dismissing the attempt by Kabbalists or any who tend to read the scriptures too allegorically and who thereby obfuscate scripture with flights of human imagination. But finally, if he did indeed know what was then known about the Caraites, he would have rejected them as exclusively literalist. Such a mode of interpretation could lead to missing such a momentous event in the divine cosmic drama as the first coming of the Messiah.[32]

Newton does not spare the Talmudic rabbis from his scorn. He observes that even in the age of the Apostles, iniquitous heresies began to undermine the pure apostolical faith of the Christian church. At first, gentile Christians were easily mixed in with Jews who followed Christ. Newton writes that:

> The law was good & was observed by the Churches of the circumcision while the Temple stood. For those with James were zealous of the law & Paul circumcised Timothy & thereby obliged him to keep the law. Everyman was to remain as he was called whether in circumcision or uncircumcision.[33]   /

In Newton's view, the initial unity of the Jewish-Christian church was shattered by the Talmudic rabbis with their seditious questions, based not upon scripture but upon what other rabbis had said about scripture in the Mishnah and the Gemara. For Newton, these Talmudists precipitated the doctrinal disputes in the early Church which ultimately culminated in the triumph of the apostate Christian church with its idolatrous, non-literal, non-scriptural doctrine of the Trinity in the fifth century.[34]

Newton writes that:

> Now the Jews who were for imposing the law upon the Christian Gentiles were apt to trouble the Churches also wth unnecessary questions about ye traditions of their Doctors & And [sic] these were thus reprehended by the Apostle. *I besought thee*, saith he, to Timothy, *to abide still at Ephesus that thou mightest charge some* [sic] *they teach no other doctrines neither give heed to fables & endless genealogies wch minister questions rather then godly edifying wch is in faith.*[35]

Do not, warns Newton, have faith in "*Jewish fables & commandments of men that turn from the truth.*"[36]

Newton believed that his own middle path through the texts is the best way to determine both what doctrinal beliefs are necessary for salvation as well as what further knowledge might then be obtainable (either literally or allegorically) concerning more speculative doctrines about which interpreters of open and charitable Christian dispositions may disagree. He is willing to listen to the evidence from whatever school in each case. Thus, in the difficult question of how exactly Eve brought unhappiness on mankind, he is happy to follow the *"opinion of the Jewish Doctors that Adam eat of this fruit by knowing his wife* ffor [sic] this is the phrase wch Moses uses for carnal copulation."[37] But exclusive allegoricism can also blind the interpreter to the literal events of the second coming. Newton's middle path best reveals an absolutely univocal God who posesses absolute freedom and infinite power. If interpreted properly (which usually means literally but occasionally means allegorically), the pertinent scripture evidences God's direct (specially provident) and indirect (generally provident) power to act throughout human and natural history.[38]

II. Newton's *Irenicum*: "Milk for Babes" and "Strong Meats for Elders"

Newton's approach to scriptural interpretation leads him to rely upon literalism first.[39] Newton's emphasis on literalism leads him to the following unique and daunting text from 1 Tim.2.5: "...there is one mediator between God and men, the man Christ Jesus." When Newton is at his most Maimonidean and is attempting to produce a creed of twelve doctrinal points roughly in the same format as Maimonides' thirteen-point statement of the Jewish creed in the Perek Helek, the first "Article" is Newton's paraphrase of the entire quotation from 1 Tim. 2.5. Newton writes:

> Artic. 1. There is one God the Father *everlasting, omnipresent, omniscient, almighty*, the maker of heaven & earth, & one Mediator between God & Man the Man Christ Jesus.[40]

In his most important theological manuscript, the *Irenicum*, Newton refines his creed into a fixed conception of three essential points (with subsidiary elements) constituting true Christian doctrine which must be taught to all catechumens prior to baptism and communion.[41] All catechumens in the first age of Christian preaching were taught that they must literally:

> (1) forsake the *Devil*, that is, all fals gods & all manner of idolatry, this being a breach of the first & great commandment.
>
> (2) forsake the *flesh* & the *world*, or as the Apostle John expresseth it, the lust of the flesh & the lust of the eye & the pride of life, that is, unchastity, intemperance, injustice, covetousness, pride & ambition, these things being a breach of the second of the two great commandments.
>
> (3) believe in one God, the father, almighty in dominion, the maker of heaven & earth & of all things therein: and in our Lord Jesus Christ, the

son of God, who was born of a Virgin, & sacrificed for us on the cross, & the third day rose again from the dead, & ascended into heaven, & sitteth on the right hand of God in a mystical sense, being next to him in honour and power; & who shall come again to judge & reign over the quick & the dead raised to life; and who sent the Holy Ghost to comfort his disciples & assist them in preaching the Gospel.[42]

Newton calls these literally derived doctrines (and the one "mystical" interpretation about the meaning of "sitting" on God's right hand) "the foundation and first principles of the doctrines of Christ" and "milk for babes."[43] These doctrines were taught prior to baptism and communion so that the Catechumen "might know before baptism why & in whose names he was to be washed, viz. in the name of one God ye Father & of our Lord Jesus Christ & c 1Cor. 8.6."[44] No other doctrines were taught by the disciples or learned by the first Christians prior to baptism or communion as none were necessary for baptism, a cleansing of the bodily flesh which symbolized the catechumen's repentance for his lust and pride and, through communion, with Christ's promise of the remission of these sins and, finally, eternal salvation.

These "first principles of Christ" are founded, not on disputable conclusions, or human reason, or rational conjecture. They rest squarely upon "the express words of Christ & his Apostles."[45] As a result, it is important to understand that these doctrines are certain and unchanging. As they are divinely instituted, they "are unalterable by men."[46] Newton emphasizes just how unbreachable these first principles are when he writes that "if an Angel from heaven preach any other Gospel then that wch the Apostles preached [imposing it as a law of God necessary to baptism, communion, and salvation] let him be accursed Gal. 1.8, 9."[47]

Beyond this crucial core of literal theological doctrine or catechetical "milk for babes," only a learned and wise scholar, a true adept who has mastered the languages, sources, and learned when to apply literal or allegorical interpretation, is duty-bound to go forward in seeking to perfect his understanding of Christian doctrine. While all Christians are enjoined to study scripture, success in perfecting knowledge of such difficult doctrines is most difficult. Newton writes that:

...since strong meats are not fit for babes, but are to be given only to men of riper years, they are not to be imposed on all men as necessary to communion, but only to be learnt by such as after admission into communion are able to learn them.

Scholarly elders capable of ingesting the "strong meats" of theological doctrines beyond those necessary to the instruction of catechumens understand that *true* Christians do not quarrel with one another over these more esoteric points of doctrine. True Christians, continues Newton:

> are not to damn or excommunicate one another or treat one another as here-
> tiques, or quarrel or reproach one another or hate or despise or censure one
> another for not knowing them. Every man after chatechizing & admission
> into communion, is to study the scriptures & especially the prophecies, &
> to learn as much as he can out of them, & may endavour to instruct his
> neighbour in a friendly manner, but not fall out with him for differing in
> opinion about any thing which was not required before baptism into the
> remission of sins, & admission into the communion of Christians.[48]

It follows that, in the spirit of Christian charity, tolerant disagreements over
the meaning of these more advanced and obscure doctrines is possible, but
no such tolerance is permitted for those who break the foundational, literally
grounded injunctions ingested as "milk for babes."

But what Newton emphasizes as legitimate grounds for tolerant and friendly dispute among adept scholars must not be confused with his exceptionally
clear descriptions of the literal "foundation and first principles of the doctrines
of Christ" necessary to receive baptism and communion in the days of the
Apostles if not in Newton's own time. Commentators are well aware of how
Newton anathematizes idolatry but do not seem to connect the implications
of Newton's harsh injunctions against idolatry with the prohibitions in the
Irenicum. Newton is not a tolerant latitudinarian theologian who believes
that Christianity reduces simply to the golden rule. Newton is unrelentingly
intolerant of anyone who embraces the Devil through any form of idolatry.
Christians of Newton's Judaized stamp, i.e., true Christians who obey utterly
the "first and great commandment,", MUST absolutely "believe in One God,
the father Almighty in dominion," and in Christ's divinely ordained mission,
i.e., his sacrifice, his promised future return, and his inevitable judgement of
the quick and those raised from the dead.[49]

Anyone who fails to adhere literally to this "milk for babes" is "accursed."
After all, Newton observes that:

> the Gospel which Christ sent his Apostles to preach is not alterable by
> humane authority. It is as much the law of God as the Law of Moses was,
> & as unalterable. The High Priest & the Sanhedrim it self had no power
> to alter the law of Moses, & if an Angel from heaven preach any other
> Gospel then that which the Apostles preached [imposing it as a law of God
> necessary to baptism, communion & salvation] let him be accursed Gal.
> 1.8, 9.[50]

Newton believes that he follows St. Paul when he argues that:

the imposing of any proposition (true or false) as an Article of Communion wch was not an Article of Communion from the first preaching of the Gospel may be preaching another Gospel, & the persecuting of any true Christians for not receiving that Gospel may be persecuting Christ in his mystical members, & the Persecutor in making war upon Christ breaks the second & third great commandments, and may deserve the name of an Anti-Christian in a literal sense.[51]

As a radical reformer, Newton believes that it constitutes idolatry when the entire Christian Church forsakes the one true Lord God of Moses and simultaneously divinizes Jesus Christ through an unwarranted allegorical reading of the texts. Newton defines "idolatry" unequivocally as a:

breach of the first & greatest commandment. It is giving to idols the love honour & worship wch is due to the true God alone. It is forsaking the true God to commit whoredome with other lovers. It makes a Church guilty of apostasy from God, as an Adulteress forsakes her husband. It makes her become the Church of the Idols, fals Gods, or Daemons whom she worships, such a true Church as in scripture is called a Synagogue of Satan.[52]

In Newton's view, just as the Lord God inscribed in the Book of Nature the vivid impression of his generally provident creative power so, too, in scripture he reveals to the Jews and their Christian successors abundant evidence of his nature as a deity who is always capable of direct involvement in his creation through particular acts of specially provident power. Prophetic history, rightly understood, supplements the generally provident God of the design argument and reveals a specially provident God who has been regularly active in the use of his specially provident, miraculous power to guide the affairs of men and nature since creation. Newton's conception of the Lord God of absolute power and dominion logically culminates in the dependence of every aspect of created nature and of human knowledge of created nature upon the will and power of the creator. God created nature, and everything in nature, in a generally provident act. Since that creation, he has providentially preserved nature in its "ordinary concourse." From time to time, as fulfilled Biblical prophecies and the corroborating testimony of the "ancient" theologians show, he has directly suspended his natural laws in a specially provident act of will. In unfulfilled "future" prophecies, he has promised to destroy both the "world natural" and the "world politick" and the "wise" have strong inductively grounded reasons to believe him. Such evidence is the metaphysical and epistemological basis for Newton's millennialism as well as the source of his interest in Judaic religion, past, present, and future. At the heart of Newton's fascination with God's continuous pattern of involvement with the

Jewish people is his utter fascination with the Lord God, the completeness and totality of whose power Newton describes in the *General Scholium* of the 1713 *Principia*. Newton's literalistic understanding of St. Paul's "milk for babes" has a decidedly Judaized flavor simply because behind all these fundamental elements of Newton's Judaized creed – including even behind the mission, ressurrection, and final return of Christ, the "son" of God – stands the supremely monotheistic Lord God of dominion, the God of Moses whom Newton emphasizes in his most famous published statement about the nature of God:

> This Being governs all things, not as the soul of the world, but as Lord over all; and on account of his dominion he is wont to be called *Lord God...*, or *Universal Ruler*; for *God* is a relative word, and has a respect of servants; and *Deity* is the dominion of God not over his own body, as those imagine who fancy God to be the soul of the world, but over servants. The Supreme God is a Being eternal, infinite, absolutely perfect; but a being, however perfect, without dominion, cannot be said to be Lord God....[53]

Newton's most famous Christian heresy, his anti-Trinitarianism, is absolutely consistent with his Mosaic conception of God and is in fact required by his literal interpretation of the Mosaic Law. In Newton's view, Jesus cannot be consubstantial with God, but *must* be a being separate both in substance and nature from the Lord God or else one would disobey the literal dictate of the first great commandment. Though not of the same substance with God and though not co-existent from eternity with God, Jesus IS God's deputed vice-regent with his divine liege. Newton writes that, because God grants it to him, Jesus shares with God:

> Unity of Dominion, the Son receiving all things from the father, being subject to him, executing his will, sitting in his throne & calling him his God, & so is but one God wth the Father as a king & his viceroy are but one king. For the word God relates not to the metaphysical nature of God but to dominion.

Newton goes on to make clear the identity of the idolaters of his own age:

> And therefore as a father & his son cannot be called one King upon account of their being consubstantial but may be called one King by unity of dominion if the Son be Viceroy under the father: so God & his son cannot be called one God upon account of their being consubstantial. The heathens made all their Gods of one substance & sometimes called them one God & yet were polytheists. Nothing can make two persons one God but unity of dominion. And if the Father & Son be united in dominion, the

son being subordinate to the father & sitting in his throne they can no more be called two Gods then a King & his viceroy can be called two kings.[54]

In one of the drafts of the *Irenicum*, Newton thus describes the sorts of worship Christians owe to the one God and to his vassal, Christ, who fully deserves reverence but only because God deputized him to suffer and die for the sins of mankind and not because he is himself God. Resorting to an allegorical interpretation of John's vision of the worship in the Temple, Newton writes that:

We are not to give the worship of the father to the son nor the worship of the son to the father but to worship each with that worship wch is proper & peculiar to him.... We are to worship the father as God almighty maker of heaven & earth & the son as the Lord Jesus Christ who was slain for us & hath redeemed us with his blood. For this form of worship is prescribed to us in the Apocalyps where the scene of the visions is in the Temple & God the father is represented sitting there upon his throne that is, above the Ark between the Cherubims, & the son is represented in the form of a Lamb receiving the book of prophecy from him that sitteth upon the throne & the Presbyters & People are represented by four & twenty Elders & four Beasts worshipping in the courts of the Temple.[55]

For Newton, in the best of all possible worlds, churches which pretend to be truly Christian would realize that the various trinitarian creeds adopted by fourth-century Church Councils are not "milk for babes" because such creeds were not necessary for salvation during the first three centuries of the Church (and, hence, were not taught to catechumens during those first three centuries.) Furthermore, they would realize that to ordain one particular interpretation of the meaning of these creeds regarding the consubstantiality and co-eternality of Christ with God absolutely and utterly breaks the first great commandment which must be taken literally. Finally, they would understand that to impose through threat and intimidation such an idolatrous interpretation upon all future Christians breaks the commandment to be charitable to those who share Christian communion. Newton writes that:

The Constantinopolitan Creed usually called the Nicene Creed & the Creed usually called the Creed of Athanasius are not therefore any part of the milk for babes in the Church of England but are to be referred to the strong meats for them that are of age, & therefore to fall out about them proceeds from the want of Charity. They are indeed appointed by the Common prayer book to be read in the Churches upon certain occasions. And so are many parts of the Scriptures wch we do not understand. As Daniel 9. & 10 v.5. Apoc. 1.& 4 & 7.v2 to v13 & 12 v. 7 to v. 13 & 14. v. 1 to v 6. & 19 v. 1 to v. 17 & 22; We dayly dispute about the meaning of these & many other parts of scripture without falling out about them & are allowed to do so, And so we may about the meaning of the two Creeds notwithstanding their being read in Churches.[56]

After all, Newton argues, the twelfth of the Thirty Nine Articles of the Church of England declares that General Councils such as Constantinople and Nicaea:

> may err & sometimes have erred even in things pertaining to God: & therefore things ordained by them as necessary to salvation, have neither strength nor authority, unless it may be declared that they are taken out of holy scriptures.[57]

Newton is, in sum, an extreme metaphysical voluntarist who Judaizes his conception of God by emphasizing in a literal sense God's supreme will and power over creation at the expense of Jesus' divinity. Newton is no liberal latitudinarian. Throughout all the versions of the *Irenicum*, he argues implicitly that the Church of England is an apostate Church, a "synagogue of Satan." Newton imparted his constructions of various problematic texts to a trusted few whom he regards as the last remnant of the "true" Christian communion. Newton writes that not everybody will understand his interpretations of prophetic doctrine but:

> If they are never to be understood, to what end did God reveal them? Certainly he did it for ye edification of ye church; and if so, then it is as certain yt ye church shall at length attain to ye understanding thereof. I mean not all that call themselves Christians but a remnant, a few scattered persons which God hath chosen, such as without being led by interest, education, or humane authorities, can set themselves sincerely & earnestly to search after truth. For as Daniel hath said that ye wise shall understand, so he hath said also that none of ye wicked shall understand.[58]

Newton's literal understanding of such an esoteric doctrine as the events connected with the millennium absolutely depends upon Newton's Judaized conception of an undiluted Lord God whose power knows no bounds. Without such a Lord God of supreme power and dominion who stands ready to usher forth the new Jerusalem and the day of judgement, Newton would undoubtedly believe himself to be alone in a world of arbitrary fate. Without the Old Testament God, the grave would indeed be an empty, cold place reminiscent of Andrew Marvell's lines about the "Deserts of vast eternity" and would justifiably evoke Pascal's trepidation at the terrifying prospect of "the eternal silence of those infinite spaces."[59] Only the Lord God of absolute power – the God of Moses, Abraham, and Isaac Newton – stands between Newton and the abyss of the modern scientific world devoid of meaning,unspeakably immense, random in its development and motion, and terminal. But stand there the Old Testament Lord God does for Newton. Such a Lord God is revealed by the twin testimonies of scripture and nature and provides Newton with hope beyond the grave, a hope directly attributable to Newton's Judaized conception of the absolute and undiluted power of the Lord God.

III. NEWTON'S GOD AND NEWTON'S SCIENCE

But, what, one may legitimately argue, does Newton's intense, and intensely private, musings about the nature of the Lord God of Israel have to do with his method in natural philosophy or with his expectations of what that method can achieve? Is not the *Principia* still the *Principia*? I believe, in particular contrast to Manuel and Westfall,[60] that Newton's metaphysical theology interacts with his scientific epistemology just as it does with all other elements of his thought. It must do so given Newton's understanding of the power and dominion of the Lord God.

Newton's literal, even Mosaic, conception of God's dominion and power cannot be, for Newton, simply divorced from the empiricist epistemology which he adopts in his empirically grounded scientific method but is entirely consonant with it. Henry Guerlac's description of Newton's *probatio duplex* remains unsurpassed in its clarity and elegance.[61] Newton's single methodological procedure for obtaining "knowledge" begins with "Analysis" (*resolutio*) and then moves to "Synthesis"(*compositio*). For Newton, in contrast to Descartes, the initial path of "Analysis" is identified with empirical experiments and observations. On the basis of this empirical starting point, Newton inductively derives probationary "Principles" such as the Inverse Square Law by "Analysis." The second part of his method is the synthetic deduction of future phenomena on the basis of these "Principles." Newton's clearest statement of his two-step procedure is in the famous Query 31 of the second English edition of the Opticks:

As in Mathematicks, so in Natural Philosophy, the Investigation of difficult Things by the Method of Analysis, ought ever to precede the Method of Composition. *This Analysis consists in making Experiments and Observations, and in drawing general Conclusions from them by Induction,* and admitting of no Objections against the Conclusions; yet *it is the best way of arguing which the Nature of Things admits of,* and may be looked upon as so much the stronger, by how much the Induction is more general. And *if no Exception occur from Phaenomena, the Conclusion may be pronounced generally.* But *if at any time afterwards any Exception shall occur from*

Experiments, it may then begin to pronounced with such Exceptions as occur. By this way of Analysis we may proceed from Compounds to Ingredients, and from particular causes to more general ones, till the Argument end in the most general. This is the Method of Analysis: And the *Synthesis consists in assuming the Causes discover'd and establish'd as Principles, and by them explaining the Phaenomena proceeding from them,* and proving the Explanations.[62]

Guerlac is correct in emphasizing that, for Newton, experiments and observations which admit of "no exception" are "certain" even though the "Principles" inductively derived from them are only "morally certain" and that such "Principles" are initially "the best way of arguing which the Nature of Things admits of." It is also the case, for Newton, that a single, well-chosen *experimentum crucis* may be the basis for the firm induction of a "Principle" or Law which governs the current natural order. Nevertheless, even the best scientific knowledge which Newton's version of the *probatio duplex* can provide is limited to the current "Nature of Things" which, in turn, is utterly dependent, both for its being and its continued operation, upon the absolute will and power of the Lord God of supreme dominion described in the *General Scholium*.

Because of God's sovereign nature as "Lord God," the laws of nature are, in an important sense, *both* necessary and contingent. They are necessary – and thus knowable by the double method – *only* while God, who created them, maintains them in operation. Newton is no enthusiast and he labors mightily to separate the few cases of genuine historical (often catastrophic) miracles from the many cases of idolatrous and false ones.[63] Nevertheless, Newton accepts the reality of direct divine intervention in nature through miraculous ("specially provident") acts of will (which are simultaneously supremely acts of power) which interrupt the ordinary coursing of nature and nature's generally provident laws. Further, his reading of prophecy leads him to expect a "new heaven and a new earth" when the laws and principles of the current system may no longer apply. For Newton, the primacy of God's power results in a distinctive contingency in the natural order even while Newton acknowledges the virtual necessity of that order in its ordinary ("generally provident") current operation and provides a unique methodology, the *probatio duplex*, for studying its operation. For Newton, the whole of creation is "subordinate to [God], and subservient to his Will."[64] This is the theological and metaphysical background to Newton's most famous methodological statement in his fourth "Rule" of reasoning:

In experimental philosophy we are to look upon propositions inferred by general induction from phenomena as accurately or very nearly true, notwithstanding any contrary hypotheses that may be imagined, till such time as other phenomena occur, by which they may either be made more accurate, or liable to exceptions.

This rule we must follow, that the argument of induction may not be evaded by hypotheses.[65]

Fifty years prior to Hume's *Treatise of Human Nature*, Newton, from a vastly different metaphysical and theological starting point, is telling us that the future need not resemble the past and that, consequently, we must mark ALL the consequences of this fact in regulating our expectations of what sort of human knowledge scientific empiricism can provide.

I wish to emphasize that I am not now arguing either that Newton's metaphysical and theological voluntarism *causes* either his Arianism, his millennialism, his method of analysis and synthesis, or his conservative view of the divine right of kings to rule (exercised through the specially provident divine cause of the "will of the people.") I *am* arguing that Newton's theory of the Lord God's supreme dominion is entirely consonant with all these aspects of his thought and that he very likely does not view them as disconnected or compartmentalized theories. Newton's Lord God of true and supreme dominion provides a crucial key for understanding the synthetic unity of his truly complex and incandescent genius.

IV. CONCLUSION: THE TESTIMONY OF HISTORY – JOHN MAXWELL AND CHAMBERS' 'CYCLOPAEDIA'

The intimate connection between Newton's metaphysical conception of the Lord God of Israel and the rest of his thought was recognized in his own time. While reading Ephraim Chambers' widely distributed *Cyclopaedia* article on, simply, "God," I was stunned to come across long quotations emphasizing Newton's voluntaristic theory of God's nature taken both from Newton's *General Scholium* and from a hitherto unanalyzed source. Chambers bases much of his article on "God" on a book by one John Maxwell entitled *Traveller in Africa. A discourse concerning God; wherein the meaning of his name, his providence, the nature and measure of his dominion are consider'd;...To which is subjoined a translation of Sir Isaac Newton's general scholium at the end of the second edition of his Principia.... As also a short account of the Cape of Good Hope* (London, 1715.) The Chambers article on God has never been noted by Newton scholars. The short book (123 pages) by Maxwell has been only listed in passing in one brief bibliographical entry.[66] Neither have ever been discussed in print.

Maxwell's work is easy to miss. First, it is quite rare in the present day. Second, it is usually catalogued simply under "Traveller in Africa." Nevertheless, because of his discussion of the significance of God's providential power in helping us to understand "the nature and measure" of God's "dominion" in the immensely popular *Cyclopaedia*, Maxwell's work and its exposition in Chambers' article can no longer be ignored because of the important light it sheds on how widely Newton's metaphysical theology is known after the publication of the *Cyclopaedia* in 1728. First, Chambers quotes long passages directly from Newton's General Scholium:

> Sir Isaac Newton chuses to consider, and define GOD not as is usually done, from his Perfection, his Nature, Existence, or the like; but from his Dominion. 'The Word *GOD*,' according to him, 'is a relative Term, and has a Regard to Servants: 'Tis true, it denotes a Being eternal, infinite, and absolutely perfect; but a Being, however eternal, infinite, and absolutely perfect, without Dominion, would not be *GOD*.'

Next, Chambers observes that:

> A late ingenious Divine [i.e., Maxwell] has wrought these Thoughts of that admirable Philosopher [i.e., Newton] into Form, and ripen'd them into a more express System; in a Discourse upon this Occasion.
>
> The great Principle or Proposition he lays down, is that '*GOD* is not rightly defined a Being absolutely perfect, but a spiritual Being endued with absolute Dominion....'[67]

The Deists, the Latitudinarians, the secularists within the Royal Society of Newton's day, and many modern scholars in the "Newtonian industry" have underestimated, it seems to me, the key theological/metaphysical element of Newton's thought as a whole, i.e., his Lord God of dominion. They have thereby reduced his theology largely to the design argument (illustrative of general providence) and judged his consuming interest in fulfilled prophecies (illustrative of special providence) either to be "important" only to his eccentric and puritanical psychology or indicative of some embryonic tension. Many modern scholars argue that Newton's Lord God may have been important, psychologically or illogically, to Newton himself, but the Lord God of Israel can be entirely disconnected from the rest of Newton's thought, especially from his natural philosophy. Modern interpreters have especially sought to divorce Newton's methodology in natural philosophy from his Old Testament Lord God of complete and absolute dominion.[68] The inevitable consequence is a truncated, sanitized deity who is merely a supreme architect skilled in geometry. Thus is Newton's universe "stripped of metaphysical considerations." But here, in Chambers' immensely popular *Cyclopaedia* article on "God" is evidence that many people in the early eighteenth century had access both to Newton's metaphysical conception of the Lord God of Israel and to the implications which this conception of the nature of God had for obtaining knowledge of, as Maxwell states in his title, "the nature and measure of God's dominion."

We must guard against the tendency among specialized scholars to see Newton through a prism, so to speak, and to study Newton's refracted parts separately just as Newton studied light in refraction. Newton has been seen, at different times, as a heretical theologian, a scientific genius, or a politically connected bureaucrat. There often seem to be as many Newtons as there are primary colors and, most frequently, the many manifestations of Newton's diverse and complex genius are studied independently as if they are actually disconnected from one another in Newton's mind. One most important key to understanding how Newton may have integrated the totality of his thought is to approach it through his own metaphysical and theological conception of the power and dominion of the Lord God of Israel. Newton's universe *cannot* be shorn of "metaphysical considerations" because he believes that its creator, owner, and operator is the Lord God of Israel, the God of Gods, the Lord of Lords. Truly for Newton, science and religion are indeed synthesized in a most "holy alliance."

NOTES

1. W. E. H. Lecky, *History of the Rise and Influence of the Spirit of Rationalism in Europe*, 2 vols. (London, 1865); John W. Draper, *A History of the Conflict Between Religion and Science* (New York, 1875); Andrew D. White, *A History of the Warfare of Science with Theology*, 2 vols. (New York, 1896.)
2. Basil Willey, *The Eighteenth Century Background* (Harmondsworth: Penguin, 1972), p. 162.
3. Norman Hampson, *The Enlightenment* (Harmondsworth: Penguin, 1979), p. 28.
4. Richard S. Westfall, *Science and Religion in Seventeenth Century England* (Ann Arbor: The Univ. of Michigan Press, 1973) p. 219.
5. I am pleased to note that this common place attitude of the past twenty years in the "Newtonian industry" may be changing in the face of efforts by a new generation of scholars, many of whose articles are published in *The Books of Nature and Scripture: Recent Essays on Natural Philosophy, Theology, and Biblical Criticism in the Netherlands of Spinoza's Time and the British Isles of Newton's Time*, ed. James E. Force and Richard H. Popkin (Dordrecht: Kluwer Academic Publishers, forthcoming, 1994.)
6. This recent statement of the "disconnectedness" thesis is by Gale E. Christianson in his book *In the Presence of the Creator. Isaac Newton and His Times* (New York: The Free Press, 1984), p. 312. In his Preface to this work, Christianson shows that he is no naive positivist. He clearly understands the importance of Newton's scientific thought for the design argument of natural theology. Nevertheless, Newton's pre-eminent "gift" to the modern world remains for Christianson a rational, mechanical, material order obedient to necessary natural laws and simply "stripped" of "metaphysical considerations." John Herman Randall, Jr., elaborates this widely shared attitude that Newton's theology is, simply, *disconnected* from the rest of his philosophy as a whole and is especially compartmentalized from his natural philosophy in an earlier statement of this general

point of view in his essay, "What Isaac Newton Started," the Introduction in *Newton's Philosophy of Nature*, ed. H. S. Thayer, 2nd ed. (New York: Hafner Press, 1974), pp. xi–xii. Cf. Edward W. Strong, "Newton and God," *Journal of the History of Ideas* 7, No. 2 (April, 1952), p. 167.

7. Newton wrote a work entitled *A Dissertation upon the Sacred Cubit of the Jews and the Cubits of the Several Nations; in which form the Dimensions of the Greatest Pyramid, as taken by Mr John Greaves, the Antient Cubit of Memphis is Determined.* This "most elusive of all Newton's published works" (to borrow Derek Gjertsen's phrase) was translated from Latin into English and published by Thomas Birch in Volume 2 of his edition of the *Miscellaneous Works of John Greaves* in 1737. See Gjertsen, *The Newton Handbook* (London: Routledge & Kegan Paul, 1986), who writes (p. 6) that it is "mysterious why Newton should pursue the matter" of "how many English inches are contained in the cubits of Egypt, Rome, Persia, Israel and other ancient kingdoms...."

8. Richard S. Westfall, *Never at Rest. A Biography of Sir Isaac Newton* (Cambridge: Cambridge University Press, 1980), p. 346, observes that Newton read Ezekiel in Hebrew in order to draw up plans for the exact shape, in cubits, of the Temple. On p. 347, Westfall reproduces Newton's diagram of the temple (now in the Babson College Library, Babson MS.434) to which Stukeley refers below. Newton almost certainly knew of contemporary attempts to build models of the Temple. He possibly was familiar with the model of the Temple exhibited throughout England in 1675 by Jacob Jehuda Leon. He possibly also knew of the many lectures William Whiston started giving about the design of the Temple in 1726 which Whiston illustrated with a scale model. See A. K. Offenberg, "Jacob Jehuda Leon (1602–1675) and his Model of the Temple," in *Jewish-Christian Relations in the Seventeenth Century*, ed. Jan van den Berg and Ernestine G. E. van der Wall (Dordrecht: Kluwer, 1988), pp. 95–115. William Stukeley, in his *Memoirs of Sir Isaac Newton's Life*, ed. A. Hastings White (London: Taylor and Francis, 1936), pp. 17–18, conveys the tone and depth of Newton's interest in the Temple when he describes a conversation he had with Newton during a Christmas "visit":

   In Christmas 1725, upon a visit I made him, we had some discourse about Solomons temple: a matter I had study'd with attention, and made very many drawings about it, which I had communicated to my Lord Pembroke (Thomas), to Mr Folkes and more of my friends. I found Sir Isaac had made some drawings of it, and had consider'd the thing. Indeed he had study'd everything. We did not enter into any particular detail, but we both agreed in this, that the architecture was not like any design or descriptions yet publick. No authors have an adequate notion of antient architecture. Sir Isaac rightly judged it was older than any other of the great temples mention'd in history; and was indeed the original model which they followed. He added that Sesostris in Rehoboams time, took the workmen from Jerusalem, who built his Egyptian temples, in imitation of it, one in every *Nomos*, and that from thence the Greeks borrow'd their architecture, as they had the deal of thir [sic] religious rites, thir [sic] sculpture and other arts.

9. Frank E. Manuel, *The Religion of Isaac Newton* (Oxford: Clarendon Press, 1974) p. 66.

10. James E. Force, "Newton's God of Dominion: The Unity of Newton's Theological, Scientific, and Political Thought," in James E. Force and Richard H. Popkin, *Essays on the Context, Nature, and Influence of Isaac Newton's Theology* (Dordrecht: Kluwer Academic Publishers), pp. 75–102.

11. As Simon Ockley writes in his Preface to his 1707 English edition of Leo of Modena's *The History of the Present Jews Throughout the World. Being An Ample tho Succinct Account of their Customs, Ceremonies, and Manner of Living, at this time. Translated from the "Italian," written by Leo Modena, a "Venetian" Rabbi. To which are Subjoin'd Two*

Supplements, One concerning the "Samaritans," the other of the sect of the "Carraites."
From the "French" of Father Simon, with his Explanatory Notes, Preface, p. iii, by
studying what is termed the "Rites, and Customs of the Jews": "we may explain several
Texts in the New Testament; and better understand several Customs in the Primitive
Church, which receeded often times from those of the Synagogue." An earlier translation
by Edmund Chilmead, with the chapter on the Caraites, had appeared in 1650. Cf. Richard
H. Popkin, "The Lost Tribes, the Caraites and the English Millenarians," *Journal of Jewish
Studies*, 37, No.2 (Autumn, 1986) p. 223. Newton owned the 1681 edition of Modena's
work translated into French by Richard Simon which had supplements by Simon which
Ockley translated and refers to in the English title above. Of course Newton's own interest
in Jewish ritual began, as Westfall observes, in the 1680's.

12. New College, Oxford, MS. 361.2, f. 132r. By permission of the Warden and Fellows, New
College, Oxford. This text is also cited in Scott Mandelbrote, "'A Duty of the Greatest
Moment': Isaac Newton and the Writing of Biblical Criticism," *British Journal for the
History of Science*, forthcoming.

13. Isaac Newton, *Observations upon the Prophecies of Daniel, and the Apocalypse of St.
John* (London, 1733), p. 12. Newton goes on to list, in this posthumously published
work, the "historical books" Joshua, Judges, Ruth, Samuel, Kings, Chronicles, Ezra,
Nehemiah, Esther, Job, the Psalms, the "books" of Solomon, and Lamentations. Westfall
has dismissed this work as "the meandering of an old man." (*Never at Rest*, p. 321.)
I agree that the heart of the book ought to have been Newton's anti-trinitarianism, but
the skeleton of Newton's methodological injunctions remains. While Newton clearly
exercised self-censorship, I do not find it to be the pointless meanderings of an old man.
As in his sly conversation with John Conduitt three years earlier, Newton may have felt
that he had said enough for the "wise" to "know his meaning." See John Conduitt's
account of a private conversation with Newton on 7th March 1724/5 about the possible
role of comets in "replenishing" the sun and fixed stars. King's College Library MS.
130.11. Cited with the permission of the Librarian, King's College, Cambridge.

14. Newton, *Observations upon the Prophecies*, p. 13.

15. *Ibid.*, p. 12.

16. *Ibid.*, p. 14.

17. Newton Yahuda MS. 1, f. 17r, at the Jewish National and University Library, Jerusalem.
Portions of this manuscript have been published as Appendix A, pp. 107–25, in Manuel,
The Religion of Isaac Newton.

18. *Ibid.*, f. 18r.

19. *Ibid.*, f. 3v. Newton's basic assumption that the key to understanding the chronological
sequence of the "synchronal" visions lies in analyzing their internal relationship regardless
of the order in which St. John relates them derives from Joseph Mede. While Newton
accepts this much of Mede's general approach to the visions of St. John, he differs from
Mede who takes the Vials and Trumpets to signify different events, i.e., the downfall of
the beast and the wars waged by anti-Christians against Christians respectively.

20. *Ibid.*, f. 12r. Newton is emphatic on the need to stick to a literal sense wherever possible.
On f. 13r, he writes: "He that without better grounds then his private opinion or the
opinion of any human authority whatsoever shall turn scripture from the plain meaning to
an Allegory or to any other less naturall sense declares thereby that he reposes more trust
in his own imaginations or that human authority then in the Scripture. And therefore ye
opinion of such men how numerous soever they be, is not to be regarded. Hence it is &
not from any reall[sic] uncertainty in ye Scripture yt Commentators have so distorted it;

And this hath been the ye door through wch all Heresies have crept in & turned out ye ancient faith."

21. *Ibid.*, f. 18r–19r. Peter Allix argued the same point about the mistake of the too-literalistic Jews in the days of Jesus. Those Jews, writes Allix, "by mistaking the Prophecies of Scripture concerning the Kingdom of their Messias, expected he should have a Temporal Kingdom; and because our Lord Jesus was not for that, therefore they would not acknowledge him for their Messias." See Peter Allix,*"The Judgment of the Ancient Jewish Church, Against the Unitarians, in The Controversy upon the Holy Trinity, and the Divinity of our Blessed Saviour* (London, 1699), p.i. In this rather astonishing work, Allix is most concerned to show that the Jewish Cabalists had always expected their Messiah, whenever he came, to participate mystically in the divinity of the Father and thus most of his analysis is devoted to analyzing the strictly allegorical school of Cabalistic Jewish interpreters who arose long after the time of Christ. Newton owned three other books by Allix and two tracts. See John Harrison, *The Library of Isaac Newton* (Cambridge: Cambridge University Press, 1978), pp. 84–5.

22. Newton, Yahuda 9.1, f. 20r, at the Jewish National and University Library, Jerusalem. This manuscript dates from the mid- to late 1680's. Mede had written much the same interpretation of the serpent who was not a *brute serpent* but was a symbol for guile. Mede also, like Newton, went on to identify the serpent who deluded Eve with the *old serpent* spoken of in Rev. 12.9 and 20.2 who, according to prophecy, will be cast down into a pit for a thousand years. [Joseph Mede, *The Works of The Pious and Profoundly-Learned Joseph Mede, B.D.. Sometime Fellow of Christ's Colledge in Cambridge* (London, 1672), p.223.] Newton, in Yahuda 9.1,f. 20r, identifies Eve's serpent with that of Revelation. In Yahuda 9.1, f. 19r, Newton analyzed the sort of knowledge which came about as the result of eating of the forbidden fruit and writes that "Tis *the opinion of the Jewish Doctors that Adam eat of this fruit by knowing his wife* ffor [sic] this the phrase wch Moses uses for carnal copulation." Westfall's emphasis upon the Temple as a "type" which prefigures, and thereby explicates, later prophecies (*Never at Rest*, p. 346) is another example of Newton's willingness to resort to allegorizing.

23. *Ibid.*, f. 3v.

24. *The Correspondence of Isaac Newton*, 7 vols., ed. H. W.Turnbull, J. F. Scott, A. Rupert Hall, and Laura Tilling (Cambridge: Published for the Royal Society at the University Press, 1959–77), 2:331.

25. *Ibid.*, p. 332.

26. Newton owned two extremely important studies which evince his interest in the Jews in general and which may have been a source of his knowledge of the Caraites. First, he owned a copy of Humphrey Prideaux's *The Old and New Testament Connected in the History of the Jews and Neighbouring Nations* in a three volume edition from 1718. This work has an extensive description of the interpretative method of the "Karraites." Second, Newton owned Richard Simon's French translation of Leone da Modena's *The History of the Present Jews Throughout the World* which had both a description of the "Jewish Heresy" of "*Carraim*" with an extensive supplement by Simon describing the interpretative method of the "Carraites." See Harrison, *The Library of Isaac Newton*, pp. 178 and 221.

27. Leone da Modena, *The History of the Present Jews Throughout the World*, trans. Simon Ockley, p. 247.

28. *Ibid.*, p. 248.

29. *Ibid.*, pp. 248–9.

30. *Ibid.*, pp. 250–1.

31. Humphrey Prideaux, *The Old and New Testament Conncected in the History of the Jews and Neighbouring Nations, From the Declension of the Kingdoms of Israel and Judah to the Time of Christ,* 4 vols. (London, 1729), 3:476.

32. Newton occasionally makes notes of interpreters who have resorted to typological interpretation against the Jews, for example Justin Martyr. *Ex Justin Martyrs Dialogo cum Tryphon's adve[r]sus Judaeos.* See for example, Yahuda MS.14, f. 14r, at the Jewish National and University Library, Jerusalem, where Newton notes that: "As ye changing of Abrams name to Abraham & of Sara to Sarra (Gen 17) was a type of their multiplication, so ye changing of Auses ye son of Nava his name to Jesus (numb 13.8 & 14.6) was not without a mystery, viz: to to [sic] typify yt name of ye Messiah who was to turn again their captivity & lead ym into ye good land wch should be for an eternal inheritance, as yt Jesus lead ym into ye temporall land. And as it was not ye lawgiver Moses but his successor Jesus wch lead ym into ye land so it must not be ye works of ye laws but of ye gospel, yt must lead us higher." p. 30F,G.

33. Yahuda MS. 15.4, f.80v, at the Jewish National and University Library, Jerusalem.

34. *Ibid.,* f. 69r.

35. *Ibid.,* f. 80v.

36. *Ibid.,* f.80r.

37. Yahuda 9.1, f. 19v, at the Jewish National and University Library, Jerusalem.

38. Cf. James E. Force, *William Whiston. Honest Newtonian* (Cambridge: Cambridge University Press, 1985), Chapter 3, where I show how Whiston attempts to preserve the rationality of scripture against the assaults of the scoffing deists by attempting to follow a middle path between literalism and allegory.

39. See Note 14 and compare what Newton writes with what WilliamWhiston writes about how to interpret the book of Genesis in the first of three *postulata*: "I. The Obvious or Literal Sense of Scripture is the True and Real One, where no evident Reason can be given to the contrary." See *A New Theory of the Earth, From its Original, to the Consummation of all Things, Where in the Creation of the World in Six Days, the Universal Deluge, And the General Conflagration, As laid down in the Holy Scriptures, Are Shewn to be perfectly agreeable to Reason and Philosophy. With a large Introductory Discourse concerning the Genuine Nature, Stile, and Extent of the Mosaick History of the Creation* (London, 1696.) The postulata are from the separately paginated "Introductory Discourse," p. 95.

40. Newton, "Twelve Articles on Religion," Keynes MS. 8, King's College Library, f.1. Cited with the permission of the Librarian, King's College, Cambridge. This manuscript has been reprinted in Brewster, *Memoirs of the Life, Writings,and Discoveries of Sir Isaac Newton* 2 vols. (Edinburgh,1855), 2:349, and Herbert McLachlan, *Sir Isaac Newton. Theological Manuscripts* (Liverpool: At the University Press, 1950), pp. 56–7. Newton owned five works by Maimonides and made notes on many of them. See Richard H. Popkin, "Some Further Comments on Newton and Maimonides," in James E. Force and Richard H. Popkin, eds., *Essays on the Context, Nature, and Influence of Isaac Newton's Theology,* pp. 1–7. Beyond his possible direct knowledge of Maimonides' thirteen-point statement of the Jewish creed, Newton may have known of it from two books in his library. It is outlined, first, in his copy of Richard Simon's 1681 French translation of Leone da Modena's *History of the Present Jews* as well as in the English translation of this work by Simon Ockley (1707) which he also owned. A more extensive listing of the thirteen articles occurs in Lancelot Addison (the father of Joseph), *The Present Stateof the Jews: (More particularly relating to those in Barbary.) Wherein is contained an exact Account of their Customs, Secular and Religious. To which is annexed a summary of the "Misna Talmud," and Gemara* (London, 1675), pp. 16–23.

41. Newton, as Derek Gjertsen has pointed out, "never seemed to tire of drawing up lists" of his own essential theological doctrines. "Whether they were theological, historical, Biblical or linguistic, he would seem to have little difficulty in conjuring up a dozen or so objections to some particular aspect of orthodox christian theology." See Gjertsen, *The Newton Handbook* (London: Routledge & Kegan Paul, 1986), s.v. "Argumenta and Twelve Points on Arian Christology," p. 33.

42. Keynes MS. 3, f. 9r. Cited with the permission of the Librarian, King's College, Cambridge.

43. Keynes MS. 3, f. 11r. Cited with the permission of the Librarian, King's College, Cambridge.

44. *Ibid.*, f. 11r.

45. *Ibid.*, f. 13r.

46. *Ibid.*

47. *Ibid.*

48. *Ibid.*, f. 11r.

49. Newton cannot find anywhere in the New Testament the literal term "homoousios." It is not in the text, he believes, but is rather manufactured by human commentators at the various councils and thus has only a human, not a divine, authority. The trinitarian doctrine, which maintains that Jesus is "consubstantial" with the the Father, thus is for Newton a Christian equivalent of the more allegorical flights of fancy in the Jewish oral tradition. In Yahuda 15.7 (at the Jewish National and University Library, Jerusalem), which dates from the seventeenth century, Newton writes (f. 154r) that: "In these disputes Arius & Athanasius had both of them perplexed the Church with metaphysical opinions & expressed their opinions in novel language not warranted by scripture."

50. Keynes MS. 3, f. 13r. Cited with the permission of the Librarian, King's College, Cambridge. Cf. citation 16 from Newton's *Observations upon the Prophecies of Daniel, and the Apocalypse of St. John* above where Newton also alludes to the accursed angel.

51. *Ibid.*, f. 14r.

52. *Ibid.*, f. 14r.

53. *Sir Isaac Newton's Mathematical Principles of Natural Philosophy and His System of the World.* Translated into English by Andrew Motte in 1729. The translations revised, and supplied with an historical and explanatory appendix by Florian Cajori. 2 vols. (Berkeley and Los Angeles: University of California Press, 1934), 2:544.

54. Yahuda MS. 15.7, f. 154r, at the Jewish National and University Library, Jerusalem. Westfall has argued that Newton's conception of God comes from his Arianism and is an "incidental acquisition by Newton." Westfall, *Never at Rest*, p. 317.

55. Keynes MS. 3, f. 48r.

56. *Ibid.*, f. 51r.

57. *Ibid.*, f. 51r. On f. 52r, Newton writes that: "The Church of England in her sixt Article declares that the Holy Scripture contains all things necessary to salvation: so that whatsoever is not read therein nor may be proved thereby, is not to be required of any Man that it should be believed as an Article of faith, or be thought requisite or necessary salvation."

58. Yahuda MS. 1, f. 1r, at the Jewish National and University Library, Jerusalem.

59. Marvell's "To his coy mistress" and this particular Pascalian pensée are explicated at length in Christopher Hill, "'Till the Conversion of the Jews'," in *Millenarianism and Messianism in English Literature and Thought, 1650–1800,* ed. Richard H. Popkin (Leiden: E.J. Brill, 1988), pp. 12–36.

60. In his pioneering examination of Newton's theological manuscripts, Manuel rightly insists that Newton achieves, in his private thought, an "intimate union of science and religion." See Frank E. Manuel, *The Changing of the Gods* (Hanover: Univ. Press of New England, 1983), p. 15. See, too, Manuel, *The Religion of Isaac Newton, passim,* and p. 49. However, in explaining the nature of this union, Manuel emphasizes that – in his view – it is Newton's scientific rationality which affects Newton's approach to interpreting biblical prophecies. The tests of truth in biblical interpretation, as in scientific demonstration, are "constancy and consistency." See Manuel, *The Changing of the Gods,* p. 23. Westfall also concludes that Newton brings the rigorous standards of scientific demonstration to the interpretation of biblical prophecies. Both Manuel and Westfall agree that it is primarily Newton's science, or his scientific rationality, which influences his theology and not his theology which influences his science. Westfall explicitly finds it "more likely to find the flow of influence moving from science, the rising enterprise, toward theology, the old and (as we know from hindsight) fading one." See Richard S. Westfall, "Newton's Theological Manuscripts," in *Contemporary Newtonian Research,* pp. 139–40.

61. Henry Guerlac, "Newton and the Method of Analysis," in *Essays and Papers in the History of Modern Science* (Baltimore: The Johns Hopkins University Press, 1977), pp.193–216. This paper was first published as an article in the *Dictionary of the History of Ideas* in 1973.

62. Sir Isaac Newton, *Opticks or A Treatise of the Reflections, Refractions, Inflections & Colours of Light,* based on the 4th London edition, 1730 (New York: Dover, 1952), Query 31, pp. 404–5 (emphasis added.) An abbreviated version of this Query was published in the Latin edition of 1706 as Query 23.

63. Newton, "Paradoxical questions concerning ye morals & actions of Athanasius & his followers," William Andrews Clark Memorial Library MS, University of California, Los Angeles. Cited with the permission of the Clark Librarian.

64. Newton, *Opticks,* Query 31, p. 403. It seems very likely that this aspect of Newton's metaphysical viewpoint is influenced by his reading of Moses Maimonides' *De Idolatria.* In addition to the immediate cultural influences shared by all writers of Newton's day, the influence of Maimonides' voluntarism and of Maimonides' concomitant view about the nature of idolatry are crucial to the development of Newton's theology as are the influences of other philosophers in the medieval nominalist tradition such as, especially, Pierre d'Ailly. Cf. Manuel, *The Religion of Isaac Newton* (Oxford: Clarendon Press, 1974), p. 87, and Brian P. Copenhaver, who corrects Manuel's overly rationalistic interpretation of Maimonides' thought, "Jewish Theologies of Space in the Scientific Revolution," p. 545. Cf. note 23. Moses Maimonides' brief tract, *De Idolatria,* was translated into Latin and edited by Dionysius Vossius, the son of the noted seventeenth-century taxonomical doxographer, Gerardus Joannis Vossius. Young Vossius died before printing his edition of Maimonides' tract. His father, G. J. Vossius, published his son's edition of *De Idolatria* with his own massive commentary on the text. Newton owned a copy of this work which is "very extensively dog-eared...." Cf. John Harrison, *The Library of Isaac Newton* (Cambridge: Cambridge University Press, 1978), p. 258.

65. *Sir Isaac Newton's Mathematical Principles of Natural Philosophy,* 2:400. This rule is not added to the *Principia* until the second edition of 1713. Newton's view about the contingency of human knowledge, in the light of God's absolute power and dominion over every aspect of creation, parallels that of Robert Boyle who writes that:

in this very phenomenal world of partial regularity, at any moment all our science may be upset by the elimination, or change of regularity through the operation of Him who is the guider of its concourse. For the most optimistic investigator must acknowledge that if God be the author of the universe, and the free establisher of the laws of motion, whose general concourse is necessary to the conservation and efficacy of every particular physical agent, God can certainly invalidate all experimentalism by withholding His concourse, or changing those laws of motion, which depend perfectly upon His will, and could thus vitiate the value of most, if not all the axioms and theorems of natural philosophy. Therefore reason operating in the mechanical world is constantly limited by the possibility that there is not final regularity in that world, and that existential regularity may readily be destroyed at any moment by the God upon whom it depends. [Robert Boyle, *Reconcilableness of Reason and Religion*, in *The Works of the Honourable Robert Boyle*, 6 vols., ed. Thomas Birch (London, 1772), 4:161.]

66. The only Newton scholars even to mention this work are Peter and Ruth Wallis in their bibliographical survey *Newton and Newtoniana 1672–1975* (London: Dawsons, 1977.)

67. Ephraim Chambers, *Cyclopaedia: or, An Universal Dictionary of Arts and Sciences; Containing The Definitions of the Terms, and Accounts of the Things signify'd thereby, in the Several Arts, Both Liberal and Mechanical, and the Several Sciences, Human and Divine*, 2 vols. (London, 1728), s.v."God."

68. See Note 6.

9. JEWS AND ROMANTICS: THE PUZZLE OF IDENTITY
RAHEL LEVIN VON VARNHAGEN

Ever her faithful recorder for the posterity she so urgently desired, August Varnhagen transcribed what Rahel said to him a few days before her death:

> What a history! – A fugitive from Egypt and Palestine, here I am and find help, love, fostering in you people. With real rapture I think of these origins of mine and this whole nexus of destiny, through which the oldest memories of the human race stand side by side with the latest developments. The greatest distances in time and space are bridged. The thing which all my life seemed to me the greatest shame, which was the misery and misfortune of my life – having been born a Jewess – this *I should on no account now wish to have missed.* Will the same thing happen to me with this bed of suffering, will I not rise once again in the same way and not to wish to miss it for anything? Dear August, what a consoling idea, what a significant comparison.... Dear August, my heart is refreshed; I thought of Jesus and shed tears over his suffering; I felt, *really felt for the first time*, that he is my brother. And Mary, how she suffered! She saw her beloved son suffer and did not succumb, she *stood* at the cross! I would not have been able to do that, I would not have been that strong. God forgive me, I confess, how weak I am.[1]

Leaving out the part about Jesus and Mary, Leon Poliakov quotes these words of a German-Jewish woman, famous for her intellectual Salon in Berlin around 1800, adding the comment: "Judaism, consolation of their ancestors, was thus becoming the very symbol of sickness and torment for Rahel Levin's generation."[2] Hannah Arendt gives the statement a prominent place in the introduction to the first chapter "Jewess and Schlemihl" of her intellectual biography of Rahel Varnhagen,[3] leaving out both the parts about Jesus and Mary and the part about her protagonist's "bed of suffering." She warns her reader that dealing with Rahel's life required her to show how the Romantic schlemihl's "struggle against the fact of having been born a Jew, very rapidly became a struggle against herself. She herself refused to consent to herself; she, born to so many disadvantages, had to deny, change, reshape by lies this self of hers, since she could not very well deny her existence out of hand."[4]

If Poliakov's use of Rahel's comparison is too generalizing and melodramaticaly simplistic, Arendt's rejection of Rahel's deathbed reconciliation

R.H. Popkin and G.M. Weiner (eds): Jewish Christians and Christian Jews, 159–187.
© 1994 *Kluwer Academic Publishers. Printed in the Netherlands.*

with her Jewishness, is too one-sided, too selectively focussed. Both have their reasons for their readings. Poliakov's focus on anti-Semitism presents the self-evidence of its victimizing power. Arendt's political-psychological analysis of an individual life initiates a process of historical reflection on the meanings of anti-Semitism and of the victim status of Jews. In Rahel's case, Arendt's reading is more useful than Poliakov's, because it does more justice to the contradictions and conflicts of a person whose highly complex individuality has been articulated and documented so exhaustively. Rahel had been writing her life in letters and diaries as she lived it, and she had married the gentile Varnhagen for the stated purpose that he would be responsible for that significant text upon her death.[5] Moreover, and more importantly in our context: it was precisely Arendt's critical focus on this individual experience of a Jewish woman of the Romantic period that enabled her to develop a more critically discerning concept of anti-Semitism.[6] But reading Rahel's life in the early 1930s, Arendt could not but read her own concerns into it. She re-wrote that life – and this has to be understood in literal terms, not in the cloudy terms of 'textuality' – from the perspective of a political-philosophical historian who happened to be a German-Jewish woman threatened by the Nazi regime.

In the preface to *Rahel Varnhagen*, Arendt states that her approach to Rahel concerned both the "Woman Problem" and, "though here with more difficulty," the "Jewish question, which in Rahel's own opinion exerted a crucial influence upon her destiny."[7] Actually, her analysis is centrally focussed on the Jewish question. Much of the conceptual grid of "Antisemitism," the first and arguably most effective part of *Origins of Totalitarianism*, owes its peculiar pointedness and clarity to the analysis which she undertook in the Rahel book of a minority's conflicted self-perception and self-presentation. In the early thirties Rahel had been for Arendt "truly my best friend,"[8] – the person in whom and against whom one can reflect oneself. So Rahel, like herself at the time, understood the Jewish question to be *the* crucial influence on the course and shape of her life. And in re-telling Rahel's life-story, that is, retracing the shape Rahel had given to this life, Arendt brilliantly illuminated such influence. More, she presented the shaping of this life by individual development and accident of birth as a historical model of the troubled social discourse of educated German Jews desiring assimilation. Here, too, her perception, her judgment was colored by her own situation, a coloring that both enlightened and obscured. In certain important ways Rahel was an ideal subject for Arendt to come to terms with her own situation by both identifying with that other German-Jewish woman who had lived more than a century before her, and distancing herself from her.

I am reading the text of Rahel's life now, in the 1990s, and here, in

Los Angeles, troubled by the difficult realities of gender and multicultural relations and hopeful for their precarious potential, and I have come away with an interpretation that asks for more tolerance of that text's opacities and obscurities, its conflicts and contradictions, tensions and lacunae. That is to say that as a reader of this lavishly documented life – first by Varnhagen, then by women and men throughout the 19th and early 20th century, and now in a modern ten volume *Klassiker* edition – I remain much more puzzled and uncertain than were Poliakov and Arendt about the cultural meanings of the historical Rahel Levin Varnhagen, a Jewish woman of the Romantic period.

In the 19th and early 20th century, Rahel's *Gestalt*, as shown in texts published by Varnhagen, could be described as a priestess and female incarnation of Goethe, in which the woman and the Jewish question were somehow sublated. These publications *of* rather than *about* Rahel[9] reflect the fascination for 19th and early 20th century educated readers, both male and female, of (Goethean) *entelechy* – an irresistible development of individual form and meaning from its core of potentiality. Clearly, this fascination provided relief from the more disturbing aspects of modernity: cultural secularity and diversity including the woman and minority questions, and the increasing importance of 'quantifying' science and technology. But recent admiring biographies of 'Rahel the Woman'[10] look at her life with their own rigorously pre-established notions of cultural meaning and significance reflecting *their* alliances, *their* anxieties and desires. Arendt's probing reconstruction of Rahel as "Jewess and Schlemihl," hovering, to the end, "between pariah and parvenu,"[11] that is, between a responsibly critical perspective on her minority group and unquestioning assimilation to the majority group,[12] is still, with all its distortions and limitations, the most thought-provoking to the historian, precisely because she held Rahel so firmly – and impossibly – responsible for the text of her life.

On September 27, 1814, at the age of 43, Rahel Levin married the Gentile Karl August Varnhagen von Ense and was baptized Antonie Friederike von Varnhagen. Born Rahel Levin on May 19, 1771 in Berlin, the eldest daughter of Levin Markus, a well-to-do Prussian Schutzjude, banker and *Muenzjude*,[13] and having adopted in 1809 the surname 'Robert' from her favorite brother Louis who had taken it upon conversion in 1800, she would from now on sign most of her letters with 'F.V.' In the marriage to a man who was 13 years her junior and, though gifted with a curiously flexible and perceptive contemporaneity,[14] has always been seen as less than an equal, this woman of great subtle social intelligence and psychological sophistication fully expected to be (literally) born again; to be given a new self.

This re-birth was to occur in the public rather than the private sphere. Rahel's Christianity, a highly individualistic Jesus-centered secularist pan-piety, was fully developed long before her conversion. Rahel's comments on her arrangements for the baptism and wedding ceremonies are ironical and matter-of-fact, framed, in her letters to Varnhagen during the last weeks before the event, between reports on favorite meals shared with friends (pike, fried potatoes and pickles) and financial transactions (changing money for the impending move to Vienna). Prediger Stegemann who was going to baptize and marry her, is more than accomodating, she writes; he receives her "as if Spinoza wanted to be baptized: crushed by the honor."[15] But during those weeks she also wrote several letters to her husband-to-be that harshly illuminate the depth of her emotional needinesss and the urgency of her socially focused desire. All spring and early summer of 1814, she had been anxiously waiting for Varnhagen to come back to her from his various adventures and assignments during the end stage of the Napoleonic wars.[16] He was held up in Paris by the war, politics and illness, and in her letters in June, Rahel writes of her waiting for him as an excruciatingly painful state of being, or, rather, of dying:

> I am sitting here – ill and in much pain – wanting that you come for me. But I understand, God wants me to die the death of hesitation and waiting; and *no* other. But even where fate is most contrary, I cannot be without active self-involvement [*Selbsttaetigkeit*]: and even if that were thwarted – the greatest misfortune – I simply must at least *co*-determine, if only that I will suffer it; and how I will suffer it. Since your departure from France is completely dependent on Emperor Alexander, that is, the revolving world-wheel itself, I have *co*-determined to stay here [in Prague] till at least June 14.... Only *come*!!! To wait, to wait any *longer, will kill me*. Keep in mind how *long* I have been waiting; and that my whole life since I have known you has been oriented towards you: and could, at least *perhaps*, have taken a totally different turn. What you have done so far, you had to do; I had to agree to it; but if the goal were to always remain inaccessible, and I in bondage to expectation [*Erwartung*], by God – since it *yet* has to happen –I would finally rather die. And what was my life like before I knew you? A blooming heart: at which everyone stabbed, threw all the weapons, everything hard; a heart that did not know its beauty, purity, fullness, youth, and suffered it: and made no claims. I cannot go on. This heart is sick and it makes the whole human being sick: it has been too much. *God knows it*. This, August, has to be my answer to your pure, divine love letter. What you are for me, what you can be for me, you know yourself. You know me completely. If human beings can know each other. Don't overlook the fact that my life – as I want to live it; the recognition of your love and nature –is *my* answer to your most intense, most exuberant expressions of love, signs of love! I will follow your life completely; but

I must be able to live *with* you.[17]

This composition of despair, panic, subtle recriminations, and solid manipulation is expressed in a language – alas not rendered in my translation – whose fluidity and inventiveness gives this complex of emotions the peculiar seductive immediacy characteristic for Rahel's "management" of her friends. Varnhagen answered at great length on June 21 from Baden where he had been detained by illness, seven of her letters in front of him, reacting anxiously to "your despairing waiting, your being so intensely frustrated" with somatic explanations of his emotional state – "how torn apart and tortured I feel" – and psychological descriptions of the experience of his illness. He is trying not so much to calm her fears, as to show her that he shares them.[18] Rahel's response is short and ecstatic, religious: she has been delivered from her panic and despair by his God-sent letter that arrived just when her anxiety was rising. They will be together; they will be married.

She will not really be able to calm down before the wedding actually takes place. The many letters that pass between them during July, August and the first weeks of September 1814 contain much information concerning their visits, arrangements of travel, purchases for their life together. On July 2 Varnhagen joins her for three happy weeks in Teplitz,[19] her beloved Spa, but they are separated again during the last weeks before the wedding and there is a rush of letters between Berlin where she is waiting for him and Hamburg, where, following her advice, he initiates the crucial career change from the Russian army to Prussian diplomatic service.[20]

From the beginnning of their relationship, she had reassured herself about that future by guiding him. She 'styled' his emotions and his intellect, oversaw his social development and directed his career goals, urging him to obtain the title of nobility,[21] to get a firm foothold in the slippery field of diplomacy,[22] and to make the best of the connections he had obtained through her or had made on his own.[23] With Varnhagen she left little to chance; she had too much to lose.

Why, being 'the famous Rahel,' admired by Alexander von Humboldt as well as Goethe, by Schleiermacher as well as the Mendelssohns, by Gentz as well as Mme de Stael,[24] did she feel so needy, so excluded? It is important to keep in mind that this feeling was most intense after 1806 – until she became Friederike von Varnhagen – when political nationalism rose in Germany in reaction to the disastrous battle of Jena. In combination with late Romantic cultural nationalism and increasing Pietism, it changed the situation in which the Salons of Jewish women like the notoriously beautiful, high-minded and well-married Henriette Herz, but also the plain-looking, original, subversive and temperamental unmarried Rahel Levin had flourished. 1806 to 1814 were the years when Rahel was feeling, like the Gentile male contemporaries who had frequented her Salon, the reduced opportunities that made even such in many ways enlightenend freethinkers as Friedrich and Dorothea Schlegel and Romantics like Clemens von Brentano seek refuge in Catholicism.[25]

It is true, some of the often quoted statements about the 'misfortune' of her Jewish birth were made early, especially to David Veit (nephew by marriage of Dorothea Mendelsohn-Veit-Schlegel), when he was a student in Goettingen and Jena[26] and she felt stifled, as if arrested or shrinking, in her parents' house in Berlin. On April 2, 1793, twenty-one years old, she writes that she shall never be able to conceive that she is "a Shlemihl and a Jewess." "Since after all these years and having given so much thought to it, it has eluded me, I will never really know it. That is why 'the clang of the murderous axe does not nibble at my *root*'; that is why I am still living. I haven't yet said all these things to you, that's why I am writing them so that you'll be amused."[27]

Veit's answer of April 14, 1793 implies that, laughing with her about her letter, he would of course be aware of its darker meanings.[28] He does not respond explicitly to either the complaint about her Jewish birth, nor to the much more emphatic lamentations about her having been born a girl into that particular Jewish family: "If my mother had been kind and hard enough and if she had been able to anticipate what I would be like, then, with my first scream she should have suffocated me in this dust here. An *impotent* being, expected to sit at home, with heaven and earth and men and beasts turned against her should she want to leave."[29] As she would lament so frequently in her letters, Rahel feared above all the sensation of being held back, the absence of motion, movement, of friends coming and going: "It is not worthwhile to dress and undress.... I am stuck in the sludge."[30]

Rahel understandably found difficult the combination of a talented but emotionally unstable, tyrannical father and a fearful weak mother.[31] But after her father's death in 1790, she always was financially independent, even if she had to be careful. And, somewhat ironically, the beginnings of her Salon which she held in her parents' house and which flourished between 1795 and 1805, are linked with the visits paid to her successful businessman father by the young intellectuals and noblemen who met her on these occasions and then proceeded to gather in her attic room.

When she writes to David Veit on March 22, 1795 that her Jewishness is at the root of all her suffering, that it makes her whole life a bleeding to death, "eine Verblutung,"[32] her despairing mood is triggered by the fact that her mother will not take her to the Leipzig fair. As usual, she is not well. All her life she would be plagued by an extreme physical irritability, which would often prove useful to getting her way. Characteristically, she describes her "suffering" to Veit in terms of her greatest frustration, her lack of social control. The desire to leave for Leipzig consumes her; being held back in

Berlin makes her literally mad: "As if an alien being had pushed these words into my heart with a dagger upon my entrance into this world: "Yes, have feeling, see the world as few see it, be be great and noble, eternal thought has not been denied you, *one thing*, however, has been forgotten; be a Jewess."[33]

Rahel's temperament and her talents had prevented her from being social-ized to accept the fact that such life was not possible for a woman, Jewish or Gentile, no matter how competent or active. If her violent reactions to the limitations imposed on her seemed to center on her Jewishness, this was a metaphor for more than she had thought to be experiences of social exclu-sion. Veit's highly articulate, sensitive, and sensible letters said as much.[34] For such a young man, he wrote her curiously reflective, both distant and pro-tective love letters. And perhaps for that reason of temperament, too, these letters show him as much more perceptive of the other person than she ever managed to be. She pours her frustrations and envies, flatters and entertains him; however, she does not really respond to him. He admires her originality and is very supportive of her talents; most of all, he is sharply aware of her great need to find a person whom she could trust completely. But, he is also aware of the fact that she is known and feared for her penetrating judgment of the people she meets: for her – though he would not put it those terms – making them manageable.[35]

Veit was aware of, but did not point out to Rahel, the one-directedness of her need for trust that was never to change. Not even during the liveliest period of her *Dachstuben* (attic) Salon, when the social intercourse between extraordinary Jews and Gentiles, playing at being outsiders, was much easier than in the period after 1815 with its xenophobic religio-political patriotism. It seems, and certainly seemed so to the participants, that everybody who was young and 'coming' in cultured Berlin society around 1800 gathered here: diplomats, officers, scholars, writers, students, actors – among them the brothers Humboldt, Tieck, Schleiermacher, Fichte, Friedrich Gentz, the brothers Schlegel, Jean Paul, Pauline Wiesel and her lover, Prince Louis Ferdinand of Prussia, the "most human prince of his time."[36]

But the places where this cultural-intellectual vanguard came together so effortlessly were also outside established 'society'. As Salons, Henriette Herz' elegant house and Rahel's modest room shared that location. In 1786 Wilhelm and Alexander von Humboldt were introduced by their tutor Kunth to Markus Herz in whose house they met Joseph and Abraham Mendelssohn, Dorothea Veit, Israel Stieglitz, David Veit, David Friedlaender, and later also Rahel Levin. The teenager Alexander referred to his parents' estate, Tegel, as "castle boredom" and thought that there was more amusement and stimulation to be found among Jewish intellectual women than at the castle of his forebears. But he knew that his parents, though approving of his admiration for the well-known physician and physicist Markus Herz, would not be thrilled by his delighting in the company of his beautiful wife and her unconventional friends.[37] Significantly, the association between these young intellectuals, aristocratic and bourgeois, Jewish and Gentile, male and female, was not transferred to the young Gentiles' family homes. Clearly, this association was of crucial importance to the development of the Humboldt brothers. Clearly, too, the male Gentile friends of Henriette and Rahel had the unquestioned choice of being outsiders on a temporary basis, while they much enjoyed the friendship of Jews in the social no-man's-land of their houses. They never had, nor could they have, given up their citizenship in the majority. In 1806, when the spirit of the times began to favor Nationalism and Pietism, Rahel wrote to Rebecca Friedlaender to whom she was close during that time, constantly complaining about her limitations:[38] "How unpleasant it is to have to legitimate oneself over and over again! That's why it is so awful to be a Jewess."[39] And in 1810, in the middle of moving into a new apartment that she does not like: "And in the end I am *mesquin*, not really, as I would like, at home in a place where I belong only because I have been there so long. I feel it eternally and deeply that I am not a citizen."[40]

Like all her lamentations about her Jewish birth, this statement was made in reaction to a specific experience at a specific moment in time: she was upset or angry, suffering because she had been denied a favor, kindness, consideration, understanding, or admiration. More, the perceived slights, and she herself often pointed out her sensitivity, were always social. But raising the issue of legitimation and of citizenship, she rightly points to the majority's power to define the social self-presentation of other groups. The situation was complicated by the fact that this majority's "customs, opinion, education, conviction" was highly attractive to Jews of her generation.[41] Doing so well in society and being so gifted for sociability, Jews, intellectuals, professionals, and businessmen, had quickly risen to prominence; but they had acquired privileges, not rights. Ironically, when the 1812 Emancipation Edict was passed as part of the Stein-Hardenberg reforms in Prussia, the social climate had changed.

The situation around 1800 did hold certain advantages for intelligent and sociable Jewish women like Henriette Herz and Rahel Levin. More 'naturally' unconventional, they could be more active social mediators than could Gentile women; it was easier for them to make themselves known within an intellectual elite on their own terms. Where other women's self-articulations in letters and diaries were not granted space in cultural memory, women like Dorothea Veit, Henriette Herz, but especially Rahel, became 'famous,' that is, they were admitted to this memory from the beginning, because of, not despite, their 'feminine' talents for sociability. Still, with all her fame,

Rahel's being *in* society continued to be a struggle – in contrast, as she saw it, to Henriette Herz. Consequently Rahel never much liked her *grossbuerg-erlich* friend Henriette Herz, at least not during the years of her own relative isolation: The "Hofraetin Herz," wife of a highly respected physician and scientist, is "sterile and affected," she writes to the young, untested Varn-hagen in a letter of September 28, 1811, wishing to reassure him about their own willingness to take risks for the sake of future greatness.[42] A year before she had punned with some bitterness "Madame Herz' lives with her pretty clothes (lebt geputzt) and does not know that one can take them off and how one feels then."[43]

It was Varnhagen who secured her place in cultivated society, the cultural elite, by marrying her, recording her and keeping her public after her death in agreement with her notions of her (exhaustively articulated) uniqueness and her editorial guidance. He was prepared for such responsibility to her 'genius' through his literary talents and interests, but above all through his participation in the Romantic form of *Geselligkeit* that was in itself literary. *Geselligkeit* as the communal explorations of emotional and intellectual experiences was realized in the *geistreich* conversation of the like-minded. This conversation was extended, "infinitely" as it were, by the sharing of long letters and diaries, often by reading them aloud in a circle of friends who could be trusted to appreciate both their congeniality and originality. In his eight volume memoirs, Varnhagen describes these experiences and activities to prepare the reader for Rahel's entrance into his circle of *Geselligkeit*, that is, his scrupulously examined life. Suddenly one evening, while he is reading aloud from Wieland to the guests gathered at the house of the wealthy businessman Cohen whose sons he tutors, she is announced:

And when the name was called, there was that sort of commotion connected with the expectation of something unusual and pleasantly stimulating. It was Rahel Levin or Robert... I had often heard her name mentioned, and by many different people, and always with such fascination that I by needs conjured up the most extraordinary, most incomparable being.[44]

He had heard of Rahel as representing "an energetic combination of mind (*Geist*) and nature in the most original, the purest power and form." There was some criticism of her, but he took it, on a higher level, as praise. He mentions her notorious passionate attachment to the Secretary of the Spanish Legation Don Raphael d'Urquijo, that, according to the stories, "surpassed all poetry in grandeur, elevation, and unhappiness." Remembering her entrance, he sees, with his mind's eye, a graceful, small but full figure, with strikingly small hands and feet, thick black hair, a face that showed mental power, dark and lively eyes that left it doubtful whether they gave rather than received, and an expression of suffering that lent a soft loveliness to her features. In her dark clothes she moved like a shadow, lightly but surely. Most striking was her voice, soft, melodious, coming from her innermost soul, and "the most wonderful way of speaking I had ever encountered. In the light, unpretentious expressions of her peculiar mind and temperament were combined naivité and sophistication, incisiveness and charm, but all of it infused with a profound truth like iron, so that even the strongest character felt unable to bend or break what she had said."[45]

This was in 1803 when Varnhagen was 20 years old, and Rahel 33; a real meeting was not to happen for another 5 years.[46] The Rahel *Gestalt* created here combines Varnhagen's youthful admiration for the famous Rahel of the early Romantic Salon with the Rahel she instructed him to construct for posterity. The real Rahel had at that time been emotionally paralysed for several years by the disastrous relationship with the handsome and immature d'Urquijo. She had made herself fall violently in love with him in 1801, shortly after she had broken off her engagement to the Prussian Count Karl von Finckenstein. The pain caused by that severing she described to a woman friend as "a kind of death." And there was another strong emotion, "Real misfortune makes one ashamed."[47]

Actually, it was not so much misfortune as bad choice: in both cases she had picked the wrong man; more, she had reacted wrongly to a bad choice. She felt unable to let go of the emotionally unstable Spaniard who appalled her with his irrationality and whom she nevertheless expected to take her into the world of pleasure. Cast away in his passionate outbursts, she had herself become fantastic. Her own passion for him was a self-consciously elaborate fiction – which does not mean that she did not suffer considerably; but here, too, she saw her suffering as fated and significant. In her relationship with the much milder, meeker Finckenstein with whom she might have lived well, she had exaggerated his sisters' resistance to the union and, by her insistence on his complete and exclusive loyalty to her, had created additional difficulties for this not very bright young man.[48] He finally shrank away from her over-powering need to be accepted and adored.

Not long after she had married Varnhagen, she wrote him a letter to be opened upon her death, a poignant and disturbing document. It shows both her great talent for drawing the other person into her experience, here of mortality and memory, and her enduring self-deception about her relation to the man who was of crucial importance to her life because he assured her immortality:

> As much as it was *possible*, possible for your temperament to understand one like mine, you did understand it; through a magnificent spirited accep-
> tance: with an insight which I cannot *grasp* as it does not come from any

similarity of temperament. There simply is no more impersonal, more grandiose, more understanding way for one human being to take in and treat another than yours to me.[49]

But Varnhagen had understood her because she had interpreted herself to him so forcefully and exhaustively, and because he had been fascinated by the contemporeaneity of this interpretation: its emphasis on personal authenticity *and* sociability. Prepared to admire her as she was, he presented her as she had made herself, fated to be immortal in her uniqueness.

In accepting life itself as her artistic assignment and achievement, Rahel, as she wrote to Veit in 1805, saw herself both unique and equal to the greatest artists, philosophers or poets. She needs to assert this connection and rank herself, she writes, because, until this century, her talent had remained a potentiality, "covered as with earth against the outside."[50] Both unwilling and willing outsider, Rahel here insists on her uniqueness and her originality as her truth, which by definition cannot be related to others, because as insiders they are all caught in the lies of social intercourse. Her exclusion is fated and self-created and transcends her Jewish birth.

Yet, since her letters and diaries tell her "poetic original life story" (*Originalgeschichte*), they must be collected and reconstructed by her friends and lovers.[51] Depressed about the difficulties with Finckenstein, she asks loyal Frau von Boye to arrange for the collection. The origin of this *Originalgeschichte* is not the fact of her suffering, but its trans-personal cultural significance.

This significance is central to Varnhagen's role in the construction and publication of her *Originalgeschichte*.[52] He is the only one who knows, understands and continuously shares her suffering, she writes in 1812. Never has there been a meaningful correspondence between her life and her nature; and he has been touched, his love for her has been shaped by precisely this rupture: "For your eye alone this terrifying spectacle."[53] She has never had a friend like him, nobody has ever been so understanding, so exclusively centered on her, she tells him in an early letter that lists all the details of her misfortune: physical, emotional, financial, father, mother, brothers, sisters in law – all of them responsible for the fact that "my history goes back before the beginning of my life."[54] But if this last remark, summing up the record of miseries that constitute her complex unhappiness, does indeed refer to her Jewishness, it does not do so exclusively. Such Jewishness is highly composite and very much hers; it, too, is unique.

From the beginning of their relationship, Varnhagen collected and sent to Rahel the brilliant utterances extracted from her letters to himself and other friends, together with the admiring reactions of those with whom he had shared them. She admonishes him to keep better track of her letters and praises him for his loyalty when he diligently asssembles and distributes the text of her life.[55] There is a note from her to the Romantic poet Friedrich de la Motte Fouqué of January 30, 1810, accompanying a letter from Varnhagen: "I share V.s opinion; I, too, wish to preserve what exists of me. It has been thrown up by explosions, there are jewels among it. Long live suffering."[56]

No wonder that she is holding fast to Varnhagen through the difficult, frequently chaotic years of the Napoleonic wars. In that web of self-quotes and admiring references to her "Goetteraussprueche,"[57] her "divine" surprising connections between the most diverse experiences, she can, in a sense, be the author of her (otherwise overwhelming) world – authorize herself through such control, write herself out of her isolation. A good example is her correspondence in 1811 and 1812 with Alexander von der Marwitz, a Prussian aristocrat whom she met through Varnhagen in 1809, sixteen years her junior and soon to be killed in the Napoleonic wars. The relationship, producing a substantial volume of letters that was to contribute significantly to the Rahel Gestalt,[58] was shaped by her characteristic intellectual-erotic intensity. Writing to her, young Marwitz, like David Veit, became her equal in their correspondence.[59] Characteristically, she presented herself to him as both supremely happy and unhappy, infinitely free and existentially imprisoned, bad and good, transcendingly useful and profoundly useless, unabashedly self-centered on her greatness and ironically self-distanced.[60]

In that duality is located her contemporaneity. Writing to Marwitz about the politically chaotic, socially fluid Romantic present, she describes it as motivated by consciousness mirroring itself into infinity, into giddiness. In this situation, the "most effective and most capable nature" will be a "dual" talent. It is this duality, a symbiotic incisive intelligence and mobile poetic imagination, that she finds "truly human." She sees herself as the priestess of a new religion revealed only to her, separating her from her friends' social vanity. The war experience is highly important to her: only battles, she writes, can re-create a *whole* world now; they require heroes like Alexander, Moses, Christ.[61] Constructing that glorious role for her young friend, Rahel is very much moved here by the greatness of the times, that is, by the experience of significant community that for the short duration of her active involvement would even remove her psycho-somatic symptoms, make her healthy, whole.[62]

But in general this wholeness needs to be redeemed, constructed out of the text of her life, and here Varnhagen is crucial, since Marwitz, handsome and heroic, is too unanchored, too exclusively Romantic. Writing to her friend and alter ego Pauline Wiesel in 1810 about the isolation they share, she talks about her love for Marwitz and his for her. But he loves her as one loves the ocean, cloud formations, grandiose mountainscapes: "That is *not* enough for me. *Not any more*. The person I love must want to live with me."[63] Like hers, Marwitz' desire was to prove himself spontaneously, in unmediated action, and the pull of war could not be resisted.[64] Varnhagen's temperament was mediation and circumspection; she could hold him to his obligations to her and simply forbid him to go to war.[65]

During the winter months 1811/12 when Rahel had disagreements with Varnhagen, she complained repeatedly to Marwitz about his behavior and their friends' expecting that she would mend the matter. She wants him to share her anger that this "crazy Varnhagen, to whom I owe an immense debt of gratitude for his love, calls me unfair, in the midst of his apotheosis of me."[66] And, as she often does when she is really upset by one of her friends, she asks another one, here Marwitz, to preserve the "image of my soul" when she is dead.[67] A few days later, still angered by Varnhagen, she decides "to use him for what he is good for, and only that." But the problem, as she now puts it, is not so much his taking from her, rather her giving to him – overgenerously and immoderately. He is on the side of the "great deficit" of the world; she on the side of the riches.[68]

This rift, the only serious one in their relationship, came about through Varnhagen's earlier exaggerated reaction to alleged anti-Semitic remarks about Rahel made by Clemens von Brentano in the summer of 1810. Brentano, in turn, had probably reacted derisively to an indeed outlandish Rahel-apotheosis that Varnhagen had come up with in his role as her "Apostle." Rahel was cast as "the third *Lichtgeburt* (birth of light) of the Jewish nation, the first and second being, chronologically, Christ and Spinoza, but you, in terms of content, the first."[69] Varnhagen had physically attacked Brentano, who had been apologetic, and everyone had been properly upset, most of all Rahel who wrote violent letters but abhorred violent scenes.

The intensely and mystically Catholic Brentano was given to religio-political anti-Semitism, unlike the sceptical Wilhelm von Humboldt, who on occasion made anti-Jewish statements concerning observed individual modes of behavior, but actively and consistently supported the political betterment of Jews as a group. The *Christlich-Deutsche Tischgesellschaft* founded by Achim von Arnim in the beginning of the Prussian-French war and counting among its members Brentano, Fouqué, Fichte, Schleiermacher, and Savigny, explicitly excluded women, Frenchmen, philistines and Jews. Ostensibly directed against France and certain tenets of the European Enlightenment, it was radically anti-bourgeois as well as against the early Romantics' androgynous fusions, their poetico-philosophical, a-political transcendence of social conventions, including gender. The intention was not so much to exclude from its fraternity women and Jews in general, as to keep a distance to specific bourgeois intellectual activities like the Salons, in which Jewish women, played an important role.

Many among the *Tischgesellschaft* patriots were old friends of Rahel's, and around 1810 her relationship to them was ambiguous. In 1809 she wrote a long letter to Fouqué, explaining how much pain she had suffered from the undeserved "misfortune" of her "wrong birth"[70]. Here she sets up the usual dichotomy between her ideal of complete happiness and her total unhappiness. Since great happiness has eluded her, nobody has ever treated her as a happy person, namely one who can make demands and who is obeyed. Therefore she has failed – important here the German phrasing: "ist mir missglueckt" – in every human relationship, and chance has never helped her. Her perception of people is sharper and truer than anyone's, she writes, and yet nothing and nobody has made her whole in the sense in which she needs and desires it. It is instructive that she insists on being "ganz Natur"[71] to the Romantic poet Fouqué, who was to achieve some fame with his Romantic fairytale of the eternally feminine mermaid, *Undine* (1811). In frequent contact with him during these years, she laments about her isolation, flattering and manipulating him, and asking for understanding and adoration. But she also complains to Varnhagen about Fouqué's religious craziness: he dares to deny that Goethe has religion, a sacrilege for Rahel, the devoted Goethe priestess. Fouqué, she reports, claims that Goethe "was speaking of Abraham's gods, not of God. Then Fouqué spoke to me about his own Christianity. The Lord Jesus will have to forgive him, since he is serious about it... In answer to one of my questions he said: there were people who were redeemed before Christ, but only in anticipation and intimation of his Coming!"[72] Clearly, Rahel did not think much of such parochial Christianity, but she still remained intrigued by Fouqué's and Brentano's religious and patriotic mysticism, if irritated by their willfully excentric behavior and opinions. Her complaints about Fouqué[73] were made in one of the many letters that went back and forth between her and Varnhagen in the winter of 1811/12 in the affair of Brentano's maliciously perceptive remarks about Rahel.

Varnhagen had written her from Prague on October 24, 1811 of his renewed friendship with Brentano who had read from his great poem, *The Invention of the Rosary*, a piece Varnhagen found deep, genuine, of a pure mysticism and pious historical Catholicism. Brentano, Varnhagen is happy to report, is not as mindlessly anti-French as is customary for the later Romantics, has changed his opinions about Rahel, and, in fact seems in certain ways close to her intellectually.[74] Rahel, in her lengthy response of November 12, 1811, lectures Varnhagen over many pages for his impulsive and sometimes fool-ishly aggressive behavior, also against Brentano, but is pleased by his good news about their changed relationship.[75] There are tensions between her and the old friends that Varnhagen, known for his impetuous and quarrelsome temperament, has made worse, notwithstanding his good intentions. In this situation his gift to her of a planned publication of passages from their correspondence that deal with Goethe's work,[76] and his sending on Goethe's positive thoughtful answer is very effective.[77] Goethe is for Rahel the measure of all creative achievement in life and through living, the divine model for the text of her life. He is also one of the most important reasons for her deliberate and consistent renunciation of authorship during her life-time: *Her* story must be kept open for the significant ending that includes her intellectual and emotional responses to the ongoing work of Goethe, the person pre-eminently contemporary to her life-time.[78]

When reassured by her positive response, Varnhagen sends on a letter from Brentano. Rahel acknowledges definite intellectual similarities between him and herself, but she also is irritated by Brentano's mystifying statements about her, Fouqué, and Arnim.[79] Varnhagen, ever the eager mediator, reports this to Brentano, who then promptly writes Rahel a letter (after showing it first to Varnhagen) that she thinks unspeakably malicious: "I cannot understand how you could have let him insult me so."[80] Varnhagen, in vain, had warned her of what was coming in a rambling distraught letter of his own, trying to read Brentano through Rahel's sensibilities.

Brentano's attacks on Rahel focus on what must have hurt her most, her desperate search for admiration, her isolation, and her manipulative addiction to suffering. Naively, Varnhagen tries to undercut Brentano's assertion that very few friends still admire her. Brentano himself, he writes, "has told me that Arnim, his God, has in the past venerated and admired you, but now, remembering that you are Jewish, has turned away from you. Why does he withhold that? he can't have forgotten it."[81] Rahel knows why; and Varnhagen's denseness must have made her even madder. Brentano takes pleasure in presenting her unhappiness exclusively as that of the plain, older woman, left by all the men she ever desired. Knowingly and pitilessly he concentrates on the most concrete, the bodily aspect of her experience of isolation and lack of wholeness. She tells Varnhagen never to speak about this letter to anyone; it contains ridicule, for her the most potent social poison. And shrewdly she explains Brentano's, and by implication Arnim's, behavior: "The French have exhausted all social relations." Sociability, the easy sophisticated *Geselligkeit* between Gentiles and Jews, men and women, has been profoundly damaged by the disastrous French victories that have undermined the self-confidence of German Gentile males.[82]

Rahel had a second Salon in Berlin from 1819 to her death in 1833; she was a success and continued to be grateful to Varnhagen, because in his total acceptance of her uniqueness he had built a permanent bridge between her and the world into which she wanted to be accepted once and for all. As she had predicted before their wedding, marriage did not change her inwardly. Things were different only on the outside, and only pleasantly so.[83] After two years of marriage Rahel re-affirmed to Varnhagen her enduring *Freiheitsstreben* (desire for freedom), deeply appreciative for his understanding.[84] In letters to friends she praises her husband for delighting in her being different, completely her own person, entirely true to herself. She could not, she asserts, be married to him in any other way. Freedom, of overriding importance to her, means to be in society on her own terms rather than have to adjust.[85] The marriage to Varnhagen has made that possible and on her own terms she wants to make him happy. She is again the famous Rahel, attracting the most interesting people, a highly skilled hostess whose charm and wit are legendary. She also runs their house smoothly if unpretentiously, keeps a good table, and creates the physical and intellectual order in which Varnhagen, now a social-political historian and critic with a growing reputation, can work on the construction of the Rahel *Gestalt*. They do not share sexual and emotional passion although they deeply enjoy their emotional and intellectual intimacy. Judging from the many letters written whenever they were apart, this mutual enjoyment increases rather than diminishes with time.

It is a working marriage devoted to Rahel's cultural immortality and they both work on it successfully, apart or together, each appreciating the other's contribution. The letters they exchanged during Varnhagen's four weeks' trip to the South of Germany in the late summer of 1827, a hundred printed pages of them, are a good example of his admiration, warmth and loyalty towards her and her consideration for him. Her letters constantly urge him to enjoy new friends, new landscapes, new cities, good talk, good food, good weather; all the not so small pleasures of living. It was her decision that he ought to go and she ought to stay, ostensibly for reasons of health. She is enjoying life with her friends at home, and she adores receiving his love letters.

August, of course, copies all the letter passages that will add to the Rahel *Gestalt* and sends them back to her. She, in turn praises him for his diligence and corrects his misreadings.[86] He also quotes in great detail the flattering remarks made about Rahel by old and new friends, tributes that she will savor and then file away for further use. Her letters are filled with news about her hectic days, often just piling up breathlessly the names of friends dropping in or luring her away from home. Clearly, he adored being included in her spirited sociability, drawn, like everyone else to this "Menschmagnate."[87] She, in turn, is profoundly attracted to her own magnetism.

The distinguished guests of Rahel's second Salon tended to be Gentiles rather than Jews, philosophers and historians, rather than poets, men rather than women. It was the time of Restauration, and around Rahel one ridiculed and was apprehensive of the ever growing nationalist Pietism and attendant parochialism. When Varnhagen visited Berlin in the fall of 1817, he complained bitterly to Rahel about his former friend Ludwig Theremin, the Hof and Domprediger since 1814, who was now hoping, as Varnhagen put it "that all Jews would be murdered promptly; I know what his Christianity is all about." Varnhagen's heated response may have been influenced by the appearance in 1816 of several anti-Semitic treatises reflecting the reactionary spirit of the Vienna Congress.[88] Rahel, more calmly, points out that Theremin was a special case, always a follower, and always looking for something, someone to adore and venerate. Shrewdly, she links such desire with a particular weakness that can produce cruelty. There is a disturbing reemergence of spiritual illnesses that had been temporarily cured by the Enlightenment intellectuals' ridicule. Troubled by the contemporary ('postmodern') intellectual demonization and rejection of everything having to do with world trade, of its effect on the voyages of exploration, and of their cultural consequences, Rahel laments:

> Ah! poor Novalis, poor Friedrich Schlegel.... You did not think your shallow disciples [the younger Romantics] would be like that. Great, dear, blindly read Goethe, fiery honest Lessing, and all you great and serene ones, you could not have thought of that. A nice mess! [*Eine schoene Saeuerei!*] But, then, we, too, looking at that situation, are not without prejudice, because we are annoyed by it: what small bends in the eternal stream of being; that is, of becoming![89]

This, in nuce, is Jewish-Christian Rahel Friederike: a highly individual symbiosis of Enlightenment and Romantic sensibilities,[90] trying to be a contemporary to and a critic of the age of Restauration.[91] Significantly, in that same letter she urges Varnhagen to push one of her pet literary ideas, to make accessible Moses Mendelssohn's translation of the Old Testament to all Germans, Jews and Gentiles by printing it in German (not Latin!) rather than in Hebrew letters. If not explicitly, then certainly by implication Rahel draws here the connection between trade, which tends to open the world rather than close it, and Moses Mendelssohn. Mendelssohn, the darling of the Enlightenment was, as everyone knew, the model for Lessing's wise and shrewd Nathan, that seafaring, prosperous conflict mediator *par excellence* and agitator for mutual tolerance. In Nathan's world there is no majority.

But unlike Mendelssohn or Nathan, Rahel also sought transcendence, impossibly desiring an immediacy of meaning in a culture that was, as she very well knew, irreversibly modern, secular. In her circle of friends it was Alexander von Humboldt, returned from his voyages of exploration, who proved to be the steadiest debunker of all those troubling spiritual epidemics of the time. He became a sort of less Olympic, shrewder, funnier

Goethe-figure, significantly on the natural sciences side of culture.[92] Goethe himself, the monumental *Urbild* of all human cultural greatness for the German 19th century, Jewish and Gentile, was Rahel's religion, the cult of both her Salons.[93] He also proved to be a useful figurehead against the irrationalist, isolationist tendencies of the Restauration age.

Yet, Frau von Varnhagen continued to find irreversible her "Uremigrantentum," as she wrote an old friend in 1825.[94] It is true, she was now entirely established in *Geselligkeit*. But if she no longer felt exiled from it, it had irreversibly changed on her. In Rahel's interpretation, her exile from luck and fortune had proved to be permanent, in profound contrast to Pauline Wiesel, one of the very few truly independent women of the Romantic period. In Rahel's scenario, they both are significant outsiders. But, Pauline "*lives* everything," because she has had courage and luck, whereas Rahel "*imagines* most of it," because she has had no luck and thus has been unable to gain courage.[95] However, Pauline, as Rahel knows very well, chose to offend society, went on the attack, made her own decisions and mistakes, was active; whereas Rahel offended inadvertently and was apssive. For Rahel, Pauline's luck is ineluctibly linked to her great beauty, whereas she herself, is "unpleasantly unprepossessing, without there being immediately apparent any striking deformities."[96] Rahel's phrasing here is highly perceptive because it stresses the social aspect of physical beauty, whereas her plainness is a negative quality signifying the lack of social power which beauty can give to women.[97] The beautiful woman can control social intercourse and thereby overcome a culturally developed and enforced female passivity and lack of control. Beauty may not go to the heart of the matter, which is the obscurity, confusion and exclusiveness of the social sphere as it presents itself to the outsider, especially of Rahel's willing-unwilling kind, but it changes the meanings of exclusiveness. In his admiring description of Rahel's first Salon, one of its most loyal visitors, the Swedish diplomat Karl Gustav von Brinckmann, took care to point out her lack of connections, wealth, and, perhaps most importantly, of the *allgueltige Freibrief der Schoenheit*, the charter of beauty that is recognized everywhere.[98] Rahel was highly sensitive to that fact. A month after the wedding she writes to Varnhagen about the importance of the burdensome and exhilarating symbiosis that is marriage. And there still remains the old anxiety: "I am terribly apprehensive (*zittere immer*) that I am not pretty, and that people might not approve of your choice. But here [she is writing from Prague, exulting in being made to feel so welcome there], too, everyone approves. Jews and Christians. The former are on my side as always."[99]

Her need for explicit social acceptance and the solidarity of her circle could not be stilled. In her view, she could never be independent because she did not have, with Pauline's *Freibrief* of beauty, her unmediated, unquestioned power over people, which for Rahel meant the freedom to take or leave society. Where the older Pauline still has that freedom through her luck and her wholeness, Rahel has admiring friends, perhaps more Christians now than Jews. Yet she shares with Pauline her religious appreciation for the "true realities" in life, all that is beautiful, moving and growing: music, flowers, trees (*Gruenes*), love, children, good weather.[100]

The great love of her later years was a grand-niece whose quite ordinary sayings and doings are adoringly described in many of her letters. Encouraging her old friend Friedrich von Gentz in what was to be his last passion, his scandalous, difficult and blissful relationship with the famous nineteen-year-old dancer Fanny Elssler, Rahel writes: "I, too, still have a *Liebeherz* [love heart]. I love with new, never-known tenderness a pure dew drop from heaven, a six-year-old niece-child.... But the child belongs to me in a higher sense. My blood, my nerves, my quickness: soft of heart and strong of heart. I call her the child of reason; pious daughter. But she is pretty, graceful; bewitching, carefree; and quite different from me; pleasing to God and men."[101] She is how Rahel would have liked to be: an *alter ego* more fortunate, more blessed, more whole. Pauline and Friedrich von Gentz, both important members of the first Salon, are contrast figures for Rahel that do not so much reflect as duplicate and thereby refract her uniqueness. Gentz wrote her subversely erotic letters when they were both young, making them change and transcend genders in their relationship; he, receptive and feminine, she, masculine and productive.[102] Their friendship lasted, in spite of his ambivalent feelings about Jews in post-Napoleonic Germany, and his frequent betrayals of her. Gentz, the highly intelligent, versatile "secretary of Europe" during the years of Restauration, an "assiduous guest" at Jewish salons in Berlin and Vienna before he became the official speaker for the Rothschilds in his article on them for Brockhaus' encyclopedia. Here, he praised them for their spiritual qualities which, in the spirit of the times, he singled out as one of the important sources for their huge financial success. In the privacy of letters, however, he expressed his mixed feelings in ways which say as much about his Romantic self-perception and self-stylization as about his views on the Jews:

> Intelligence – that is the mortal sin of the Jews. All of them are more or less intelligent; but only let one be born in which a spark of heart, a spark of true feeling can be found. The curse pronounced on them, and it pursues them to the ten-thousandth generation, is that they can never leave the sphere of intelligence, in the narrower meaning of the word, to their own detriment and that of the world, but must make endless circles in it until their black souls descend into hell. That is why the monsters are at home everywhere

where intelligence, stupid and criminal intelligence arrogates the right to govern alone; born representatives of atheism, Jacobinism, Enlightenment and so on. No Jew has yet believed seriously in God! No Jewess – I make no exception – has ever known real love! All the misfortune of the modern world, if it is traced to its furthest roots, comes manifestly from the Jews, they alone made Bonaparte emperor.[103]

Rahel's turbulent relationships may not have let her know "real love" in his sense; and she never left the sphere of intelligence, neither did he. Toward the end of their lives – both died within a year – they again became emotionally very close, supporting and consoling each other in their religious feelings toward life. He would have adored what Rahel wrote after his death to Leopold von Ranke about her admiration for his great talents and her love for his luck – and like Pauline's, the lightness, in fortune, of his being:

His *Perfidien* – there were plenty against me – are different from those of others. He glided, soared in Fortune's toboggan, down a track that he alone followed; and no one can rightly compare himself with him. On this path he saw, as if no longer on earth, neither right nor left. When he was in pain or contradicted, he was no longer on this path. And then he asked for help and consolation that he himself never gave. Nobody may do so and yet be lovable. And as long as he was alive I did not let that pass unpunished. But now, in sum, there remains to me only pure living love. Let this be his epitaph: he always stirred me to love; he was always receptive to what struck him as true. He seized upon untruth with a passion for truth. Many people must be praised item by item; and they do not arouse love in our hearts; others, a few, can be reproached for much, but they always open our hearts, move them to love. Gentz did that for me: and he will never die in me.[104]

Again, she admires the whole, the *gestalt*, of a life. What she understood and therefore loved in this complex, uniquely and typically Romantic diplomatic ideologue was much more important to her than his betrayals. He had been more than charmed by her; she fascinated and threatened him with her, as he put it, "infinitely productive" intellectuality.[105] He had put her into the male role because she had asked too urgently that, opening the world for himself, he include her.

If, in her gallant summing up the beauty of Gentz' life, Rahel stressed the fortune of his exhilarating worldliness: did she adore him in spite or because of her own inability to share it? I think it is here, in this uncertainty of motivation, that the attempt to understand the historical Rahel has to be centered, and that the difficulties of this attempt are illuminated. Public and private identities merge in the unique Rahel *Gestalt* that she herself removed to posterity, still wishing not to be answerable for the entangled symbiosis of nature and nurture, of accident and choice. She, of course, was very well aware of that: "We really are how we would like to be, and not how we are," she wrote in her diary in 1825.[106] The Romantic desire, especially in its German provenance, for ongoing, infinite self-creation and self-presentation, had honed the young Jewish woman's unhappiness with *how* – rather than *what* – she was *in the world*. This desire had stayed with her, notwithstanding political and social changes, and prevented her contentment, or confinement, in middle-aged Christian Friederike von Varnhagen. "All my life I have taken myself for Rahel and for nothing else," she wrote to her sister Rose in 1829.[107] And so she had, evading historical time and transformation.

NOTES

1. Varnhagen quotes his wife in the introduction to *Rahel. Ein Buch des Andenkens fuer ihre Freunde* ed. Karl August Varnhagen von Ense, Three Parts (Berlin: Duncker und Humblot, 1834, rprt Bern: Lang, 1972) I, 43–44. The text was reprinted again in *Rahel Varnhagen Gesammelte Werke* 10 vols, ed. Konrad Feilchenfeldt, Uwe Schweikert, Rahel E. Steiner (Munich: Mathes & Seitz, 1983), vols I–III. References to any of the three editions since they share pagination. Unless stated otherwise, all translations from the German are mine and the emphasis is Rahel's who liked to underline.

2. Quoted in Leon Poliakov, *The History of Anti-Semitism* (New York: The Vanguard Press, 1975 (French 1968)) III, 200f.

3. Hannah Arendt, *Rahel Varnhagen: The Life of a Jewish Woman* (New York: Harcourt Brace Jovanovich, 1974); all references are to this edition.

4. *Rahel Varnhagen*, 13.

5. Rahel's general control over this text was assumed by her contemporaries and by the many editors of her letters and diaries based on Varnhagen's collections throughout the 19th and early 20th centuries, though Varnhagen's interference in details was known. Arendt thought that Varnhagen had interfered systematically to overemphasize Rahel's relations to German aristocrats, but her own active editing has has been reaffirmed by the recent discovery in Krakov of the Varnhagen papers presumed lost from the Berlin Staatsbibliothek at the end of the war. See Deborah Hertz, "The Varnhagen Collection is in Krakow," *The American Archivist*, 44/3 (summer 1981; Jutta Juliane Laschke, *Wir sind eigentlich, wie wir sein moechten, und nicht wie wir sind* (Frankfurt, Bern: Lang, 1988), 63–67; Ursula Isselstein, "Rahels Schriften I. Karl August Varnhagens editorische Taetigkeit nach Dokumenten seines Archivs," *Rahel Levin Varnhagen Die Wiederentdeckung einer Schriftstellerin*, ed. Barbara Hahn und Ursula Isselstein (Goettingen: Vandenhoeck & Ruprecht, 1987), 16–36.

6. See the argument in Dagmar Barnouw, *Visible Spaces Hannah Arendt and the German-Jewish Experience* (Baltimore: Johns Hopkins, 1990).

7. *Rahel Varnhagen*, XVII.

8. Letter to Heinrich Bluecher, August 12, 1936 (unpublished).

9. This is true for the many different letter and diary selections based on Varnhagen's published and unpublished collections, as well as the different spiritual (rather than intellectual) biographies of Rahel, among them notably Ellen Key's *Rahel Varnhagen A*

Portrait translated from the Swedish by Arthur G. Chater, introduced by Havelock Ellis (New York and London: G. P. Putnam's Sons, 1913). 10. See here Lotte Koehler, "Rahel Varnhagen," *Deutsche Dichter der Romantik Ihr Leben und Werk*, ed. Benno von Wiese (Berlin: Erich Schmidt, 1983), 290–316. Impressed by Rahel's subtle social intelligence and sympathetic to her claims to unique individuality, Koehler, who translated Arendt's Rahel book into German, rightly judged Arendt's perspective onesided in its conceptual emphasis on the Jewish question (295) and tried to balance it with the woman question. For a rigidly exclusive feminist perspective see Marlis Gerhardt, "Ich ist eine andere Ueber die Briefe der Rahel Varnhagen," *Stimmen und Rhythmen Weibliche Aesthetik und Avantgarde* (Darmstadt und Neuwied: Luchterhand, 1986), 20–61.

10. Arendt found this distinction in Bernard Lazare's 1894 two volume *L'Antisemitisme: Son Histoire and Ses Causes*, which criticized, too, the victims of prejudice, the Jews, for their lack of social and political responsibility. Lazare confronted anti-Semitism by calling on all groups, including the Jews, to share the world equitably and responsibly – a position which would be particularly accessible and attractive to Arendt's intellectual temperament. Self-confidently and self-consciously a French Jew, Lazare advocated using an intentional – in contrast to imposed – outsider or "pariah" position in fighting one of the most virulent cultural-racist prejudices of the 19th and 20th centuries. He was able to do so because he had found his Jewish identity in confronting the challenge of anti-Semitism.

11. On Arendt's use of these concepts see my *Visible Spaces*, 38–41.

12. Belonging to the group of Jewish businessmen who were responsible for the quality of coins in the Prussian State and involved in the silver trade. One of the best accounts of Varhagen's career as diplomat and social intellectual historian of his time is still Carl Misch, *Varnhagen von Ense in Beruf und Politik* (Gotha / Stuttgart: Friedrich Andreas Perthes, 1925).

13. Rahel also mentions here that the government offices in Potsdam and the *Konsistorium* (administrative office of the Protestant Church) in Berlin move very slowly – the latter, she jokes, because it is so "mystisch neuchristlich": to Varnhagen Sept. 9, 1814, *Briefwechsel zwischen Varnhagen und Rahel*, 6 vols (Leipzig: Brockhaus, 1874, rprt Bern: Herbert Lang, 1973 and *Rahel Varnhagen Gesammelte Werke*, 1983) (*Briefwechsel*) 4, 54, abridged in *Rahel Varnhagen, Briefwechsel*, 4 vols. ed. Friedhelm Kemp (Munich: Koesel, 1967) (Kemp) II, 294.

14. During those months Varnhagen was close to military action and her letters clearly reflect her nervousness, especially as news were sparse: *Briefwechsel* 3, 306–377. On Varnhagen's maneuvering himself into appointments in the fluid situation of the Napoleonic wars see Misch, 17–30.

15. Rahel to Varnhagen, June 3, 1814, *Briefwechsel* 4, 1–2 and 4–5, abridged Kemp II, 284f.

16. *Briefwechsel* 4, 9–17.

17. See Rahel's memory of these days as having enabled them to be together undisturbed and whole (*unzerstueckelt*): to Varnhagen September 21, 1814, *Briefwechsel* 4, 75.

18. See Rahel's and Varnhagen's letters of September 6, 9, 13, 15, 16, 1814, *Briefwechsel* 4, 47–74.

19. See her letters to Varnhagen of December 15, 1811 and January 11, 1812, *Briefwechsel* 2, 199 and 219: "Please, dear friend, try to have your title confirmed this winter. It is necessary and I insist on it. Since you sign yourself that way, and aristocracy has survived. Won't Graf Bentheim be able to help you with this through his influence,

rank, decoration and birth? Tell him, I have asked him to do so. Use all you have; all acquaintances." (199).

20. In the matter of titles in general, see Rahel's letter to Varnhagen of October 27, 1814, *Briefwechsel* 4, 102: Varnhagen had preceded her to Vienna to establish himself in a still rather floating diplomatic career, and she urges him to insist on a title, "because it is too precarious and not decent to work in a department without a title. (By the way, you know, I hate all titles that are not either inherited or bestowed for life achievement: for instance Judge, etc.)." Varnhagen, who by temperament was liberal and anti-aristocracy (see here Misch, 90–136) was to advance, in Rahel's scenario, through social rather than professional connections, mostly aristocratic.

21. She used the connections she had made in her first Salon, especially also the Humboldt brothers. See here Misch, 19f; Otto Berdrow, *Rahel Varnhagen Ein Lebens- und Zeitbild* (Stuttgart: Greiner & Pfeiffer, 1902), 173–187.

22. Rahel had met Mme de Staël in 1800/01 at the Humboldt's in Paris and was re-introduced to her by their mutual friend Karl Gustav von Brinckmann, the Germanophile Swedish diplomat, who praised Rahel's "genius" to Mme de Staël in 1804. Brinckmann wrote an account of their meeting shortly afterwards, and of Mme de Stael's fascination by Rahel, that was preserved in Varnhagen's memoirs (quoted in Berdrow, 64f and Kemp III, 428f). Rahel met Goethe in the summer of 1795 in Karlsbad, and David Veit reported on Goethe's being very impressed by the peculiar intensity of her feelings and her intellect: letter to Rahel of August 14, 1795, Kemp III, 64. The combination of remarkable individual talent and cultural 'groupiness' in German intellectual life at the time is noteworthy and, willing or not, Goethe in Weimar was at the center of it. When Varnhagen made a trip to Southern Germany in the early fall of 1827, the pull of the "magic place" Weimar could not be resisted: meeting Goethe again and receiving the gift of his praise for Rahel was the high point of the journey: see Varnhagen's long letter to Rahel of September 19, 1827, *Briefwechsel* 6, 183–188, especially 187.

23. Dorothea Mendelssohn Veit Schlegel had first converted to Protestantism in Paris on the day of her marriage to Friedrich Schlegel, April 6, 1804, and then in Cologne, together with her husband, to Catholicism, on April 16, 1808. Authors of the tediously rambling but potentially subversive gender 'deconstruction' *Lucinde* (1799), both had become increasingly pious, anti-French, and mystically nationalist. See here Dorothea's letters to Rahel during 1815–17, complaining about Wilhelm von Humboldt's "paganism" that made him ban religious ritual from political celebrations (November 6, 1816), and about Henriette Herz' "stubborn" resistance to baptism (January 11, 1817)– she was to give in and convert in 1817. Dorothea felt close to Rahel despite their different religious temperaments, since Rahel seemed to share her own appreciation of Christianity as "the most precious gift of the eternal father in heaven" (April 16, 1817). (*Caroline und Dorothea Schlegel in Briefen*, ed. Ernst Wieneke, (Weimar: Kiepenheuer, 1914) 482f, 488, 492). Before her conversion in Paris where both she and Friedrich were quite unhappy, she wrote to her old friend Schleiermacher on November 21, 1802 that she was reading the bible in Luther's translation: as an "antidote" to life in Paris." Reading both testaments, she finds Protestantism purer and preferable to Catholicism, which "bears too much resemblance to the old Judaism which I loathe." Protestantism seems to her "entirely the religion of Jesus and the religion of culture (*Bildung*); in my heart I am, as much as I can understand from the bible, Protestant." Public profession of one's creed seems to her unnecessary, indeed "Catholic ostentation, desire for domination and vanity." (*ibid.*, 357f) This describes important aspects of Rahel's enduring position. Dorothea, of course, was to change her mind dramatically.

24. See his remarks on his life in Jena in his letter to Rahel of October 23, 1794: "I take my meals with a Professor (for money) in so-called very good society.... I am not trying to go into society here, though that would be easy, because I am bored in anticipation." Complaining about the habit of people to play silly games to amuse themselves, he still appreciates the "great qualities" of Jena. "I am the only Jew here. One very much misses the more sophisticated amusements where there are no Jews; I *am* pleased that there are no *Jewish students* here" (Kemp III, 41; Veit's emphasis).

25. Kemp III, 20. See this passage in English in Arendt, XIV–XV making Rahel sound more unambiguously in despair. There is also a suggestion in Arendt's text – rendering as "es wird mir nie einkommen" "be convinced" – that Rahel was repressing that knowledge deliberately. The quote is from Goethe's *Egmont*: his monologue in the dungeon (Act V). Significantly, Arendt does not quote the last sentence where Rahel refers to Veit's being amused by her lamentations.

26. Kemp III, 21.

27. Kemp III, 19.

28. To David Veit December 12, 1794., Kemp III, 48. See here also Henriette Mendelssohn's letter to Rahel of April 8, 1800, complaining of stagnation: in, *Galerie von Bildnissen aus Rahel's Umgang und Briefwechsel* ed. K.A. Varnhagen von Ense (Leipzig, Gebrueder Reichenbach, 1836), 67.

29. See Rahel's description of her development in her long letter to Varnhagen of March 28, 1814: she analyses her flaws and her strengths and describes what she perceives to be a unique combination: nature has given her "one of the finest and most strongly organized hearts on earth" and this sensibility was *broken* – she emphasizes this word and repeats it several times – by her "rough, strict, violent, moody, *genialisch*, almost crazy father" who thereby "broke," without being able to weaken her character, any "talent for action" she might have had, making it impossible for her to have luck (*Briefwechsel* 3, 310–314, 11, abridged Kemp II, 258). See her also her letter of March 12, 1810 to her friend Pauline Wiesel, Kemp III, 228–231.

30. Kemp III, 54.

31. Kemp III, 52–54.

32. See especially his long letter to Rahel of December 24, 1793, encouraging Rahel to demand more, be more assertive, not be so accomodating, such a "noble being." Here he also makes some very perceptive remarks on Lessing's *Nathan der Weise* and on Mendelssohn's oriental self-stylization: "He wanted to show that a Jew formed by the spirit of his fathers and by the model of the orient can reach the highest degree of freedom. He wanted to show what can be achieved by the Jew as Christian *and* Jew; he has always tried to swim between both parties; and sometimes even the most experienced, most skilled swimmer is deserted by the strength of his arms and breaks out into a sweat of anxiety" (*Galerie*, 16–28, 20; this passage not included in the very much abridged version in Kemp III, 30f).

33. *Galerie*, 25–26.

34. Rahel to Fouqué after the death of the Prince, November 29, 1811, Kemp III, 309.

35. See Hanno Beck, *Alexander von Humboldt* 2 vols (Wiesbaden: Franz Steiner, 1959), I, 12–14.

36. Habitually in letters to Varnhagen, referring to Rebecca Friedlaender as G.= "die Gute," i.e. endlessly trying, not succeeding: see here to Varnhagen November 12, 1810, where she also criticises Henriette Herz for her bourgeois superficiality, declares her great love for the unconventional 'authentic' Bettina Brentano-Arnim, and complains about "Madam Frohberg-Friedlaender" resting on the laurels provided by Goethe and

the philologist Wolf, namely their praise for her "abysmally bad writing, called novel...
We are not mad at each other. I don't fight with her anymore. She is not open to rational
argumentation (*ueberzeugungsunfaehig*)" (Kemp II, 157). See also Rahel to Pauline
Wiesel March 12, 1810: "I am not going to see Friedlaender anymore – she has taken
the name Frohberg – she is too too intolerable, unnaturally *pauvre* in character, and
pretentious" (Kemp III, 231).

37. Rahel to Rebecca Friedlaender, Summer 1806, Kemp III, 273.
38. To Rebecca Friedlaender, September 6, 1810, Kemp III, 287.
39. See Rahel's letter to Ernestine Goldstuecker, May 16, 1818, *Buch des Andenkens* II,
    537: she points out this situation to her friend in Dresden who is planning to convert,
    advising her strongly to change her name: " I think this change of name extraordinarily
    important. It will make you a different person externally; and this is really necessary."
    (536). Rahel thinks that it is precisely that external, visible attachment to the "great
    class" ("grosse Klasse") that will prevent Ernestine from agreeing with the new hatred of
    Jews ("neuerer Judenhass") and enable her to be the support of the "unhappy remnants"
    of a great, talented, highly religious nation "in a *human*, that is *Christian* way." (537)
40. *Briefwechsel* 2, 157.
41. Letter to Varnhagen November 12, 1810, *Briefwechsel* 2, 109.
42. Karl August Varnhagen von Ense, *Denkwuerdigkeiten des eigenen Lebens*, 2 vols, ed.
    Joachim Kuehn (Berlin: Wegweiser-Verlag, 1922) I, 105–125.
43. *Denkwuerdigeiten* I, 125f.
44. Varnhagen saw Rahel again in the winter of 1807 in the house of Henriette Herz (there is
    a nice description of Rahel's animating effect on Schleiermacher in *Denkwuerdigkeiten*
    I, 255), and then met her properly in the early spring of 1808, establishing immediately
    the shared intellectual context marked by literary figures like Friedrich Schlegel, Tieck,
    Mme de Staël, Goethe: see his extravagantly praising, thoroughly Romantic portrait of
    "this genuine human being," "marvelous creation of the divine," a sort of pneumatic
    pan-creative nature-spirit who for him is "grandiose in her innocence and her profound
    intelligence" in *Denkwuerdigkeiten* I, 256–267. This portrait combines many of the
    terms and concepts used by Rahel in the endless self-explorations of her letters.
45. Letter to Frau von Boye, July 1800, Kemp I, 303; diary entry fall of 1801, *Buch des
    Andenkens* I, 248.
46. See Kemp I, 408–410: Kemp quotes Varnhagen who tells the story in the version
    of Rahel's friend, the sophisticated and experienced Countess Josephine von Pachta,
    quoting her comment that Rahel's and the young Count's happiness could have been
    secured with some shrewdness and consistency on Rahel's part. Characteristically,
    Varnhagen disagrees with Pachta; he not only refrains from blaming Rahel, but sees
    "the full greatness and beauty of Rahel's soul" precisely in wanting complete – i.e.
    non-negotiated – happiness, or none at all.
47. April 24, 1816, *Briefwechsel* 5, 116, abridged Kemp II, 393. 50. To David Veit,
    February 16, 1805, Kemp III, 83: "I am as unique as the greatest phenomenon on this
    earth. The greatest artist, philosopher or poet is not above me. We are of the same
    element. Of the same rank, and belong together.... But my assignation has been life."
    See here also her diary entry of 1801: "The human being as human being itself is a work
    of art and its essence is an alternation of consciousness and non-consciousness. That's
    why I love Goethe so!" (*Buch des Andenkens* I, 226).
48. Letter to Frau von Boye, July 1800, Kemp I, 304.
49. See her letter to Varnhagen of June 20, 1815, *Briefwechsel* 5, 143, abridged Kemp II,
    306, thanking him for his love as "elucidation" of her acceptance of her "pure misfortune."

50. Rahel to Varnhagen February 27, 1812, *Briefwechsel* 2, 258. See here also Varnhagen's long letter to Rahel of October 24, 1811, *Briefwechsel* 2, 167–174 on the greatness of her suffering, promising to revenge her on all those who don't understand her, and Rahel's irritated answer of November 12, 1811, ibid., 175–180, pointing out that her suffering is increased by his lack of judgment as to who are her friends and her enemies.

51. Letter to Varnhagen of February 26, 1809, *Briefwechsel* 1, 307–312. See also her letters to him of March 4 and 7, 1809, and his consoling, sympathetic answer to her lamentations, reassuring her of his unwavering love, of March 27, April 2 and 4, 1809 (*Briefwechsel* 1, 317–324).

52. See here her letter to Varnhagen of November 25, 1808: she lists all the letters she had written to Tuebingen, "and all of them great. Where are they?" (*Briefwechsel* 1, 158). See also her letter to him of September 28, 1811, where she reassures him they will both be great together and tells him that Count Marwitz is going to send him a list of all the witty things she said on her visit in Dresden: "And there were an awful lot." At the end of this letter she advises him not to call her life "a great one" in his preface to their little book on Goethe: "Leave it out; even if it seems so to myself and to you" (*Briefwechsel* 2, 157f.).

53. Letter to Fouqué, January 30, 1810, *Buch des Andenkens* I, 461.

54. This is what her friend Friedrich von Gentz called Rahel's famous utterances in a letter to Gustav von Brinckmann, December 28, 1803, *Briefe von und an Friedrich von Gentz*, ed. Friedrich Carl Wittichen (Muenchen und Berlin, 1919), II, p.179.

55. See here *Rahel und Alexander von der Marwitz in ihren Briefen Ein Bild aus der Zeit der Romantiker*, ed. from the original texts by Heinrich Meisner (Gotha: Leopold Klotz, 1925). The texts were in the Varnhagen collection in the Prussian Staatsbibliothek; Varnhagen had published some of them in *Galerie* and *Buch des Andenkens*.

56. Marwitz, she writes after his death rather opaquely, "was the last one whom I placed above myself; he has atoned for it with tears, and this angel, who was not more than I, found me of stone" (quoted *Rahel und Alexander von der Marwitz*, 14).

57. Letter to Marwitz, November 5/6, 1811, Kemp I, 123.

58. Letter to Marwitz, May 16, 1811, Kemp I, 38f.

59. See here her letter to Varnhagen April 20, 1813 (Kemp II, 207) about her work for Berlin military hospitals, collecting clothing and bedding and money, running about, exhausted but healthy ("aber ich *bin* gesund") and exhilarated by the citizens' generosity and community spirit: everybody gives, especiall ythe Jews, whom she hits for contributions first ('an die wandt' ich *mein* Geschrei zuerst"), including her brothers. She even praises Henriette Herz for her tireless activities. "How I am delighted by the city! it finally has found itself; finally doing good in the spirit of Jesus; and how it pains me when it does not happen. Oh dear, dear God. If only the Christians gave like the Jews! Then there wouldn't be any suffering here." Varnhagen included this letter in *Buch des Andenkens* II, 90–93, leaving out that last sentence.

60. Letter to Pauline Wiesel, March 12, 1810, Kemp III, 231. See here also her reaction to the news that Alexander has been killed in action in her letter to Varnhagen of April 22, 1814, *Briefwechsel* 3, 329: she is deeply shocked, sick at heart, but enormously relieved that it was Marwitz rather than Varnhagen whom she needs so much more because he won't fail her. A few days earlier, not yet sure that Varnhagen is alive, she writes to her brothers in Berlin about the bad news of Marwitz and her anxiety about Varnhagen, pressing them to write to friends for news: "I *must* know where he is, whether he is alive, suffering. This is not a lover who can be replaced, this is my *only* friend in the world. I can prove it. A husband" (April 18, 1814, *Buch des Andenkens* II, 204).

61. Rahel understood that very well, writing to Pauline on March 12, 1810: "One would like to go to *war*, me too, to seek nourishment for the claims with which nature has sent us into being." (Kemp III, 229).

62. See here his letter of May 27, 1810: "Shall I join it, this war?" and her incensed "No" of June 6, 1810, *Briefwechsel* 2, 67, 75. She was successful in keeping him away from action till the chaotic spring of 1814; and even then, as it turned out, he was not really in danger.

63. January 9, 1812, Kemp I, 158–159.

64. March 11, 1812, Kemp I, 177.

65. Letter to Marwitz of March 17/24, 1812, Kemp I, 182. Rahel gives an interesting reason for her interrupting this letter: she had been reading Mendelssohn's translation of Manasse Ben Israel's *Conciliator[sic., Esperanza Israel]*, explaining to the British govermnent why they ought to welcome Jews in England and (only half) jokingly she compares herself to Ben Israel, mentioning that she "wrote a great original-German letter to Frau von Fouqué that prevented me from writing to my friend, the Cavalier von der Marwitz)"(180).

66. Varnhagen quotes what he had said to admiring friends, nicely framed by two items of gossip: letter to Rahel of May 27, 1810, *Briefwechsel* 2, 69; abbridged Kemp II, 133. In her answer of June 6, 1810, *Briefwechsel* 2, 74–78 Rahel discusses all the news his letter contains, but not this passage.

67. July 26, 1809, Kemp III, 295.

68. Kemp III, 296.

69. Letter to Varnhagen, January 30, 1812, *Briefwechsel* 2, 233.

70. In this letter, Rahel mentions also that "Fichte, my dear lord and master, has sent greetings through Fouqué, blaming me that I haven't been seeing him: I am pleased, but I can't go out in the cold right now." (*Briefwechsel* 2, 235).

71. *Briefwechsel* 2, 171. On November 24, 1804, Brentano reported to his wife on his first visit to Rahel's Salon: the "famous Mlle. Levi" looks younger than her age, is unpretentious, good-hearted and extremely witty. She is not impressed by the princes and dukes who visit her – they might as well be intelligent lieutenants or students. (quoted Berdrow, 187f from a letter that had been forcefully edited (cut up) by Varnhagen).

72. *Briefwechsel* 2, 179.

73. He sends her the letter he had written to Goethe of November 20, 1811, and includes, with delighted, affirming commentaries, Goethe's answer of December 10, 1811 in his letter to Rahel of December 19, 1811, *Briefwechsel* 2, 193–95, 200–202. Goethe's letter in Kemp II, 438: he characterizes here the two correspondents/readers whose identities he does not know at that point: holistically understanding in Rahel's, ordering, distinguishing, evaluating in Varnhagen's case. See also Varnhagen's answer to Goethe of February 3, 1812, *Briefwechsel* 2, 243–246. He tells Goethe that the correspondents are Rahel Robert and himself and, over several pages, extolls Rahel's uniquely beautiful humanity, deepness, delicacy, lamenting a lack of general appreciation for her greatness.

74. See Rahel's letters of December 15 and 26, 1811, *Briefwechsel* 2, 199, 206.

75. On the news of his death, a year before her own, she writes in her diary: "Milder than the May rains are the kisses of children. The scent of roses, nightingales, the warble of larks. – Goethe won't hear it anymore. A great witness is gone." (*Buch des Andenkens* III, 573).

76. January 11, 1812, *Briefwechsel* 2, 215–217.

77. February 1, 1812, *Briefwechsel* 2, 236–237.

78. January 24, 1812, *Briefwechsel* 2, 228–230.

79. February 1, 1812, *Briefwechsel* 2, 236–237.
80. See here her letter to Varnhagen September 13, 1814, two weeks before their wedding, which she projects as "a thoroughly entertaining and enjoyable *Evenement* and it will only make a *pleasant* outward change and no inner change at all." Here she also distinguishes her serene friendship with Varnhagen – she feels light-hearted, nothing but optimistic about the impending marriage – from her troubled love relationships with d'Urquijo and Finckenstein (*Briefwechsel* 4, 62).
81. To Varnhagen September 26, 1816, *Buch des Andenkens* II, 419, abridged *Briefwechsel* 5, 157. As she would tell him repeatedly, his "knowing" her in this respect was of the greatest importance to her in their relationship: "You know me: I am not a mystery to you; and the condition, the element of happiness in the relation to you is that I don't *have* to be: that I am not shy with you in anything..." (ibid.).
82. To Pauline Wiesel September 1815, Kemp III, 237; to an unnamed friend April 21, 1816, *Buch des Andenkens* II, 388.
83. To Varnhagen September 14, 1827, *Briefwechsel* 6, 173.
84. Rahel to Varnhagen/Varnhagen to Rahel August 21 – September 19, 1827, *Briefwechsel* 6, 95–189.
85. Jacob Friedrich Fries, *Ueber die Gefaehrdung des Wohlstandes und Charakters der Deutschen durch die Juden* (Leipzig, 1816); Friedrich Ruehs, *Ueber die Ansprueche der Juden an das deutsche Buergerrecht* (Berlin, 1816) and *Die Rechte des Christentums und des deutschen Volkes, verteidigt gegen die Ansprueche der Juden und ihrer Verfechter* (Berlin, 1816).
86. Varnhagen to Rahel October 21, 1817; Rahel to Varnhagen, October 28, 1817, *Briefwechsel* 5, 246, 264–267.
87. She does not say so, but she might have had in mind an essay written by the young critic Friedrich Schlegel that is still (almost two centuries later) one of the most intelligent appreciations of the circumnavigator, explorer and revolutionary Georg Forster: Friedrich Schlegel, "Fragment einer Charakteristik der deutschen Klassiker," *Kritische Schriften*, ed. Wolfdietrich Rasch (Munich: Hanser, 1964, 2nd ed.). "Klassiker" means for Schlegel the writer as exemplary interpreter of (Enlightenment) modernity. 91. In reaction to physical attacks on Jews in 1819, Rahel complains to her brother Louis on August 29, 1819 about the (younger) Romantics' "hypocritical new-love for Christian religion," their fascination by medieval art and horrors, with which they incite uneducated people (Kemp IV, 504f).
88. On the cultural-political implications of Alexander von Humboldt's *Kosmos* lectures and of his presidency of the first all-German association of scientists and physicians see Beck II, 80–87.
89. See here Varnhagen's remarks in his lengthy introduction to *Buch des Andenkens* I, 22: "Through Rahel, the love and veneration for Goethe had become a cult in her circle." Varnhagen approves totally, pointing out that Friedrich and August Wilhelm Schlegel were guided by Rahel in their affirmation of Goethe's literary fame: "It seems noteworthy that these men practised their adoration not entirely without some hope of being rewarded, whereas Rahel did so completely without self-interest." Varnhagen's introduction to Rahel's circle did not take place until 1808, when she was relatively isolated, and this may be the reason for his emphasizing Rahel's incomparable position in her circle regarding genuine humanity, superior insight and intelligence (ibid. 17). It may also have influenced his listing her guests as aristocratic diplomats, scholars like the Humboldts, some poets and critics like the Schlegels and Tieck, no Jewish intellectuals (ibid., 19).

90. Letter to Wilhelm von Willisen November 11, 1825, Kemp IV, 284f.
91. Letter of March 12, 1810, Kemp III, 228–231. See here also her letter to Varnhagen of March 28, 1814, *Briefwechsel* 3, 310–314.
92. To Varnhagen March 28, 1814, *Briefwechsel*, 310, abbridged Kemp II, 256.
93. In her letter about Brentano's letter (see above), she is clearly hurt by his calling her "nicht schoen" – not beautiful – which she translates into "haesslich," ugly (*Briefwechsel* 2, 236).
94. Quoted Berdrow, 75.
95. To Varnhagen, October 27, 1814, *Briefwechsel* 4, 101, abridged Kemp II, 298.
96. See her letter to Pauline of June 8, 1826, Kemp III, 258. *Gruenes* had become a code word used between them for the pleasures of daily life: see also August 1, 1818, ibid., 243.
97. To Gentz October 3, 1830, Kemp III, 173.
98. Letter to Rahel in 1803, Kemp III, 121f.
99. Letter to Gustav von Brinckmann, quoted in Franz Kobler, *Juden und Judentum in deutschen Briefen aus drei Jahrhunderten* (Vienna, 1935), 149f; this excerpt is quoted in Leon Poliakov, *Anti-Semitism* III, 297. Note the list of conventional late Romantic attacks on the Enlightenment that would re-surface in wave after wave of reactions to the difficult ongoing process of modernity, notable recent examples being Adorno-Horkheimer's *Dialectic of Enlightenment*, and current celebrations of a "postmodern," anti-logocentric, anti-Western condition of knowing.
100. To Leopold Ranke June 15, 1832, *Buch des Andenkens* III, 577.
101. Kemp III, 122.
102. May 18, 1825, *Buch des Andenkens* III, 203: "Wir sind eigentlich, wie wir sein moechten, und nicht so, wie wir sind."
103. May 13, 1829, Kemp IV, 314.

10. SEPHARDIC PHILO- AND ANTI-SEMITISM
IN THE EARLY MODERN ERA:
THE JEWISH ADOPTION OF CHRISTIAN ATTITUDES

A unique situation arose beginning in the sixteenth and seventeenth centuries when Sephardic Jews who left Spain and Portugal encountered central and east European Jews from whom they had been separated for over fifteen hundred years. In Europe, their initial reunion was laden with reactions characteristic of Spanish anti-Semitic racial policy which somewhat bizarrely they accepted. However, this was also the age of Philo-Semitism, and it will also be shown that when Sephardic and Ashkenazic Jews encounter one another in a frontier atmosphere, as was the case in Ireland, Brazil and the English colonies in the New World, a more tolerant attitude developed among them.[1] This essay will document the philo- and anti-Semitic attitudes of Jews during the early modern reunification in Europe and frontier areas, and it will attempt to explain the opposing responses according to the natural, social and religious environments in which the reencounters occurred.

By now we are familiar with the type of anti-Semitism that emerged as part of the Protestant and Catholic Reformations.[2] However, anti-Semitism also appeared among Jews, a fact thus far largely ignored by both Jewish and secular historians.[3] In 1597, Cornelis Pieteresz Hooft, a Regent of Amsterdam remarked in a speech on religious toleration, "....Also among the Jews, with whom we so much like to compare ourselves, especially among them too, there are several sects living together in the greatest of harmony...."[4] Unfortunately, Hooft's claim was incorrect for the European setting. During the sixteenth and seventeenth centuries there emerged such a level of hostility on the part of wealthy Sephardic Jews towards their poorer Ashkenazic brethren in the Northern European urban centers that the term "Jewish anti-Semitism" is not an overstatement.[5] But this hostile reaction was virtually absent in the newer frontier areas of Europe and the New World, or what were considered to be so, where an altogether different set of Jewish responses set in. Not only did this more tolerant treatment reflect the Philo-Semitic Christian attitudes, but they also mirrored much of what is alleged to have occurred as part of value changes in the Turner Frontier Thesis. The scene of the hostile developments lies largely in northern Europe, and especially the cities of Amsterdam, Hamburg, Bordeaux and eventually London. After the Inquisition began in

R.H. Popkin and G.M. Weiner (eds): Jewish Christians and Christian Jews, 189–214.
© 1994 *Kluwer Academic Publishers.   Printed in the Netherlands.*

earnest in Portugal in 1536, and especially after the unification of the Spanish and Portuguese crowns in 1580, there was a dramatic increase in Sephardic migration. It was to these northern cities that many of the wealthy Sephardim migrated, either as Jews or still as conversos. Salvadore de Madariaga noted that when the Jews were expelled from Spain they "left behind a deeply judaized Spain; and they went abroad no less hispanified."[6] Yosef Yerushalmi and Yosef Kaplan have argued convincingly that a significant element of this Hispanic legacy consisted of racially motivated anti-Semitism.[7]

The history of the admission of Jews into Amsterdam is filled with a mixture of fact and fiction in regard to the original group of refugees.[8] The rationale for their formal admission was premised on Calvinist logic and economic pragmatism: the group's wealth was indicative of God's blessing and this, of course, would be beneficial to the new republic.[9] Recent research has indeed revealed that the Jews brought Amsterdam new trade which the city lacked.[10] Understandings reached between the Jews and the Christian authorities at the end of the sixteenth and the beginning of the seventeenth centuries made it clear that no Jews were to become public charges. This caused no initial concern on the part of the wealthy Sephardim. After all, their ranks consisted largely of individuals who had prospered during the Portuguese imperial expansion. Further, many of them were successful in removing their assets from Portugal, under the guise of on-going trading activities, prior to their escape from the Inquisition.[11] As the seventeenth century progressed, there was an increase in the number of indigent Sephardim who entered Amsterdam; however, these poor people are never considered as burdensome as the Ashkenazim.[12]

Notwithstanding their prosperity, the admission of Sephardic Jews into Dutch society created a number of problems. As elsewhere in the north, they were barred from guild membership. This exclusion was formalized by the Regents in 1616, along with a ban on intermarriage, conversionist activity, and the right to employ Christian servants in Jewish homes.[13] This discrimination, though minor when compared with Jewish restrictions elsewhere, caused a level of concern among the Sephardic leadership. They attempted to limit the visibility of the Jews, something they were skilled in doing given their previous experiences in Portugal. Thus, the council leaders, called *parnassim*, promulgated formal edicts (*ascamot*, literally meaning agreements or decisions) designed to have the Jews maintain a low profile.[14] One of these stated:

Bridegrooms or mourners must not travel in procession lest they cause accidents through crowding or arouse unwelcome attentions from the inhabitants of the city.[15]

Their desire for caution in displaying their Judaism was further linked to political and economic concerns. The records of the Inquisition of the Canary Islands indicate that many Sephardim in Holland (as well as elsewhere) maintained numerous aliases so that they could continue to participate as ostensible Catholics in the Spanish trade.[16] Their caution would also enable them to maintain a Christian identity should the Spanish ultimately prove successful in defeating the Dutch.

These Jewish leaders were politically conservative, supporting the ruling Calvinist party and the House of Orange in return for their early support and because the leaders were convinced this was in their own best interest. Their communal power had municipal authority behind it, as the constitution of the Amsterdam Sephardic synagogue was approved by the Regents in 1616. Because of all they had experienced as crypto-Jews in Portugal and because of the novelty of the tolerance in Amsterdam, they ran a very tight ship, to the point that dissent was effectively stifled. Apparently, they felt it important to maintain a united position and this spilled over into politics, economics, and even theology itself. *Ascamah* five of the synagogue council in Amsterdam stated that members in dissent could not even withdraw and establish their own house of worship as no new synagogue could be built within six miles of the old one. It was this group that would later excommunicate Uriel da Costa and Baruch Spinoza.

It is not known exactly when the first Ashkenazim entered Amsterdam. There were large scale expulsions of Jews from imperial cities in the second half of the sixteenth century. It is presumed that most of these individuals moved east to Poland, Bohemia and Hungary. Within the Netherlands proper, the remnant of the Ashkenazic Jews had been expelled in 1550 when the Spanish crown realized that they were there. Like Spain itself, the Netherlands were to be *Judenrein*. It is likely that a few Jews remained even after this expulsion, for in 1559 an order was issued that forbad sexual relations between male Jews and female Christians, including Christian prostitutes.[17] However, news of the establishment of the Sephardic community in Amsterdam in the 1590's, and the comparatively liberal environment in which they were allowed to function spread rapidly in central and eastern Europe. A German Jewish magician visited Amsterdam in 1610, two Ashkenazic Jews were married there in 1617, and the first recorded Ashkenazic birth in the city occurred in 1626.[18] The Mocotta library of the University of London has preserved a number of Jewish travel guides from the early seventeenth century that detail the restrictions in the various imperial cities. The last chapter in virtually all of these works is a description of conditions in Amsterdam. The clear implication is that persecuted Jews would find the most tolerant situation in the United Provinces, and indeed large scale Ashkenazic migration commences. In 1612, there were five hundred Jews living in Amsterdam. The overwhelming majority of them were Sephardim. Sixty years later, in 1672, there were 7,500 Jewish residents, 2,500 Sephardim and twice as many Ashkenazim.[19] In the mid 1630's, it is estimated that the average Sephardic Jew in Amsterdam was twice as wealthy as the average Dutch citizen.[20] Indeed, the Sephardim fared very well from an economic perspective. They were engaged in large-scale international trade especially within the Spanish and Portuguese empires and the newly emerging Dutch colonies in the Caribbean and South America.[21] With Cossack uprisings in Russia and Poland, the number of Ashkenazic refugees finding their way to Amsterdam increased. The Sephardim then faced a situation that would be repeated in London, Hamburg, Bordeaux, and other cities where contact was established or re-established between the Sephardim and Ashkenazim. Most of the Ashkenazic immigrants were poverty stricken, escaping from persecution literally with the clothes on their backs. The general reaction to these newcomers by the established Sephardim was "Jewish Anti-Semitism." Further, after the re-admission of the Jews to England, many of the wealthy Sephardic *parnassim* sent their younger brothers and cousins to London to establish branches of their businesses, and thus to hedge their bets on the outcome of the growing Anglo-Dutch rivalry. We will see that the new London community will mirror the older Amsterdam base in the growth of this elitism and hostility.

The Sephardim began to refer to themselves as *la nacion* (the nation), viewing themselves as being essentially different from the Ashkenazim. These alleged differences went far beyond the separate geographic areas of origin. In some cases it went so far as to suggest that they were of a different skin color than the Ashkenazim.[22] By the terms of their admission, the Sephardim were held responsible for the poorer Ashkenazim. The question of what type and how much poor relief (*sedaka*) should be administered quickly surfaced. One novel solution adopted would kill two birds with one stone. After the re-admission to England, it was decided to help many of these Ashkenazim by buying them a ticket there, thus removing them from the need for further relief. However, the younger brothers and relatives of the wealthy Dutch Sephardim that had been sent over to England for commercial reasons would now have to deal with the identical problem. They complained to the government in London about the swarms of poor Ashkenazic Jews who were entering the country. They received permission to order all indigent Jews (i.e., Ashkenazim) out of the country within five days. *Ascamah* forty six of the London synagogue reads:

In the Name of the Blessed God.
The Senores of the Mahamad ordered announcement to be made in the

Synagogue that all foreigners [i.e., Ashkenazim] who were in this city and those who should come in the future in expectation that Ceddacka [poor relief] would support them, should within five days depart from the country; and in case they should not do so, that they should not come to the Synagogue; and for their passage the Ceddacka will aid them with what may be possible. And this was so ordained for the benefit of all this Kaal Kados [holy congregation] which God prosper.[23]

Thus, there emerges an intriguing situation where the wealthy English Sephardim begin sending the poorer Ashkenazim to Ireland (the cheapest ticket), and the Jewish situation begins to parallel Anglo-Irish Christian relations. Now there were wealthy and "superior" Sephardim in England and poor, "lower class" Ashkenazim in Ireland. It is ironic that when Cromwell summoned the re-admission conference in December, 1655, the English spokesmen for the chartered companies argued that if any Jews were to be admitted, they should be confined to the provincial ports and barred from foreign trade.[24] By the end of the seventeenth century, the "superior" London Sephardim had done precisely this. They successfully removed many of the "inferior" Ashkenazim to these same provincial ports and Ireland (perhaps the most provincial of all from the English perspective). Further, these individuals largely restricted their economic activities to local or regional retail trades. We will see later that when some of the Sephardim themselves decide to go to Ireland largely for economic reasons a decided change occurs in their attitude to the Ashkenazim who are also settling there.

Not only were the Ashkenazim shipped out of Amsterdam to England and then to Ireland, but attempts were also made by the Dutch Sephardim to resettle them in the Holy Roman Empire and Poland. In 1656 an estimated three hundred Polish and Lithuanian Jews arrived in Amsterdam. They were persuaded by the "Portuguese elders to leave, [and] many of them accepted the Portuguese offer of passage to Frankfurt."[25] Unfortunately, the Frankfurt community was impoverished as a result of the Thirty Years War and were unable to aid them. The city council intervened and informed them that only a few new arrivals would be allowed to establish residence in the city, and this could be done only if they swore not to engage in trade or lend money. Evidently, none of the newcomers took up this generous offer, and all trace of them has been lost. Also in 1656, the Amsterdam Sephardim sent approximately 170 new arrivals from Poland to Mainz and Deutz (near Cologne).[26] There is no doubt that the double-edged sword of Sephardim returning from a re-conquered Brazil and an influx of Lithuanian Jews arriving after the Russian conquest of Vilna put severe strains on Sephardic poor relief coffers. Richard Popkin has shown that:

Their number became so great that major efforts had to be launched to resettle them in German cities. In the two weeks before the date of Spinoza's excommunication, records show that the congregational leaders were engaged in obtaining boats to take hundreds of Ashkenazi refugees from Amsterdam to places in Germany. The problems of the Brazillian colonists, most of whom were "people of the nation", Sephardim, related to the proud Portuguese of Amsterdam, and the problems of the poor Ashkenazim from Vilna needed immediate attention, financial and logistic.[27]

In both the Amsterdam and London communities the problem of synagogue usage had to be resolved. After all, the buildings had been erected for Sephardic worship. Should Ashkenazic Jews therefore even be allowed in? In the long run, the decision was made to "help" the Ashkenazim obtain a structure of their own as soon as possible. Until that time, however, the Ashkenazim were restricted only to the side aisles in the synagogue. Indeed, both the London and Amsterdam Sephardic communities wax poetic about the aid they provided for Ashkenazic synagogue construction. Needless to say, the synagogues that were constructed showed considerable differences in their level of grandeur. The following discussion appeared in a 1662 description of Amsterdam:

> The Jews, too, have their Churches or Synagogues, as they call them: The Portuguese have the largest, next comes that of the Germans.... while the Polish Jews have tiny little churches, or large halls and rooms suited to the purpose.[28]

Until the separate structures were constructed, however, a wooden barrier was placed in the Sephardic synagogue, beyond which it was forbidden for Ashkenazim to proceed.[29] A fascinating incident occurred in 1772 when the Ashkenazim in Amsterdam were admitted to the Sephardic synagogue to observe the competition for a new *hazan*, and they broke through the barriers that had been erected to keep them in their place.[30] A similar situation prevailed in terms of cemetery usage prior to separate burial sites. The Ashkenazim are given a row of adjoining graves along the back fence.[31] The wealthy Sephardic synagogues hired physicians to attend to the poor and the sick of the congregations. What was to be done with sick Ashkenazim? The decision was made to refuse to allow the Sephardic physician to attend to the Ashkenazic sick.[32]

While the Sephardim did not like their poorer relations from the ghettos of eastern Europe, they found that they could not do without some of them. This need extended beyond the menial duties performed by the Ashkenazim in the Sephardic homes or businesses. The Sephardic synagogues were often forced to employ Ashkenazic officials. This can be explained simply by the greater Judaic knowledge of the Ashkenazim who had not been forced to live as crypto-Jews. For example, the Sephardim in Hamburg did not kindle Hanukkah candles until the Ashkenazim arrived and instructed them in this observance.[33] In many cases these Ashkenazic officials were not paid by the Sephardic congregation, and attempts were made to replace them with "pure" Sephardim whenever possible. The Sephardic synagogue in London was successful in "cleansing" itself of Ashkenazic officials by 1678.[34]

The level of hostility on the part of the Sephardim became so intense that they actually refused to sanction marriages with Ashkenazic Jews. The treasurer of the Sephardic synagogue in London had to resign his post in order to marry a German Jewess. While the elders gave their consent in this case, they laid down certain conditions, including the demand for his resignation, in an attempt to discourage further "intermarriage."[35] This policy continued into the eighteenth century when an *ascamah* was issued that forbad a Sephardi from marrying an Ashkenazi; and the wife or widow of such a union was not to be eligible for poor relief.[36] This practice was also continued into the eighteenth century in Amsterdam. On May 20, 1762, the famous economist and banker Isaac de Pinto, wrote to the duke of Richelieu:

> The Portuguese and the Spanish, who have the honor of being descendants of the tribe of Judah or believe to be such, have never mixed, through marriage, association, or in any other way, with the children of Jacob known under the name of German [Tudesques], Italian, or Avignonese Jews.[37]

Still, the burden of providing poor relief to indigent Ashkenazic Jews continued. In an attempt to control this aid and create a deterrent to further Ashkenazic migration, another *ascamah* ordained that no member of the Sephardic community in London "could intercede for any foreigner [Ashkenazi], under penalty of 20 s[hillings], and to the same penalty shall be liable any who may go drawing alms for them...."[38] Hostility had reached such a level that the Sephardim outlawed the purchase of Kosher meat from an Ashkenazic butcher.[39] Foreshadowing the events that would occur in late eighteenth Poland between the Hassidim and the *mitnagdim*, it was alleged that Ashkenazic butchers in Amsterdam employed defective *shechita* knives.[40] Two Sephardim were even excommunicated for purchasing Kosher meat from the Ashkenazim.[41]

The group hostility that we have been describing certainly was reinforced by economic and social factors. When they were allowed to remain in established Sephardic centers the immigrant Ashkenazim were employed in the most menial jobs. They became household servants for the wealthy Sephardim or were employed at the lowest levels in Sephardic business concerns. Their housing was located among the least desirable neighborhoods in Amsterdam (Marken and Uilenburg) which have been described as "the shabby district of the Ashkenazic proletariat."[42] These deplorable conditions lasted well into the eighteenth century. In 1749 a group of gentile diamond merchants petitioned the town council to allow them to establish a guild and thus exclude the Jews. They argued that the Jews could offer lower prices because they lived:

> like pigs, ten or twelve to a sty, as anyone can ascertain in Marken and other places where five or six householders with their women and children live under one roof....[43]

While socio-economic differences clearly prevailed between the various groups of Jews who encounter each other in the 16th and 17th centuries, is this sufficient to account for the level of hostility that has just been documented? It has been suggested that these same wealthy Sephardim acted as cultural sponges, absorbing most easily and readily new ideas and novel aspects of culture because of their long experience in living as false Christians in Spain and Portugal.[44] Clearly they gained tremendous economic advantage from their ability to participate in the Spanish and Portuguese overseas expansion and to build on these experiences and contacts in the Netherlands and England. Could it be that their anti-Ashkenazic hostility resulted simply from embarrassment over their poorer, more pious, and less culturally assimilated co-religionists? One notes similar embarrassment within the ranks of the German Ashkenazim from the eighteenth to twentieth centuries when they react in horror to the immigration of poverty stricken Polish Jews into the cultured cities of Berlin and Vienna.[45] Whatever the origin, it is high time that this neglected aspect of Jewish history be brought to light. It is all the more important to do so because of the apparent twentieth century reversal of the situation and the subjection of Sephardim from Arabs countries to similar hostility on the part of the more "cultured" Ashkenazim from Europe.

However, hostility or "Jewish anti-Semitism" was only one of the responses that the Sephardim exhibited as a Jewish mirror of Christian attitudes. In the age of developing Philo-Semitism, one also sees a decided change in Sephardic values when the older, more established urban areas of northern Europe are left behind. In Ireland, New Amsterdam, the English colonies in America and Brazil, one sees some of the early Sephardic communities reach out to the Ashkenazim in their midst and overtly refuse to continue the older hostile reactions. While many of the new immigrants obviously bring the European mind-set to their new environment, there is much that has to be changed. It is only in the Hispanic communities of Curaçoa, Surinam, and the new English colony of Savannah that attempts are made to continue Sephardic elitism and racism. In the New World Jewish settlements outside of the areas of Hispanic influence and control a much more tolerant situation prevails. Something akin to Frederick Jackson Turner's frontier thesis appears to be operating among these "frontier" Jews. Jonathan Israel has suggested that in a later period there was a lessening of hostility between the Sephardic and Ashkenazic communities in western Europe partly due to the impact of the enlightenment and the increased numbers from both groups, but especially the Ashkenazim, who obtained university educations.[46] While this narrowing of the socio-cultural differences between the two groups may have had some impact in certain quarters of Western Europe, this does not explain the situation outside of Europe. The broader picture that emerges is more complicated.

CURAÇOA

On July 29, 1634 the Dutch West India Company seized the island of Curaçao from the Spanish. It was their intention to use this island as a base to make further inroads into the Spanish empire and as a possible center for the slave trade. As had become traditional, the Dutch *conquistadores* took a Jewish interpreter, Samuel Cohen, along with the initial raiding party. Cohen returned to Amsterdam sometime before 1642 when Peter Stuyvesant was appointed governor. It is likely that Cohen left both Jews and *conversos* on the island when he left.[47] In June of 1651, a group of approximately twelve Sepahrdim received permission to settle on the island. There is even some suggestion that an Ashkenazic Jew who left Curaçao for some unknown reason and was subsequently captured by English pirates and ransomed by the Sephardic community of Hamburg in 1654 may have been among them.[48] One of the early leaders of this initial group of settlers, João de Yllan, also left the island and returned to Amsterdam, where he became one of the prominent followers of Shabbatai Zevi, and even petitioned Charles II of England to grant him special permission to have a Dutch ship take fifty Jewish families to Jerusalem.[49] It has been suggested by Scholem that the news of Shabbatai Zevi reached the West Indies. Whether this prompted de Yllan or others to return to Amsterdam to make their preparations must be left as an open question at this point.[50]

The Portuguese re-conquest of Brazil provided the impetus for the further settlement of Jews on Curaçao. After returning to Amsterdam, many of the Brazilian refugees embarked for other areas in the expanding Dutch empire and this island was one of them. In the summer of 1659 seventy of these Jews, having obtained a *sefer Torah* from the Sephardim in Amsterdam, departed for Curaçao.[51] It is with the arrival of this group that the

Jewish settlement there dates its official founding. The earliest *hascamoth* were promulgated in 1671, and there is no mention of Ashkenazim or of the treatment to be afforded to foreigners. Evidently, the community was composed entirely of Sephardim. Unlike other areas of initial Sephardic settlement, Curaçao did not attract sizeable Ashkenazic settlement until the twentieth century. While a few scattered early references exist to individual Ashkenazim who visited or settled the island, they never amount to a separate community and never exceeded ten people.[52] Notwithstanding the small number of these "foreigners," they were prevented from becoming members of *Mikvé Israel*, the Sephardic synagogue: "The *Mikvé Israel*, like the mother community of Amsterdam, could not accept the Ashkenazim as members of their congregation lest at some future election an Ashkenazic majority might change over to the Ashkenazic rite."[53] While this statement was made in reference to twentieth-century Ashkenazic migration, it will be shown below that this concern was a dominant one for the Curaçao Sephardim in the seventeenth and eighteenth centuries. It should also be noted that it was only in the 1950's that Ashkenazim were granted synagogue membership on the condition that they not stand for election as *parnas* for ten years. Ironically, the Sephardic and Ashkenazic synagogues on the island recently merged and adopted the "Ashkenazic Reconstructionist-Reform ritual."[54] Although refused synagogue membership, visiting Ashkenazim were, according to the *Ascamot* of 1721, to be subject to the $\frac{1}{4}$% *imposta* (sales tax) that the congregation levied on all Jewish businesses.[55]

On January 3, 1729, the mixed Sephardic and Ashkenazic congregation of *Shearith Israel* in New York wrote to the *parnassim* of *Mikvé Israel* in Curaçao requesting aid for the construction of their first synagogue building. One hundred and thirty-six pounds sterling was raised, but it was made conditional on the "ritual and *minhag* of the synagogue remaining Sephardic."[56] Further, it was specified that the Ashkenazic votes could not exceed those of the Sephardim, even though by 1728 it appears that the Ashkenazic members outnumbered the Sephardim. While these events will be more fully discussed below in the section dealing with the settlement of New Amsterdam and New York, let us quickly note that the Ashkenazim apparently accepted these conditions. It has been suggested that the reason they did so was the alleged long-standing tradition that "newcomers" should not interfere with the established ritual in the congregation that they find:

> The prevailing ritual was Sephardic (Spanish-Portuguese), and the Ashkenazim or "German" Jews, although already in the majority, accepted the ritual because by 1720 it had been the only one in use in North America for over sixty years. It was tradition and common practice in Jewish life for the newcomers to accept the liturgy of the host community.[57]

However, the Sephardim did not universally adhere to this alleged common practice. Indeed, the Talmudic discussions of the Mishnaic passage (*Pesachim* 4:1) cited by Jacob Marcus as the source for long-standing Jewish custom produces quite enough variation in opinion as to leave a somewhat open question regarding changing ritual practices and the retention of old customs. The conclusion of the Mishnaic passage dealing with the adherence to new *versus* old customs specifically adds, "But a man must not vary any customs which might lead to discord."[58] However, when the Sephardim who were expelled from Spain came to Ioannina in northwest Greece and encountered the established Romaniote (Greek speaking Jews descended from those in the Byzantine Empire) community, they refused to change their *minhag* (customs). Rabbi's Elijah Mizrachi and David ben Judah Messer Leon stated:

The Talmudic priciple is that Jews always adopt the prohibitions of the place they move to. However, the Spanish-speaking rabbis adopted the stance that wanderers from place to place may continue the practices of the country from which they came. The Sephardim adopted little from the Romaniote Jews.[59]

While this clearly is not the place to get into an argument over the correct interpretation of the Talmud, it should be noted that the Talmudic interpretation given above was taken somewhat out of context. The continuation of the customs when an individual is moving *from place to place* was permitted only when those people intended to return to their place of origin, which clearly the Sephardim in the Ottoman Empire did not intend, Yosef Kaplan's recent work notwithstanding.[60] Thus, it appears as if the Sephardim operated on yet another double standard when it came to non-Sephardic Jews: when they were the established group, the newcomers were made to adopt their liturgy and customs, and when the situation was the other way around, they refused to do the same. An additional element in the Ottoman situation was that while some hostility occurred between the Sephardim and the Romaniotes, the later acceded to the Sephardic interpretation and customs because they "recognized the higher Talmudic knowledge of the Sephardim and agreed to adopt the basic prayers of the Sephardim so they could be united as Jews."[61] While this may have been the case with Sephardic exiles from Spain in the sixteenth century, this was not the situation with the former Portuguese *conversos* of the seventeenth century. It is commonly agreed that the levels of Judaic, i.e., Talmudic, knowledge among the Ashkenazim was far superior to that of the former crypto-Jews.[62]

SURINAM

Jews were present in Surinam as early as 1652. In 1665, the Jews received settlement privileges from the English, and they were granted a charter by the Dutch West India company, allowing them to settle in Cayenne under basically the same status that they enjoyed in Amsterdam,[63] but they moved to Surinam in 1664 when Cayenne was taken by the French. By 1694 there were 92 Sephardic and 10–12 Ashkenazic families in residence. Similar to the experiences in Amsterdam and London, the Sephardim aided the Ashkenazim in obtaining a synagogue of their own at the earliest opportunity. In this case, the Sephardic synagogue which was built in 1720 was turned over to the Ashkenazim in 1735 when new construction on a grander building was undertaken.[64] Contrary to the experiences elsewhere in the New World, the rise of Christian anti-Semitism that occurred in Surinam did not act as a binding force between the Sephardic and Ashkenazic communities. Relations were clearly hostile among the small settlement of Jews. When the charter was granted for Jewish settlement, it made specific reference to the "Hebrew Nation." Evidently, the Sephardim interpreted this to mean that they, and they alone, were the chartered community, for in the mid-eighteenth century the Ashkenazim had to petition the Directors of the Society for equal status, which was granted.[65] Interestingly, the only early records that are extant show Ashkenazic regulations aimed at the Sephardim. However, it is quite likely that these promulgations were reactive in origin. The Ashkenazim refused to allow any of its members to attend a Sephardic service, and fines were established in the unlikely event that this should occur. Further, like the Sephardic restrictions in seventeenth century London, intermarriage between the two groups was strongly discouraged. An Ashkenazi who intermarried would be liable to "having his name struck off the list of members and demoted to associate members [status]."[66] It is fascinating to note that this same penalty was imposed for marriages to *mulattoes*, reinforcing the notion raised earlier regarding the racial nature of this hostility. Yosef Kaplan has shown that there were similar regulations in Amsterdam that lumped Ashkenazim, Blacks and mulattoes all together.[67] Whereas we suggested that it was Sephardim in Amsterdam and London that exhibited these attitudes, perhaps we now need to broaden this and suggest that even Ashkenazim living in a Hispanic environment and subjected to Sephardic racism reacted in similar fashion. In the specific case of Surinam, there is no doubt whatsoever that this attitude towards intermarriage was shared by the Sephardim. Over the course of the community's history, there were only five recorded marriages between a Sephardic man and an Ashkenazic woman, and only three for an Ashkenazic male marrying a Sephardic female.[68]

SAVANNAH

The Jewish settlement in Savannah, Georgia represents the one English colonial experience where the Sephardic-Ashkenazic hostility manifested itself in a non-Hispanic environment. George II of England chartered the Georgia colony on June 9, 1732, to act as a safety valve for excess British population, to create a buffer zone between the Spaniards in Florida and the more established colonies of the Carolinas, and to engage in silk and wine manufacturing.[69] This era coincided with an upsurge in *converso* emigration from Portugal to England, and the Sephardic leadership of the Bevis Marks synagogue appointed three of its wealthiest members to raise funds to underwrite the sending of both Sephardic and Ashkenazic indigents to the new colony. When permission to send the Jews was requested from the trustees of the colony in January of 1733, it was initially refused. Almost immediately, the normally law-abiding members of the Sephardic synagogue hired a ship and dispatched forty-two Jews to Georgia, sometime in late January. Three Ashkenazic families were included among the larger number of Sephardic passengers. They arrived on July 10, 1733, and caused something of a debate regarding whether they should be admitted. It was finally decided that since the colony's charter only excluded "papists", the Jews could stay.[70] This decision displeased the trustees back in England, but Jews had already been allotted land in Georgia, so there was little that could be done.

By 1735 the community had grown and in response to greatly increased Protestant missionary activity aimed specifically at the Jews, it was decided to form a congregation in order to provide the individual Jews with an institutional buffer and unifying force. A *sefer Torah* had been supplied by the Sephardic synagogue in London, and a second one arrived in 1737. However, from the very start of the organized Jewish community, a rift appeared between the Sephardim and Ashkenazim. In 1735, an Anglican minister, the Reverend S. Quincy wrote, "We have two sorts of Jews, Portuguese and German." He then suggested that the Sephardim was far more non-observant than the Ashkenazim because of their "having professed Christianity in Portugal or the Brazils."[71] The best description of the emerging hostility between the two groups comes from a letter written by the Lutheran pastor, the Rev. Bolzius, to the head of the mission in charge of converting Jews and other infidels. It reads in pertinent part:

Some Jews in Savannah complained to me the other day that the Spanish and Portuguese Jews persecute the German Jews in a way no Christian would persecute another Christian. He asked me to use my influence with the authorities on behalf of the German Jews.

The Jew did not answer much, but promised to tell me sometimes the reason why there is so much bitterness among themselves. They want to build a Synagogue, but the Spanish and German Jews cannot come to terms. I do not know the special reason for this.

The Spanish and Portuguese Jews are not so strict insofar as eating is concerned as the others are. They eat, for instance, the beef that comes from the warehouse or that is sold anywhere else. The German Jews, on the other hand, would rather starve than eat the meat they do not slaughter themselves.

They do not know if they will ever get permission from the Trustees to build a synagogue. It will be quite some time; as I mentioned before, the Spanish and Portuguese Jews are against the German Jews and they are going to protest the petition by the German Jews to build a synagogue.[72]

Most of the Sephardim left Savannah in 1740 when the colony's attack on Spanish St. Augustine failed. The Spanish counter attacked at Frederica in Georgia and rumors swept through the Sephardic settlers that a Spanish victory was at hand. Most of the Sephardim left the colony, and by the spring of 1741, only one or two Jews remained, both of them Ashkenazim. It appears that the Sephardim made their way to other English colonies. Malcolm Stern has traced them to New York, Charleston, Philadelphia, and several West Indian islands.[73]

The Savannah experience illustrates that recently escaped *conversos* from Portugal who came as a group to the New World still maintained their Hispanic racial value system. While the records are sparse, this situation seems to uphold Yosef Kaplan's notion that Sephardic hostility was premised on the acceptance of Spanish racial notions by the *conversos* themselves.

RECIFE AND NEW AMSTERDAM/NEW YORK

The settlement of the original group of Jews in New Amsterdam included both Sephardim and Ashkenazim who escaped from Recife.[74] New Christians from Portugal had settled in Recife beginning in 1507 after they were permitted to emigrate. In 1568, further *converso* settlement was banned, but in 1577 this ban was lifted after the payment of 1.7 million *cruzados*.[75] After the union of the Spanish and Portuguese crowns in 1580, many of these individuals were subject to increasing scrutiny by the Inquisition, which evidently followed the old Spanish saying: "In three cases water has flowed in vain: the water of the river to the sea, the water in wine, and the water at a Jew's baptism."[76]

The emigration of the approximately 150 Jewish families that left Brazil in 1654 after the Portuguese re-conquest has been amply described by Arnold Wiznitzer.[77]

Apparently the twenty-three Jews that escaped from Recife and then from the scrutiny of the Inquisition in Spanish Jamaica arrived in New Amsterdam after a journey that had taken over half a year. The length of the trip and the stops that were made in first Jamaica and then Cuba had exhausted those resources the Jews were able to bring with them. Thus, upon their arrival in New Amsterdam their possessions were offered at public sale to pay for their voyage's expenses.[78] An interesting sidelight to the departure of the Jews from Brazil comes in the form of a letter sent to Oliver Cromwell dated May 16, 1654 wherein three Englishmen, Mathew Goodwin, Will Searchfeild and John Mallorie describe the departure of the Jews:

> ....Jewes of that nation, dwellinge in the Recife at the surrender therof, wherein they have embarked verry much wealth, in Jewils, golde, and plate, besides sugar etc to a greate vallew, which by the articles made with the Portuguezes were freed to them.[79]

This description of the Jews' great wealth may have helped to reinforce some of Cromwell's economic motives for the re-admission of the Jews.[80]

Shortly before the Portuguese re-conquest of Brazil, the Jews of Recife had gathered on November 16, 1648 for a revision of their communal regulations. It is this revised Minute Book of the combined congregations of *Zur Israel* and *Magen Abraham* that illustrates one of the earliest examples of New World cooperation between the Sephardim and Ashkenazim. Contrary to virtually all past dealings between the two groups, the overwhelmingly Sephardic dominated congregations included the following as *ascamah* 10:

> That all the inhabitants of our nation who assist in the present publication of the regulations in this Resiphe and in the whole state of Brazil, as well as those newly arriving shall become Yahidim of this K[ahal] K[adosh] and subject to its Eschamoth and orders. For this purpose there will exist a book which everyone now present and also the newcomers will have to sign. They will be liable for debts and general Fintas made for the benefit of the nations, in exactly the same manner as the other members of this K[ahal] K[adosh] whether they live in Parayba or in any other part.[81]

While the meaning of this regulation might be open to debate, given the past usage by the Sephardim of *our nation* as a term that excluded Ashkenazic (or Romaniote) Jews, it has been established that in this case the community in Brazil was talking in a broad national sense that included all types of Jews.[82] In point of fact, Ashkenazic Jews are signatories to this revision of the congregations' regulations. It should be pointed out that the number of Ashkenazic Jews resident in Brazil in the 17th century was tiny when compared to Sephardic numbers. This is the usual reason given for the lack of discrimination in this instance.

With the Portuguese re-conquest of Brazil, one observes the emigration of both Sephardim and Ashkenazim. Naturally, it was former *conversos* from Portugal who had openly professed their Judaism who had most to fear from the Inquisition. Indeed, when the ship that brought the first twenty-three Jews to New Amsterdam was blown off course and forced to stop at Spanish Jamaica, the Inquisitorial authorities there made a concerted effort to separate out former *conversos* before the ship was allowed to proceed.[83] Something of a debate exists about whether, upon their arrival, the Recife Jews met one or two Ashkenazim that had arrived there shortly before them. In any event, the important point from our perspective is that both Sephardim and Ashkenazim are represented in the original group that received, after some initial problems, permission to settle in New Amsterdam. Further, with the majority of the new community having come from Brazil, they continued the non-discriminatory recognition of both Sephardim and Ashkenazim as being equal partners in their community.

It appears that this first organized Jewish community faded away during the 1660's and was not reorganized until the 1690's.[84] A new synagogue constitution was prepared in 1706, which unfortunately has not survived, and another revised one was promulgated in 1728. As will be shown below, while certain practices were questioned by more rigorous Sephardic-dominated communities elsewhere, the regulations of the Jewish settlement in New York (after the English conquest) known as *Shearith Israel* continued the early tradition of not differentiating between Sephardim and Ashkenazim. Indeed Jacob R. Marcus has even suggested that the Ashkenazi Nathan ben Moses Samson, whose communal ledger for 1720 and 1721 is the earliest extant congregational document we possess, may even have served as *parnas*.

Samson's ledger indicates that in the early 1720's there were thirty-seven active members of the congregation. Fifteen were Sephardim and the remaining twenty-two were Ashkenazim.[85] It is also suggested that there were other Jews resident in New York who had not yet become fully active members. As has already been pointed out, although the Ashkenazim arrived at the same time as the Sephardim and by 1720 were clearly in the majority, it was decided to adopt the Sephardic liturgy. Clearly, it was this state of affairs that concerned those Sephardim in Curaçao. We have already touched on Marcus' explanation that the Sephardic *minhag* was of longer standing in the Americas, and thus the Ashkenazic newcomers had to adopt it according to *halacha*. However, a somewhat different perspective on this is presented by David de Sola Pool. He described the building campaign of 1728 and suggested that:

We may, therefore, finally accept the conclusion that as early as 1728 the Ashkenazim were somewhat more numerous in New York, more recently immigrated, and therefore predominately younger than the Sephardim, while the Sephardim were more settled, more prosperous, and more influential. These conclusions are entirely compatible with the fact that the earliest extant regulations of the community, also dated 1728, are signed by nine Sephardim and six Ashkenazim.[86]

While it remains somewhat unclear why there was a statistical shift between 1721 and 1728, it should be pointed out that a rather broad fund raising campaign was undertaken by the community. Numerous requests for help in the construction of the synagogue were made to older and more established Jewish communities. Obviously, the wealthiest communities at that time were Sephardic. Could it be that the continuation of the liturgy and some possible numbers juggling occurred so as to take advantage of potential Sephardic support? Clearly, many of New York's Ashkenazic arrivals had passed through Sephardic centers in Europe and had seen or experienced firsthand the type of aid that was distributed. Funds were actively solicited and received from the Sephardic centers in London, Curaçao, Jamaica, Barbados, Surinam.[87] Further, why was the Curaçao congregation so concerned? What we did not mention earlier was that they even insisted on having a copy of the appropriate regulations sent to them before that would release their donation.

...Know that the asquenazum or Germans, are more in Number than Wee there, [New York] the[y] desire of you not to Consent not Withstanding thay are the most, to Let them have any More Votes nor Authority than they have had hitherto and for the performance of Which you are to get them to Signe an agreement of the Same by all of them, and that one Copy of Sayd agreement Remain in the Hands of Mr. Luis Gomez as the Eldest Member, and another to be Sent to me for the Treasurer of this Congregation to Keep in his Books, and as this request is funded In Solesiting the Peace and Unety of that Holy Congregation I hope that you as Well as the Asquenazim, Whom all I wish God may bless, Will Comply with this my Petition...[88]

While many sources mention this request and while many of the documents housed in the congregational archives in both New York and Curaçao have been reprinted, there is no evidence that these assurances were ever sent. This is reinforced by an examination of the various revisions to the *Ascamot* of Shearith Israel. One does not see any reference to the mandated Sephardic voting majority nor even to the required assurance that the Sephardic liturgy would be retained. Instead, from all the extant records it appears as if membership with regular voting rights was open to all.[89] The revised constitution of 1761 speaks directly to the membership and voting issues:

12. To prevent any dispute that may arise concerning who is properly a

YACHID [member/subscriber] and entitled to a Vote, Each YACHID who hath formerly signed as such, is to renew the same unto these present Regulations, in this Book. A native here shall be admitted to sign and become a YACHID at the age of twenty one years. No Stranger to be admitted until he has resided here at least one Year. Then with the approbation of the PARNASIM and Assistants, shall pay twenty shillings, sign the list of YECHIDIM and shall be admitted to Vote, three months after signing.[90]

In 1817 a second appeal was made to the various Sephardic centers for aid in the reconstruction of the original building. Again, there is nothing in the various revisions to the synagogue constitution to indicate that the original Curaçao requirements were met in any way. To the contrary, a review of the material indicates that on numerous occasions, Ashkenazim were appointed to the position of *parnas*, and the voting regulations remained as broad as those quoted above. Between 1729 and 1825 there were forty-two Ashkenazic *parnassim* and only ten Sephardic ones. Thus, we are left with the possibility that the cooperating Sephardim and Ashkenazim who were members of the New York congregation obfuscated the concerns and demands of more racist Sephardic centers elsewhere. This line of interpretation is supported by Malcom Stern's suggestion that the adoption of the Sephardic *minhag* by the newly founded mixed congregations in Newport and Charleston, to which we might add Montreal, Philadelphia and Richmond as well, may have been primarily motivated by the recognition of where the most funds from outside sources could be obtained.[91]

In addition to the shared membership and congregational officer duties, apparently most other aspects of social and religious life exhibited this broad cooperative approach. Thus, all Jews prayed together, contributed to poor relief, and were buried together in the synagogue cemetery. As yet there has been no detailed analysis of the early marriage patterns, an area where one might expect some of the longer standing traditions to be upheld.

Similar cooperative and non-hostile group interaction between Sephardim and Ashkenazim is the norm in the communities founded in Philadelphia, Charleston, Richmond, and Providence.[92]

IRELAND

As in the case of England, there was no formal admission or re-admission of Jews to Ireland in the seventeenth century. It is now known that certain Sephardic Jews settled as Jews, and not as *conversos*, in Dublin around 1660. These people were from former *converso* families and most came by way of Amsterdam and London. The exact size of this community is not known, nor whether they established a synagogue.[93] However, the records of the Inquisition in the Canary Islands indicate that these Irish Sephardim were quite active international traders.[94] For rather obvious reasons, the Dutch and London based Sephardic firms were interested in having an entrepreneurial base in Catholic Ireland for easier entry into the Spanish and Portuguese trade. The English mercantilist acts of 1663 and 1666 allegedly put an end to the expansion of international commerce that was taking place in Ireland. However, important Sephardic economic activity continued in Ireland for the remainder of the seventeenth century, and it was the Dutch firm of Machado and Pereira that played a very prominent role in William of Orange's seizure of the throne from James II and the subsequent Boyne campaign in Ireland. A significant number of Sephardim accompanied Isaac Pereira to Ireland when he was made Commissary General of the Bread for their Majestys' Forces in Ireland.[95] All the important Sephardic Jews were said to have left Ireland around 1730 because of bank failures and the increasingly oppressive English economic discrimination. However, an entry in *Faulkner's Dublin Journal* of 1747 stated, "Last week some Jew Merchants of Great Wealth arrived here from Holland in order to settle in Ireland."[96] Given their Dutch origin and the alleged great wealth, it is a fair assumption that they were Sephardim.

During this same time, Ashkenazic migration to Ireland, via London, was also increasing. By the first decade of the eighteenth century the size of this community in Dublin had grown to the point where an Ashkenazic rabbi, Aaron ben Moses, from Poland was hired. This individual was the head of the one synagogue in Dublin that had both Sephardic and Ashkenazic members. As in the other English "colonial" areas, the traditional enmity between the two groups was lacking. They prayed together in one synagogue, in a unique experiment they even combined their different liturgical rites, and they were buried together in the one Jewish cemetery.

Thus, as we step back from all of this material, I think it is possible to argue that a number of interesting patterns seem to be emerging. In Amsterdam, London and the other urban centers in Northern Europe where the Sephardim settled in the late sixteenth and seventeenth centuries, they developed or carried with them such strong anti-Ashkenazic racial notions that the term Jewish anti-Semitism may not be an overstatement. Elsewhere in the Hispanic New World, where the Sephardim made up the overwhelming majority of the Jewish settlers, and where on-going close relations with Amsterdam or London were maintained, the local Sephardim continued their elitist and hostile behavior towards their less fortunate co-religionists. However, in non-Hispanic portions of the New World, and particularly in the English North American colonies, as well as in Ireland (which might also be classed as an English colony at this time) this Sephardic behavior underwent a fundamental change. A much more egalitarian situation emerges, with Ashkenazim being allowed full membership in the synagogues, full access to the Jewish cemetery, and apparently more or less full social equality with the Sephardim. What explains this dramatic difference? The few Jewish historians who have commented on this phenomenon raised common sense references to the New World frontier situation:

> People from different countries, of different beliefs, arrive and settle whether by design or accident. At first the "different" may be resented and rejected as intruders; but soon, because they are needed, they are grudgingly accepted and later made welcome....America was the frontier of Europe. Life on the frontier is precarious. Man is dependent upon his neighbor. Interdependence leads to acceptance, camaraderie and social integration.[97]

While the above description was applied to all Jews in terms of their ultimate acceptance into American society, it might well be applied to the in-group relations between the Sephardim and Ashkenazim. While I am not supporting the full-blown impact of Frederick Jackson Turner's thesis regarding the significance of the frontier for American history, clearly something of the sort is guiding the altered Sephardic-Ashkenazic relationships. Perhaps it is the colonial situation as opposed to the formal frontier, or the imposition of economic discrimination through the extension of imperial mercantilism, but something is bringing these two groups together in ways unknown in Europe (with the exception of Ireland where we already have noted its colonial status) and in Hispanic America.

There may well be certain problems raised with this sort of theoretical overview. Why did not the frontier impact occur within the Hispanic environment? We have suggested that by its very nature this Spanish influence in these areas perpetuated the racial notions that were carried by the Sephardim. More interesting is the question of why the tolerant, egalitarian feelings among Jews in the non-Hispanic New World lasted such a relatively short time? For when the flood of Polish and Russian Ashkenazic immigration commences in the 1880's, the mixed Sephardic and primarily German Ashkenazic community reacts in a manner not different from the earlier Sephardic reactions in the Old World. To the degree that the exigencies of the frontier produced a communality of experience and an overcoming of previous prejudice, we may declare the American Jewish frontier east of the Mississippi River closed by the 1880's.[98] In an ironic and largely false twisting of the historical record, many German Jews in the late nineteenth century attempted to justify their hostility to the Ashkenazic *ostjuden* by making reference to the alleged discrimination that they had faced from the Sephardim.[99] Further, it has been suggested that the acceptance of the German Jews by the colonial Sephardim transformed them into a kind of pseudo-Sephardim. Rather than emphasizing the egalitarian aspects of the American Sephardic tradition, by the nineteenth century these "new Sephardim" were desperate to maintain their high standing and successful assimilation.[100] Therefore, when they perceived both of these to be threatened by the unassimilated, and from their perspective the unassimilatable, Ashkenazim from Eastern Europe, they reacted with much the same hostility as the "old Sephardim" in Amsterdam and London. However, in yet another ironic twist it has been shown that the "old Sephardim" in Amsterdam differentiated between the German and the Polish/Lithuanian Ashkenazim. As Yosef Kaplan has shown in their view, the Jews from Eastern Europe were far superior to those from Germany.[101]

NOTES

1. An early analysis of the Sephardim in Amsterdam, London, and Ireland is contained in my "The Settlement of the Sephardic Jews in Ireland," *Varieties of Ireland* (B. Touhill ed.), St. Louis, University of Missouri Press, 1976.

2. See, for example, Heiko A. Oberman, *The Roots of Anti-Semitism in the Ages of Renaissance and Reformation*, Philadelphia, Fortress Press, 1981; Shimon Markish, *Erasmus and the Jews*, Chicago, The University of Chicago Press, 1986; R. Po-chia Hsia, *The Myth of Ritual Murder: Jews and Magic in Reformation Germany*, New Haven, Yale U.P., 1988; and, Jerome Friedman, *The Most Ancient Testimony: Sixteenth Century Christian Hebraica in the Age of Renaissance Nostalgia*, Athens, Ohio U.P., 1983.

3. Even the new work by Daniel J. Elazar, *The Other Jews: The Sephardim Today*, Basic Books, New York, 1989 which focuses in, part on the hostility shown towards Sephardim in Israel today states: "from the late tenth and early eleventh centuries, when the Sephardim and Ashkenazim emerged as the two main groupings of the Jewish people, until the twentieth century, each developed its own world within the larger Jewish whole. This does not mean that over the years Jewish unity has not prevailed above all else. *The occasional stories of internal discrimination among Jews are the exception; generally, Jews, whatever their origins have felt – and continue to feel – responsible for one another* (emphasis added, page 17).

4. Quoted in K.C. Meinsma, *Spinoza und sein Kreis*, Berlin, Karl Schnabel Verlag, 1909, p. 113.

5. The term *sephardim* as used in this paper refers to Jews of Spanish and Portuguese origin. The actual word *sepharad* first appears in *Obadiah* (chapter 20) in the Bible. By the end of the first century it has come to mean Spain (*Targum Jonathon*, where it is translated as "Ispamia" or "Spamia" in Aramaic). The term *Ashkenazim*, as used herein refers to Jews of central or east European origin. The word *Ashkenaz* first appears in Genesis (10:3) and in 1st Chronicles (1:6) where up until the 11th century it had been used to designate northern Jews in a variety of geographical locations. It was the famous Rashi in his Talmudic commentaries of the 11th century that set the primary meaning of the word as referencing the Jews of Germany. By the end of the 13th century this had been broadened to include all the Jews of central and eastern Europe.

6. Salvador de Madariaga, *The Fall of the Spanish Empire*, Rev. ed., New York, 1963, p. 226.

7. Yosef Hayim Yerushalmi, *Assimilation and Racial Anti-Semitism: The Iberian and the German Models*, The Leo Baeck Memorial Lecture No. 26, Leo Baeck Institute, New York, 1982; Yosef Kaplan, "The Portuguese Community in 17th Century Amsterdam and the Ashkenazi World," *Dutch Jewish History* (Jozeph Michman, ed.), Volume II, Van Gorcum, Assen/Maastricht, 1989, also see his "The Attitude of the Spanish and Portuguese Jews to the Ashkenazi Jews in 17th Century Amsterdam," *Transition and Change in Modern Jewish History: Essays in Honor of Shmuel Ettinger*, (Hebrew) Jerusalem, 1987.

8. See: Mozes H. Gans, *Memorbook: History of Dutch Jewry from the Renaissance to 1940*, Bosch & Keuning, Baarn, 1977, pp. 15–23; Salo W. Baron, *A Social and Religious History of the Jews*, volume 15, New York, Columbia University Press, 1973, pp. 22–24; and Werner Keller, *Diaspora: The Post-Biblical History of the Jews*, London, Pitman House, 1971, pp. 317–320.

9. Herbert I. Bloom, *The Economic Activity of Jews of Amsterdam in the Seventeenth and Eighteenth Centuries*, Port Washington, Kennikat Press, 1969, p. xv.

10. Jonathan I. Israel, *European Jewry in the age of Mercantilism, 1550–1750*, Oxford, Clarendon Press, 1989, p. 62.

11. See: Ellis Rivkin, "Marrano-Jewish Entrepreneurship and the Ottoman Mercantilist Probe in the Sixteenth Century," paper presented at the 3rd International Conference on Economic History, Munich, 1965, and reprinted by Hebrew Union College - Jewish Institute of Religion, Cincinnati, 1967.

12. Yosef Kaplan, "The Portuguese Community and the Ashkenazi World," *op. cit.*, pp. 28–36.

13. Bloom, *op. cit.*, p. 20.

14. *Parnassah* in Hebrew means livelihood. The members of the Sephardic synagogue councils were called *parnassim*, those with the livelihood, thus establishing the firm linkage between wealth and communal control. As will be shown below, this group was very anxious to preserve the status quo and not jeopardize their wealth, standing and power.

15. Gans, *op. cit.*, p. 33.

16. See: Lucien Wolf, *Jews in the Canary Islands*, London, Oxford University Press, 1926.

17. H.J. Zimmels, *Die Marranen in der rabbinischen Literatur*, Berlin, 1932, p. 69; and, S. Ullmann, "Geschichte der spanisch-portugiesischen Juden in Amsterdam im 17 Jahrhundert," *Jahrbuch der juedisch-literarischen Gesellschaft*, Frankfurt, 1907, p. 28.

18. Baron, *op. cit.*, p. 35.

19. Gans, *op. cit.*, p. 29.

20. Lewis S. Feuer, *Spinoza and the Rise of Liberalism*, Boston, Beacon Press, 1958, p.. 6; and, Bloom, *op. cit.*, pp. 11–12.

21. For a fuller discussion of the economic activity of the Dutch Sephardim see H.I. Bloom, *op. cit.*, and J.I. Israel, *op. cit.*, esp. pp. 106–09 and pp. 176–79.

22. A.S. Diamond, "The Community of the Resettlement, 1656–1684," *Transaction of the Jewish Historical Society of England*, volume 24, p. 149.

23. Lionel D. Barnett, *El Libro de los Acuerdos*, Oxford University Press, 1931, p. 28.

24. Marcus Arkin, *Aspects of Jewish Economic History*, Philadelphia, Jewish Publication Society, 1975, p. 107.

25. Baron, *op. cit.*, p. 36.

26. Bloom, *op. cit.*, p. 26.

27. Richard H. Popkin, "The Marranos of Amsterdam," in Popkin, *The Third Force in Seventeenth-Century Thought*, Leiden, Brill, 1992, p. 162. Yosef Kaplan points out that the Sephardim collected 3,375 florins in 1656 for the Lithuanian Ashkenazim and 3,947 florins for them in 1657 (Kaplan, "The Portuguese Community and the Ashkenazi World," *op. cit.*, p. 37).

28. Gans, *op. cit.*, p. 55.

29. H.J. Zimmels, *Ashkenazim and Sephardim*, London, Oxford University Press, 1958, p. 62

30. Eli Faber, *The Jewish People in America: A Time for Planting, The First Migration, 1654–1820*, Baltimore, Johns Hopkins U.P., 1992, p. 61.

31. Diamond, *op. cit.*, pp. 134 and 142.

32. *Ibid.*, p. 144.

33. Zimmels, *op. cit.*, p. 290

34. Diamond, *op. cit.*, p. 150; and A.S. Diamond, "Problems of the London Sephardic Community, 1720–1733: Philip Cartet Webb's Notebooks," *Transactions of the Jewish Historical Society of England*, volume 21, p. 41.

35. In 1763 the *Monthly Review* of London published an article detailing the refusal of the Sephardim to sanction marriages with Ashkenazic Jews. For a discussion of similar policies aming the Sephardim in Amsterdam, see Y. Kaplan, "The Portuguese Community...," *op. cit*, pp. 43–44.

36. Zimmels, *op. cit.*, p. 62.

37. Baron, *op. cit.*, p. 36.

38. Barnett, *op. cit.*, p. 79.

39. Albert M. Hyamson, *A History of the Jews in England*, London, Chatto & Windus, 1908, p. 288.

40. See, Yosef Kaplan, "The Portuguese Community in 17th Century Amsterdam...", *op. cit.*, pp. 31–2.

41. *Ibid.*, p. 43.

42. Gans, *op. cit.*, p. 29.

43. Gans, *op. cit.*, p. 198.

44. Jakob Petuchowski, *The Theology of Haham David Nieto*, New York, Ktav Publishing House, 1954, p. 4.

45. See, Jack Wertheimer, *Unwelcome Strangers: East European Jews in Imperial Germany*, New York, Oxford U.P., 1987.

46. Jonathan I. Israel, *European Jewry in the Age of Mercantilism, 1550–1750*, Oxford, Clarendon Press, 1989, pp. 254–5.

47. Isaac S. and Suzanne A. Emmanuel, *History of the Jews of the Netherlands Antilles*, volume I, Cincinnati, American Jewish Archives, 1970, p. 38

48. Max Grünwald, *Portugiesengräber auf deutscher Erde*, Hamburg, n.p., 1902, p. 24

49. Emmanuel, *op. cit.*, p. 42; also see Cecil Roth, *A History of the Jews of England*, Oxford, Oxford U.P., 1941, p. 175 and, Gershom Scholem, *Sabbatai Sevi: The Mystical Messiah*, Princeton, Princeton U.P., pp. 531–2. João de Yllan is not the same person as Don Garcia d'Yllan who was a communal leader in Antwerp, held the chocolate monopoly for Europe, and was one of Queen Christina's bankers and the person with whom she lived in 1654 (see, Susanna Åkerman, *Queen Christina of Sweden and Her Circle: The Transformation of a Seventeenth-Century Philosophical Libertine*, Leiden, Brill, 1991, pp. 187–88). There is firm evidence of João in Curaçao at the same time that Don Garcia is active in Antwerp. What little is written about both men mentions their extensive family connections especially for business matters, and there is a good likelihood that they are indeed related. However, there seems to be no doubt that it was the Curaçoan

João de Yllan who became the Shabbatian in Amsterdam and the author of the petition to Cromwell. Scholem states categorically that "The Public Record Office in London preserves a petition presented on February 5, 1666 to the king of England by a Jew of Amsterdam, Jean d'Illan, requesting a pass for a Dutch ship," and continues in fn. 158, "...C. Roth...gives the Portuguese form of the petitioner's name as João d'Illhão." (Scholem, *op. cit.*, pp. 531–532). However, what really clinches this identification is the fact that Don Garcia De Yllan died in Antwerp in 1655 (Åkerman, p. 188).

50. Scholem, *op. cit.*, p. 549.
51. West India Archives at the Hague 243, no. 127, p. 17; also see Isaac S. Emmanuel, "New Light on Early American Jewry," *American Jewish Archives*, Cincinnati, 1955, (7:57).
52. I.S. and S.A. Emmanuel, *op. cit.*, v. I, p. 496.
53. *Ibid*, p. 497.
54. *Ibid*, p. 497
55. I.S. and S.A. Emmanuel, *op. cit.*, v. II, p. 561.
56. *Ibid.*, p. 131; also see David and Tamar de Sola Pool, *An Old Faith in the New World: Portrait of Shearith Israel, 1654–1954*, New York, Columbia U.P., p. 42
57. Jacob R. Marcus, "The Oldest Known Synagogue Record Book of Continental North America, 1720–1721," *Studies in American Jewish History: Studies and Addresses by Jacob R. Marcus*, Cincinnati, Hebrew Union College Press, 1969, p. 52; also see Mishnah, *Pesahim*, IV,1.
58. Mishnayoth, Order Moed, volume II, *Pesachim*, IV,1, (ed. Philip Blackman), Gateshead, Judaica Press, Ltd., 1990, p. 178, with the footnote to the relevant sentence explaining, "i.e, behave differently than local practice."
59. S. Rosanes, *Divre Yeme Yisra'el be Thogarma I*, Tel Aviv, 1930, p. 216, quoted in Rae Dalven, *The Jews of Ioannina*, Philadelphia, Cadmus Press, 1990, p. 19.
60. The Babylonian Talmud, *Seder Mo'ed*, volume II, *Pesachim*, 51a, London, The Soncino Press, pp. 249–51; also see, Yosef Kaplan, "The Travels of Portuguese Jews from Amsterdam to the 'Lands of Idolatry'(1644–1724), *Jews and Conversos: Studies in Society and the Inquisition*, (Yoesf Kaplan, ed.), Jerusalem, The Magnes Press, 1985, pp. 197–224.
61. Rae Dalven, *op. cit.*, p. 19.
62. H.J. Zimmels, *Ashkenazim and Sephardim*, London, Oxford U.P., 1958, p. 62
63. See, R.A.J. Van Lier, "The Jewish Community in Surinam: A Historical Survey," (Robert Cohen, ed.) *The Jewish Nation in Surinam, Historical Essays*, Amsterdam, S. Emmering, 1982, p. 19.
64. See, Van Lier, *op. cit.* p. 20; H.D. Benjamins and J.F. Snelleman, *Encylopaedie van Nederlandsch West-Indie*, The Hague, 1914–17, p. 386; and J. Wolbers, *Geschiedenis van Suriname, van de ontdekking van Amerika tot op den tegenwoordigen tijd*, Amsterdam, 1861 (reprinted 1970), p. 36.
65. Robert Cohen, *Jews in Another Environment: Surinam in the Second Half of the Eighteenth Century*, Leiden, E.J. Brill, 1991, pp. 126–7.
66. Benjamins and Snelleman, *op. cit.*, p. 386, and quoted in R. Cohen, *op. cit.*, p. 20.
67. Y. Kaplan, "The Portuguese Community and the Ashkenazi World," *op. cit.*, p. 40.
68. Robert Cohen, "Patterns of Marriage and Remarriage among the Sephardi Jews of Surinam, 1788–1818," R. Cohen, *op. cit.*, p. 93.
69. Malcolm H. Stern, "New Light on the Jewish Settlement of Savannah," *The Jewish Experience in America: Selected Studies from the Publications of the American Jewish Historical Society, Volume I, The Colonial Period*, (Abraham J. Karp, ed.), New York, KTAV Publishing House, Inc., 1969, pp. 69–70.

70. *Ibid., pp. 71–74.*
71. Quoted in A.J. Karp, *op. cit.*, p. xx.
72. W. Gunther Plaut, "Two Notes on the History of the Jews in America," *Hebrew Union College Annual*, volume 14. part 2, "Early Settlement in Georgia," pp. 580–81; also quoted in translation by Stern, *op. cit.*, pp. 82–83.
73. M. Stern., *op. cit.*, pp. 91–2.
74. Arnold Wiznitzer, "The Exodus from Brazil and Arrival in New Amsterdam of the Jewish Pilgrim Fathers, 1654," A.J. Karp, *op. cit.*, pp. 19–36; also see his *Records of the Earliest Jewish Community in the New World*, New York, 1954; and his *Jews in Colonial Brazil*, New York, Columbia U.P., 1960.
75. For a fuller discussion of early Portuguese *converso* migration to the New World see Robert Weisbrot, *The Jews of Argentina from the Inquisition to Perón*, Philadelphia, Jewish Publication Society, 1979, pp. 15–57; Ellis Rivkin, "Marrano Jewish Entrepreneurship and the Ottoman Mercantilist Probe,"; and Seymour B. Liebman, *New World Jewry, 1493–1825: Requiem for the Forgotten*, New York, KTAV Publishing House, 1982.
76. Solomon Ibn Verga, *Sefer Shebet Yehudah*, (Azriel Shohat, ed.), Jerusalem, 1947, p. 38.
77. Arnold Wiznitzer, *op. cit.*.
78. A. Wiznitzer, "The Exodus from Brazil...," *op. cit.*, p. 30.
79. British Museum, Add. Ms. 18896, folio 126, and reproduced as an appendix to Wiznitzer, *ibid.*, pp. 35–36.
80. David S. Katz, *Philo-Semitism and the Readmission of the Jews to England, 1603–1655*, Oxford, Clarendon Press, 1982, pp. 164–5 and 192–3, briefly discusses some of the economic arguments that had been put forward as motives for the re-admission.
81. Reprinted in *The Jewish Experience in Latin America: Selected Studies from the Publications of the American Jewish Historical Society*, Volume II, (Martin A. Cohen, ed.), New York, KTAV Publishing House, 1971, p. 274.
82. Arnold Wiznitzer, "The Minute Book of Congregations Zur Israel of Recife and Magen Abraham of Mauricia, Brazil," *ibid.*, p. 237.
83. A. Wiznitzer, "Exodus from Brazil...," *op. cit.*, p. 30.
84. J.R. Marcus, *op. cit*, p. 44.
85. *Ibid.*, p. 50.
86. David de Sola Pool, *Portraits Etched in Stone: Early Jewish Settlers, 1882–1831*, NY, Columbia U.P., 1952, p. 171.
87. David and Tamar de Sola Pool, *An Old Faith in the New World: Portrait of Shearith Israel, 1654–1954*, New York, Columbia U.P., 1955, p. 40
88. Letter (c. 1729) to Rodrigues Pacheco & Daniel Gomez in New York sent by a representative of the Sephardic community in Curaçao in response to a request for aid for the construction of a synagogue, reproduced in, David de Sola Pool, *op. cit.*, p. 171
89. The various revised synagogue constitutions of Shearith Israel are reproduced in *A Double Bond: The Constitutional Documents of American Jewry*, (D.J. Elazar, J.D. Sarna, and R.G. Monson, eds.), Lanham (MD), University Press of America, 1992, pp. 103–111.
90. *Ibid.*, p. 105
91. Malcolm H. Stern, "Two Jewish Functionaries in Colonial Pennsylvania," in A.J. Karp, *op. cit.*, p. 121 and Jacob Rader Marcus, *American Jewry: Documents, Eighteenth Century: Primarily Hitherto Unpublished Manuscripts*, Cincinnati, Hebrew Union College Press, 1959, pp. 105–14.
92. See *ibid.* for a reproduction of the various synagogue constitutions in Philadelphia, Richmond, and Charleston.

93. A controversy exists on this point between Louis Hyman, *The Jews of Ireland: from Earliest Times to the Year 1910*, Shannon, Irish U.P., 1972, p. 12 and Bernard Shillman, *A Short History of the Jews of Ireland*, Dublin, Cahill & Co., 1972, pp. 13–17.

94. See, Lucien Wolf, *Jews in the Canary Islands*, London, Jewish Historical Society of England, 1926; and, Maurice Woolf, "Foreign Trade of London Jews in the 17th Century," *Transactions of the Jewish Historical Society of England*, v. 24.

95. See, Cecil Roth, *History of the Jews in England*, Oxford, Clarendon Press, 1964, pp. 185–86; Hyman, *op. cit.*, p. 20; and, Shillman, *op. cit.*, pp. 47–8.

96. *Faulkner's Dublin Journal*, October 6, 1747, item number 2145.

97. A.J. Karp, *op. cit.*, pp. xiii–xiv.

98. The various dispersal projects aimed at removing the Polish and Russian Jews to the trans-Mississippi West did result in the creation of a new Jewish frontier where one sees a repetition of in-group Jewish tolerance.

99. Rudolf Glanz, *Studies in Judaica Americana*, New York, KTAV Publishing House, 1970, pp. 11–13.

100. Stephan Birmingham, *The Grandees*, New York, Harper and Row, 1971, pp. 120–21; and Stanley Feldstein, *The Land That I Show You: Three Centuries of Jewish Life in America*, New York, Doubleday, 1978, pp. 118–173.

101. Y. Kaplan, "The Portuguese Community and the Ashkenazi World," *op. cit.*, p. 36 and 40. Kaplan does note that after the merger of the Polish and German communities in 1673, the Sephardim in Amsterdam stop differentiating between them.

INDEX

Abner (Alphonsus) of Burgos, 15
Aboab, Isaac, 60, 83
Abrahamsz, Galenus, 84
Abravanel, Judah, 17, 21
Abulafia, Abraham, 18
Abulfaraj, Samuel ben Nissim, 17
Adam Kadmon, 79 *ff.*
Adelkind, Cornelius, 43
Adrian, Matthew, 43
Agobard of Lyons, 13
Alan of Lille, 14
Alemanno, Johanen, 17
Alfonsi, Petrus, 12, 14, 16, 20
Altmann, Alexander, 84
Arama, Isaac, 44
Arendt, Hannah, 159 *ff.*
Arianism, 132
Aristotle, 98
Arnold of Vilanova, 15
Ashkenazim, 8, 64, 189–214
Aylmer, John, 107

ben Asher, Bahya, 20
ben Israel, Menasseh, 59, 61 *ff.*, 127
ben Judah Messer Leon, David, 199
ben Yohai, Simeon, 25
Benz, Erst, 77
blood libel, 73
Boreel, Adam, 59, 84
Bownde, Nicholas, 122
Brabourne, Theophilus, 126
Brawe, Justus, 76
Brayne, John, 120
Brightman, Thomas, 109
Broughton, Hugh, 109
Bucer, Martin, 40, 114
Buchanan, George, 7, 97 *ff.*
Budny, Symon, 45
Bullinger, Heinrich, 42

Buraeus, Johannes, 109
Busale, Bruno, 42

Calvin, John 42, 121
Cant, Andrew, 110
Capito of Strasbourg, 39
Caraites, 138
Carmelites, 3
Cayenne, 200
Chambers, David, 100
Chambers, Ephraim, 149
Charles I, 123
Charles II, 197
Christian August, of Sulzbach, 74
Cohen, Samuel 197
Columbus, Christopher, 3
Comenius, Jan Amos, 58
Conway, Anne, 83
Council of Nicea, 40
Council of Trent, 73
Cromwell, Oliver, 61
Cromwell, Thomas, 100
crusades, 12
Curaçao, 197

da Costa, Uriel, 84
David, Frances, 45
de Costa, João, 101
de Gouvea, André, 100
de Gouvea, Diogo, 100
de Heredia, Paul, 15
de Pinedo, Thomas, 74
de Pinto, Isaac, 195
de Rocamora, Isaac, 74
de Sola Pool, David, 204
de Valdez, Juan, 41
de Valladolid, Alfonse, 87
de Vieria, Antonio, 61
de Villafrancha, John, 42